G000139232

A FELL
PARSON

Joseph Brunskill and his Diaries
1826–1903

by

The Revd John Breay, MA

The Canterbury Press
Norwich

© John Breay 1995

First published 1995 by The Canterbury Press Norwich
(a publishing imprint of Hymns Ancient & Modern Limited,
a registered charity)
St Mary's Works, St Mary's Plain,
Norwich, Norfolk, NR3 3BH

British Library Cataloguing in Publication Data

A catalogue record for this book is available
from the British Library

ISBN 1–85311–104–X

*Typeset by Waveney Studios
Diss, Norfolk, and
printed and bound in Great Britain by
Antony Rowe Ltd.
Chippenham, Wiltshire*

In friendship to
John Langhorne of Levens, Westmorland,
and
Alan Brunskill Webster of Norwich

PREFACE

WHEN THAT excellent scourge of bishops the Revd Sydney Smith (1771–1845) made his public comments on the church reforming zeal of Lord John Russell and C. J. Blomfield bishop of London in his letters to archdeacon Singleton, he supported the design to abolish sinecures in order to improve the wages of the poorer clergy, but opposed any move to reduce the number of well-paid working posts in order to encourage hard-working men to aim for the plums at the top of the tree. He added this: 'If these men are degraded, capital is withdrawn from the church, and no one enters the profession but the sons of farmers and little tradesmen, who would be footmen if they were not vicars – or figure on the coach-box if they were not lecturing from the pulpit.'[1]

This is the story of the son of a small farmer, whose father sold butter and bacon in Penrith market, but whose grandson rose to be dean of St Paul's. But the son remained a footman in the church, always at the bottom of the ladder, and in his early years often receiving far less in salary than the minimum £80 laid down in the Curates Act 1813. His second disability was that he was trained for two years at the St Bees Clerical College in contrast to the three years for university graduates; no matter how thorough his own training, a non-graduate remained at the bottom of the lists for promotion. His third disability in the eyes of his bishops was that he was trained in the tradition of the Caroline Divines, a learned moderate high-churchmanship. His early ministry coincided with the episcopate of two bishops of Carlisle, H. M. Villiers (1856–1860) and S. Waldegrave (1860–1869), men of such narrow evangelical views that they would not countenance nor promote clergy of high church leanings, however moderate. So great was this distrust between Joseph Brunskill and the bishop of Carlisle, that when the former was curate of Askham and in 1860 was appointed headmaster of Lowther Grammar School for boys, the bishop was never told, and for ten years he remained nominal curate of

Askham, while actually working as an headmaster. Not till the episcopate of bishop Harvey Goodwin from 1869 was any serious attempt made by a bishop to bridge the gulf between himself and the grossly underpaid and very lonely country clergy.

The life story of Joseph Brunskill raises some puzzling questions. During his first ten years as a clergyman he had seven curacies, some of a few months duration. Why? He worked very hard; he took great trouble over his sermons; he was a constant visitor; and as a controversialist he loved debate, and giving a reasoned account of his faith. But sooner or later he would have bouts of ill-health, and the tell-tale sore throat. He would have a day's rest, or a few days' holiday, or an even longer absence which would incur the anger of his vicar. Then he was either dismissed, or he would resign. Why?

When he left Mr Threlkeld's school at Milburn at the age of 15 he wrote that he weighed 6 st. 8 lbs. Did his constant assertiveness stem from his slight stature? He never had a degree, though a BA was attached to his name for ten years in the Clergy Lists. Did he also have to combat the snobbery of university graduates who insinuated that you had to be a 'gentleman' born and have a degree to be a successful parson? Or, did he qualify for one of the sayings of Dr W. F. Hook, the famous vicar of Leeds, who said: 'Stick to your principles, but don't have too many of them. No man is more tiresome than he who makes a *principle* of everything which he happens to *like*, and therefore won't yield'. Or, was he possessed of a perpetual restlessness; must he be always busy? Or, and this is a strong point, had he to fight against an old tradition in the church that the clergy schoolmasters who served the average small parochial schools were often a poor lot, best left to themselves? One can select any combination of these questions and be right only to this extent; that Brunskill was a man of spirit working in an age when the gross inequality of remuneration in clergy pay, and the survival of pluralities, and the poverty and insecurity of the lower clergy were a scandal. He was always at the bottom of the ladder, always battling against the system.

He stuck doggedly to his prime belief in the glory of Christ's Church, and the high privilege of being a priest. His life was a continual battle amid hardship to prove his capacity in parish or school; he never spared himself. In the church he well knew the miseries of the lower clergy, their poor housing, and the poverty of their churches. From his early days in Sunderland he knew the suffering of the poor. As the son of a farmer he loved horses, and fought for years against their ill-usage. As a schoolmaster he gave of his best to the boys in his care. He may not have been brilliant, but he was tough, a fighter, and his pen became his sword. He was fearless, often tactless against stupid bishops, unjust poor-law guardians, patrons of livings, idle clergy, and those who laid hands on old endowed church schools, though the system was out of date. Indeed, he opposed and exposed all who denied the poor their birthright to a decent home, a living wage, and free access to the privileges of Christ in his Temple. As his letters will reveal he was a great battler, sometimes wrong-headed, but no-one doubted his honesty or moral fibre. He often took an unpopular line, even in politics, if he thought that the needs of working people or the poor demanded it. Many times he faced hot opposition in church or politics; but he never bore a grudge against an opponent. Often he won respect by his kindness. In short he was a pillar of Christ's Church, a man of principle, and very kind. The family tells this story from Threlkeld. There was a number of poor families in the parish, whose children did not have enough to eat. He went to a large farmer who used to feed his skimmed milk to the calves and asked him to consider setting aside some of this milk for some poor families. The farmer refused, and cursed the rector from his land. He had done his duty, and he accepted the curses.

What did he achieve? First, he set high standards for himself, in church and school. He rescued his churches from the squalor and filth to which the spent force of the evangelical movement had reduced them. He was a good pastor, especially to the poor. But he was not an introspective churchman. He was concerned with the needs of working people, the miners, the farmers, homeless unemployed men wandering the roads seeking work and shelter, and the need of the children of the poor to receive a sound schooling. The centre of his life was his church, with its doors wide open to receive all who would enter without distinction of wealth or rank. There was also a measure of pugnacity about him, giving an edge to his churchmanship, which was expressed through his children. While his daughter Lydia was a teenager at Threlkeld she would cycle through Keswick on a Sunday with a racquet, and dressed for tennis in order to shock the godly attending the evangelical Keswick Convention. That aside, the nearest contemporary to express his ideals was R. S. Hawker, the Cornish priest. In his poem 'The Poor Man and his Church' he wrote:

> The Poor have hands, and feet, and eyes,
>   Flesh, and a feeling mind;
> They Breathe the breath of mortal sighs,
>   They are of human kind ...
>
> They should have roofs to call their own,
>   When they grow old and bent;
> Meek houses built of dark grey stone,
>   Worn labourers' monument.
> There should they dwell, beneath the thatch
>   With threshold calm and free;
> No stranger's hand should lift the latch,
>   To mark their poverty.
>
> Fast by the church those walls should stand,
>   Her aisles in youth they trod:
> They have no home in all the land,
>   Like that old House of God.
> There, there, the Sacrament was shed,
>   That gave them heavenly birth;
> And lifted up the poor man's head
>   With princes of the earth.[2]

Those old-time parsons were tough and true; their priorities were right!

NOTES

1. Works of the Revd Sydney Smith 1839, vol. III, p. 89. Second letter to archdeacon Singleton.
2. Cornish Ballads & other Poems, R. S. Hawker, ed. C. E. Byles, 1904, p. 61. The Poor Man and his Church, written 1840.

CONTENTS

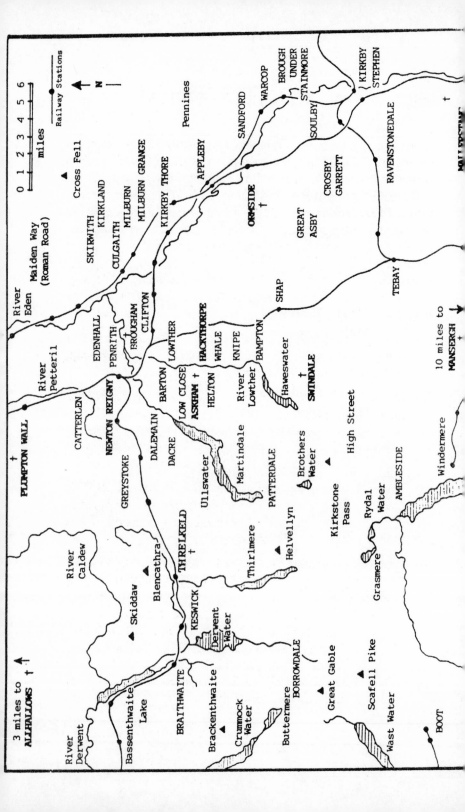

Primary Diary Sources

Apart from a number of letters, papers and press cuttings owned by John Langhorne, and Alan Webster, there are two surviving diaries in memorandum books belonging to Alan.

Joseph Brunskill was a fitful diarist with large gaps in the narrative. The diaries were mostly written at times of stress, and on one occasion he inserts a retrospective account of an earlier experience. The purpose of these diary accounts is to record events and people at times of stress; when he settles to continuous work the diary stops. Two of the memorandum books contained lecture notes, either from his tutors at St Bees, or from Dr W. F. Hook at Leeds.

(1) Ten leaves cut from *a small notebook* covering years 1841 to 1850, referring to his leaving school, his apprenticeship, and testimonials for his entering St Bees.

(2) *Diary.* 21 May 1850 to 31 Dec. 1851, covering his ordination to his curacy at Ocker Hill.
January 1851 to October 1851, Ocker Hill.
January 1852 to March 1852. Temporary curacy at Horbury, and starting at St Mary's, Leeds.

(3) *Diary* in missing memorandum book, ? March 1852 to October 1853 covering Leeds, Mansergh, and early weeks in Mallerstang. This was formerly in the possession of Mrs I. M. Langhorne of New Hutton.

(4) *Diary.* 5 November 1853 to December 1853, Mallerstang.
1 January 1855 to 8 July 1855, Mallerstang & Barton.
14 July 1855 to 26 July 1855, All Hallows.
28 April 1856 to 12 November 1856, All Hallows.
6 January 1857 to 22 April 1857, All Hallows.
23 April 1857 to June 1857, Askham.
3 October 1859 to 22 December 1860, Askham, and Lowther (Hackthorpe).

(5) *A volume of notes* made by Brunskill for his lectures on Lady Anne Clifford & family (printed in the *Penrith Observer*) covering George, Francis & Henry third, fourth and last earls of Cumberland, taken from the records of Lady Anne Clifford. Also a few extracts from her later diaries, which were later printed by Dr G. C. Williamson. The reverse of this volume has a note of the names on some engraved wine glasses, the property of the Revd W. J. Monkhouse DD, fellow and tutor of The Queen's College, Oxford, 'now in the possession of his g.g. nephew the Revd Jos. Brunskill'.

Also reading extracts: from *Orlando Furioso*, Kingsley's *Memoirs*, & *Scenes in Wordsworthshire*.

Papers by the Revd Joseph Brunskill.

1871. Letters of Commendation. A Paper read at the Penrith branch of the English Church Union, at Penrith 1867, pub. 1871.

1884. The Helm Wind. A Paper read before the Royal Meteorological Society June 1884. I have not found this in the printed proceedings.

1895. Roadmakers. A Paper read at the Meeting of the Cumberland & Westmorland Antiquarian Society 10 July 1895.

1901. Ormshed and its church. By the Revd Joseph Brunskill. Cumb. & Westmorland Antiq. Soc. N.S. 1901.

1903. The Brunskills, by the Revd Joseph Brunskill. Cumb. & Westmorland Antiq. Soc. N.S. 1903.

Abbreviations

C.R.O.	The County Record Offices at Kendal or Carlisle.
C.U.L.	The Cambridge University Library.
C. & W.	The transactions of the Cumberland & Westmorland Archaeological & Antiquarian Society. Also the Parish Register Section.
D.N.B.	The Dictionary of National Biography.
I.G.I.	The micro-film Digest of parish registers compiled by the Church of Jesus Christ & Latter Day Saints.
L.M.	The MSS and printed materials belonging to Mr John Langhorne of Levens.
N. & B.	*The History of Cumberland & Westmorland*, by J. Nicolson & R. Burn, 1777.
W.M.	The MSS & printed materials belonging to the Very Revd Alan Brunskill Webster of Norwich.

Acknowledgements

My grateful thanks are due to:

Mr John Langhorne of Green End, Levens near Kendal, and the Very Revd A. B. Webster DD, KCVO of 20 Beechbank, Norwich, grandsons of the Revd Joseph Brunskill who generously placed the family papers at my disposal.

The late Mrs Mary Mortimer and her family of the Old Rectory, Newton Reigny near Penrith for her meticulous reading of the text, and several learned suggestions.

Miss Rena Beech of Ickleton near Cambridge for patient typing; and to Mr & Mrs David Lilley also of Ickleton for photocopying.

Mr Leonard Beard MA FRPS, of Cambridge and Barrington for photographic assistance, particularly for re-photographing from family records the front cover photograph.

Mrs Jill Butterworth MA, of the Cambridge University Library for the recovery of old photos of Mallerstang Church.

Canon J. K. Byrom MA, of Cambridge for several corrections and suggestions.

Mr Chris Fisher of Norwich for the map, and to my proof readers for their alertness and help.

J. B.

1

The fellsider

AT THE foot of the western slopes of Cross Fell in Cumbria lies the ancient parish of Kirkland. It is basically a fellside parish, mostly pastoral, and, until these tenures were abolished, was composed of customary tenants paying rents, fines and services to whomever owned the lordships of the several parts of the parish. In 1777 there were 145 such tenants occupying the 6361 acres, divided between the hamlets of Kirkland, Culgaith, Blenkarn and Skirwith. The rectory belonged to the Dean & Chapter of Carlisle, who appointed their vicar, who in 1847 enjoyed the quite good stipend of £220 a year, subject to the vicissitudes of harvests and tithes. A Roman road, called the Maiden Way, runs through the length of the parish; and near to a place called Ranbeck there are three raised terraces enjoying the curious name of The Hanging Gardens of Mark Antony.[1] It was, until the coming of the railway and improved roads, a lonely place, with the farmers confined to their ancient lands, their heaf-going flocks of sheep, trade by packhorse, the pack-men coming to the farms, the intercourse of neighbours, and the weekly market at Penrith. The only educated men in the parish were the parson and the schoolmaster; and often loneliness ground them down to a condition little better than that of their neighbours.[1]

On the 20 December 1785 one Joseph Brunskill aged 30,[2] a bachelor from the parish of Kirkland was married at Milburn church to Isabella Atkinson of Milburn, a spinster aged 24. Isabella came from a Milburn family whose forebears figure regularly in the parish registers. Where Joseph Brunskills family came from is not known; there were Brunskill's in Kirkland, Milburn Grange, and a number of other villages in the upper Eden valley; but their main concentration was in the ancient parish of Brough under Stainmore. There may have been other links with Milburn for, on 1 December 1785, Richard Atkinson aged 28 and Hannah Brunskill aged 23 were also married at Milburn. Indeed, Joseph gave the name Richard Atkinson to

1

one of his sons born in 1801. Joseph and Isabella had nine children, the first four of whom were born at Kirkland.

> Elizabeth (Betty) born 11 January 1787, and baptised at Kirkland 14 January 1787.
> Mary born 19 October 1788, and baptised 1 January 1789.
> John born 28 November 1790, and baptised 13 January 1791.
> Ann born 11 January 1793, and baptised 25 April 1793.

Joseph and Isabella then moved to the hamlet of Sandford in the parish of Warcop, where he may have been a small tenant-farmer, or a farm worker, where five more children were born and baptised at Warcop:

> William born 14 December 1795, and baptised 11 February 1796.
> Joseph baptised 18 July 1797.
> George baptised 2 July 1799.
> Richard Atkinson baptised 15 June 1801.
> Isabella baptised 6 August 1803.[3]

Little is known of Joseph Brunskill except that in the years 1810 and 1811 (when he was aged 55/6) he was a churchwarden of Warcop.[4] Nothing more is known of him, or the early years of the family.

The third child John Brunskill was married on the 3 August 1824 at Newton Reigny to Mary Ann, the sole child of the Revd John Pearson, perpetual curate of Newton Reigny from 1805 to 1831. John Brunskill was then described as living at Sewborwens in the parish of Newton, while Pearson lived at Middlegate, Penrith,[5] as Newton Parsonage was not built until 1825. John Pearson was the second son of Henry Pearson of Bawness in the parish of Bassenthwaite, Cumberland, and Grace Wane the daughter of Joseph Wane of Scarness, Bassenthwaite, and latterly of Lissick in the parish of Crosthwaite. John Pearson had been ordained deacon by the bishop of Carlisle in 1788, and priest in 1789. In 1788 he was curate of Bassenthwaite, and from 1798 to 1805 curate of Newton Reigny, and thereafter perpetual curate or rector of the parish until 1831. On the 25 November 1798 he was married at Newton at the age of 34 to Mary Monkhouse aged 39, the second of nine children of William Monkhouse of Catterlen Hall and Elizabeth Bowerbank his wife. It is not clear how long Pearson lived at Newton, for in 1814 he was living at Middlegate in Penrith, and died there in 1831.[6]

Pearson's marriage in 1798, and John Brunskill's marriage in 1824 introduced Brunskill to the Monkhouse family, which for generations had been substantial yeoman farmers at Catterlen Hall, five of whose sons in turn went to Queen's College, Oxford. They held fellowships before being advanced to college livings; Thomas Monkhouse, fellow 1759; Isaac, fellow 1786; John, fellow 1792; William, fellow 1840; and John, fellow 1858.[7]

Mary Pearson's father William Monkhouse died in 1812, and one of the properties owned by Mary's mother Elizabeth was Bankfoot in Newton parish. When Elizabeth died in 1832 it descended to her youngest child Jane Monkhouse, who died in 1862. One of the unsolved problems is when Bankfoot became the property of John Brunskill. In Mannix & Whellan's History, Directory and Gazetteer of Cumberland, 1847, among the residents at Newton are Miss Jane Monkhouse, John Brunskill yeoman, and Joseph Brunskill of Sewborwens. Both were farmers; John is described as yeoman,[8] that is he owned his farm, while his brother Joseph is tenant of Sewborwens. Thus John had bought Bankfoot before 1847. As Jane Monkhouse's Will of 1859 is badly drawn up, none of her properties are named, and we cannot tell when she sold Bankfoot to John.[9]

John Brunskill and Mary his wife produced five children, two of whom died soon after birth. John Pearson was baptised 22 September 1824; Joseph 25 September 1826; and Isabella 27 July 1828. (The two who died were Mary Ann who was born 1832/3, and lived six months; and another Mary Ann who lived four days from the 18 to 22 March 1834.) Their mother Mary died after childbirth, and was buried at Newton on the 3 April 1834.[10] John remarried on the 28 March 1836 Hannah Leach of Cumwhitton, near Carlisle. A daughter Hannah was born in the following year, and was baptised at Newton on 31 July 1837. The daughter Hannah died at Bankfoot in 1877.[11]

At the same time as John and his wife lived at Bankfoot, his brother Joseph and his wife Agnes lived at Sewborwens, and had at least two children; Joseph in 1826, and Sarah in 1828.[12] Thus by the time that John was well established at Bankfoot with three children, he had extensive connections with the Pearsons, the Monkhouses, and Bowerbanks, and, through his mother, the Atkinsons of Milburn. In addition there were the families springing from John's eight brothers and sisters, in north Westmorland and Cumberland.

John's son JOSEPH BRUNSKILL born 22 February and baptised 25 February 1826 is the subject of this short biography. Being the second son, by the customary manorial laws of the time, he could not expect to inherit the farm – that went to the eldest after paying off the 'child's portion' of any brothers or sisters. Joseph would have to make his way in the world with what help the parents could afford. In this case they sent Joseph to a private boarding academy at Milburn House, Milburn, near Appleby, run by the Revds Philip Threlkeld, father and son.[13] The father had been perpetual curate of Milburn from 1786 to 1831 on a stipend of £85 a year, and the son from 1831 to 1843. These perpetual curacies were created out of parochial chapelries under the provisions of Queen Anne's Bounty. The Bounty, by its system of doubling donations for the buying of land, had increased the endowment of these small cures, and given them security of tenure within the mother parish ... in this case of Kirkby Thore. Very often the endowment of these perpetual curacies was scarcely more, and often less than the stipend of a curate at will. In order to make good the deficit, perpetual curates took to teaching, often in opposition to a local dame or charity school of doubtful quality. Joseph seems to have been given a fair schooling at Milburn, including a knowledge of Latin. In his memorandum book he says that he left school at the age of 15 weighing 6 st. 8 lbs![14] He must have been a wisp of a lad; and this may perhaps account for his assertiveness in later life. After leaving school he went from midsummer 1840 to midsummer 1841 as a pupil of the Revd J.

T. Ward, vicar of Askham, and former headmaster of Lowther Grammar School. Joseph's father, probably determined from his own days of poverty not to have an idle son on his hands, quickly arranged with an old friend, Mr John Ritson, chemist, apothecary & druggist of Sunderland to take Joseph as an apprentice. This is what Joseph wrote:

> July 17th 1841. Arrived in Sunderland, at which time & place an agreement was made contrary to my wishes between my Father and Mr Ritson, Chemist & Druggist of No. 4, High Street, the conditions being; that in consideration of paying the latter £80.0.0 I should be allowed the high privilege of serving him 'by *night* & by day' for five years and a half, or, as the Indenture expresses it be taught the Arts & Mysteries of Mr R's. profession. I was an associate of the Royal Pharmaceutical Society of Great Britain from its foundation.
>
> At the expiration of the term Mr Ritson gave me unsolicited along with my Indentures and a handsome Present the following letter addressed to my Father. [This will be given later].[15]

On a personal level Brunskill's connection with the Ritson family had an almost common root in the Penrith area. The Ritson family came from Hackthorpe. Christopher Ritson of Hackthorpe (1640–1706) had six children, of whom Thomas, the fifth, was born in 1673. His son the Revd Thomas Ritson (1705–1762) was perpetual curate of Cumwhitton near Carlisle. His eldest son John Ritson (1738–1773) was educated at Carlisle Grammar School, and was schoolmaster at Aikton. His second son John Ritson (1762–1814) was a hatter and glover at Hexham, and his first wife was Ann Ramsay. His son John Ritson (1794–1857) was the chemist and druggist of Sunderland. John Ritson was also a founder member of the Pharmaceutical Society, and with other members of his family had shipping interests. John was twice married, first in 1816 to Lydia Jane Oliver, and second in 1829 to Alice Bywater. Among the children of the first marriage, Francis, and among the children of the second, William, were co-founders of the F. & W. Ritson Shipping Company of sailing ships.[16] It was at a time when many of the shopkeepers and tradesmen of the town took shares in sailing ships and, most particularly in Sunderland, in shipping coal to London.

One of the nostrums sold by Ritson the chemist was Ramsay's Spice Nuts from Penrith. George Ramsay of Market Place, Penrith was a druggist and vendor of patent medicines; his spice nuts were for stomach disorders. George was the son of 'Mr Ramsay' of Middlegate, Penrith; he was born on the 11 February 1796 on Ludgate Hill, London, and was received into Penrith Church on the 16 February 1801.[17] At the same time as Joseph was in Sunderland his father attended the weekly market on Tuesdays at Great Dockray in Penrith, selling butter and bacon. One gets the clear impression that though Cumbrian families were widely dispersed over the north, they were still a close-knit community, maintaining strong connections.

The Ritson connection was to prove lasting. In the second generation, one of John Ritson's sons, Henry, became a solicitor in Sunderland, a director of the Nautilus Shipping Company, and a firm friend to Joseph Brunskill. Henry's influence on Joseph seems to have been strong politically, confirming him in that radical Toryism which lasted all his life.

When Brunskill went to Sunderland in 1841 it was a time of the most dreadful poverty, unemployment and suffering. In 1834 the new Poor Law abolished the old 'Speenhamland' system of parish relief, which supplemented the half wages of the poor to a minimum of 3s. a week out of the rates. Every other member of the family received 1s.6d. a week at a time when the loaf cost a shilling. Thus large families received a modest relief from the poor rates. As the price of bread rose under the restrictions of the Corn Laws so the dole rose with it, all paid for out of the rates. The new Poor Law abolished this system of institutionalised pauperism, and established boards of guardians for each Union of parishes who administered the work-houses. At a stroke large families lost the basic subsistence which had kept them going. Women and children were driven into the factories where they existed. The new Poor Law did nothing to soften the blow to the poor who were driven to sweated labour, and absolute poverty. The humiliation of going to the work-house was the final blow to the poor. As long as Parliament levied duties on manufactures, and imported materials, trade collapsed, with thousands sitting in the work-houses, and millions outside starving. It was Peel's liberal Tory budget of 1842 which abolished these restrictions, which the Whigs had failed to do, and the loss to the Treasury was made good by the revival of income tax.[18]

The best illustration of the scenes of poverty which the young Brunskill saw in Sunderland comes from a speech of Henry Grey, Viscount Howick in the House of Commons on the 13 February 1843. It was a debate on the depression of the manufacturing interests of the country. He took his main facts from the town of Sunderland. In 1839 there were 80 shipbuilders in the port of Sunderland of whom 36 had failed to the total of £320,000, and five had declined business, leaving 39 out of the 80. Twenty merchants, and chain and anchor smiths had failed to the sum of £100,000. A great number of grocers, publicans and others had failed. There were in the High Street (where Ritson had his shop) 40 to 50 shops unoccupied in consequence of the previous tenants having failed. The quantity of meat sold in 1842 was half what it was in 1841. In 1837 the amount spent in poor relief was £7,035, and in 1842 £14,232. Even this large sum proved inadequate to meet the pressure of distress in the town, and the wealthy inhabitants were compelled to subscribe £2,192, and give away 800 to 1,000 tons of coal to relieve distress. The increase in distress in Sunderland had been aggravated by the (impolitic) tax on the export of coal.

Grey then described the condition of the farming districts of Northumberland, with whole families, and groups of families hardly covered by their miserable rags, suffering from cold and hunger, wandering from place to place, with hardly a hope of finding work; many of them begging their way back to the place whence they came, more broken down in health and hope, and more destitute of clothing than when they left it.[19] When, therefore, in the 1850s, the tradesmen, the butchers, innkeepers, fruiterers, drapers and printers began to take out shares in small sailing ships, William and Francis Ritson began to build up their small sailing fleet as part of the recovery of trade.[20]

In the next generation, when shipping had developed from sail to steam, the Ritson family founded, on the 21 March 1881, the Nautilus Steam Shipping Company of Sunderland;

the directors were F. & W. Ritson, and the secretary was F. W. Ritson. The first ship was delivered in 1881 of 1,700 tons, and named the Palm Branch. The company employed the suffix 'Branch' to the names of each of their ships, the Olive Branch in 1887, the Myrtle Branch in 1889, the Willow Branch in 1893, and the Cherry Branch. Latterly the company engaged in shipping nitrates mainly from South America, but owing to the depression after the 1914–1918 War, and the fall in the value of their ships, the company went bankrupt in 1931 to the tune of £439.16.6d. Due to the depression the ships were unsaleable, and the winding-up order was made in the High Court on the 13 October 1931.[21]

I have already referred to the friendship of Joseph Brunskill with Henry Ritson (the son of his master John Ritson), later to become a solicitor in Sunderland and a director of the Nautilus Company. Among the remarkable evidences inherited by Alan Webster is a large bundle of printed tracts written by Richard Oastler (1789–1861) called The Fleet Papers, issued from the 2 January 1841 to July 1843. Oastler had been imprisoned for debt in December 1840 by his former employer Thomas Thornhill of Riddlesworth in Norfolk. Oastler and his father had been stewards for Thornhill on his Yorkshire estate at Fixby, and Richard had not been able to redeem his debts as quickly as Thornhill his master would have wished. From his cell No. 12 in the Coffee Gallery in the Fleet Prison Richard issued weekly Fleet Papers addressed mainly to Thornhill and other leading politicians. He described the lot of the poor, the women and children under the factory system, and the Poor Law of 1834. His exposure from 1830 of the cruelties suffered by children in the factories, and their increased suffering following the withdrawal of relief under the 1834 Poor Law, earned for him the title 'King of the Factory Children'. Oastler was a liberal Tory in the same vein as Lord Howick, in contrast to the Whigs, who had failed to pass the Factory Bill which aimed to relieve the condition of women and children in conditions of sweated labour in the factories. The Poor Law of 1834 had forced women and children into conditions of slavery which Oastler exposed, and earned for him the undying gratitude of the poor. He also took up the cause of the Chartists.

In the Fleet Paper of 18 February 1843 Oastler took up the case of Thomas Dixon of Calthwaite, Cumberland, recently imprisoned in Carlisle Castle for debt. In an open letter to Sir James Graham of Netherby, then Home Secretary, Oastler repeated a report in The Carlisle Patriot that on one day Dixon (with the permission of the gaoler) had lunch brought to him from the nearby Bush Inn to share with a visiting friend. The tray was seen by a visiting magistrate, who ordered the gaoler to stop the practice. The magistrate (a Mr Johnson) on another occasion heard another prisoner playing the flute, and ordered it to be stopped. On another day Mr Johnson entered a prisoner's cell without knocking, when the prisoner's wife was visiting her husband. Johnson requested that the Inspector of Prisoners should be sent down to examine the irregularities 'impartially'. Johnson was a small-minded tale-bearer, and his request was rightly refused by Sir James, who replied that the visiting magistrates were competent to deal with irregularities. These were the vindictive cruelties inflicted by small men of authority on the poor, which men like Charles Dickens and Oastler exposed so effectively. Oastler was often visited by poor men from the north who had tramped unsuccessfully to London seeking work, who would not return without visiting their champion in his cell. After Oastler had spent four years in the Fleet the working men of the north raised £2,500, and he was released in February 1844. Henry Ritson's bundle of Fleet Papers was handed to his friend Brunskill, and in turn to his daughter Lydia, and then to her son Alan Webster. The Papers had a lasting effect on Brunskill.[22]

The other influence on Brunskill was the church. He was addicted to church papers from his apprentice days. Among the Webster papers is this receipt:

Received from Mr J. Brunskill, London Jan. 23. 1846
One pound five shilling ... for subscription to the English Churchman, viz. No. 157 to No. 208. Midsummer 1846.
£1.5.0. For the Proprietor: S. Smith.

Joseph was then aged 20, and he remained an avid reader of that paper and the church *Guardian* paper till his death in 1903. The rector of Sunderland at that time was William Webb MA, on a stipend of £264; he was also perpetual curate of St John's, Sunderland on £122. He had one curate Joseph Law, and these two men served a population of 17,060.[23] With a large proportion of the population in destitution, and country people coming to the town seeking work the church was incapable of meeting their needs. In addition, education was grossly inadequate, depending on old endowed schools, and a small number of 'dame' schools of inferior quality.

On Brunskill preparing to leave Sunderland in January 1847, his master handed him this letter for his father:

Sunderland, Jany. 16. 1847
My dear Sir,

Your Son's Apprenticeship with me will expire tomorrow, and it seems he intends to return to you on Monday. And I think I should be short in my duty to him and to you, did I neglect to say something to you as to the opinion I have formed of him during the time he has been a Member of my family.

To say he is without faults would be wrong; he has faults, and I have never failed to point them out to him, I hope generally with kindness and temper; but I fear I may some times have got out of temper with him, but you know this is a fault we all fail in.

So far as his years and experience have extended I consider he has made fair progress in his profession, and as such, I can with confidence recommend him to any situation, which I am ready to do at any time. His honesty of conduct and integrity of principle I have never in any case had occasion to question, and from the day of his coming under my roof, to this moment, I have never had to charge him with any deviation from the rule of my household, and I unhesitatingly say, after thirty years' experience of young men, I have never had charge of a better, or one that myself & family part with, with greater regret. You will find, too, he remains what you wish all your family to be, a sound Churchman, and a good Concervative [sic], quite a chip off the Old Block. And I have told Joseph, what I repeat to you, when I can at any time render him service or assistance, he can command me, and when it suits his pleasure, convenience or pleasure, to visit this place or part of the Country, he will always find a knife and fork at my table. I have no doubt Joseph will prove a comfort to you.

And I feel confident that he will do credit to my training, and I shall be glad indeed if I have the good fortune to have a similar young man as his successor.

My wife joins me in kind regards, and every good wish to you & yours, and

> I remain,
> Mr Dear Sir
> Yours truly,

> JOHN RITSON[24]

From January 1847 until July 1848 Brunskill was a frequent visitor to Mr Ward at Askham Vicarage, but there is no indication that he went to him for tuition.

By now it was clear that Brunskill intended to study for the church, and, from the autumn of 1847 he went to the Revd J. B. Whitwick, perpetual curate of Newton, for instruction in the Gospels of St Mark and St John in Greek, and also the work of Hugo Grotius, *de Veritate Religionis Christianae* in Latin. Grotius (1583–1645) was an influential Dutch jurist and theologian who adopted the liberal Protestant teaching of Jacob Arminius (1560–1609) as distinct from the exclusive Calvinist doctrines of election and predestination. The Arminians insisted that the Divine sovereignty was compatible with a real free-will in man, that Jesus died for all men, and not only for the elect. Grotius' book *de Veritate* was designed to uphold the evidences of natural theology, and to establish the superiority of the Christian faith to all other creeds. He taught that the essential of the Gospels is a perfect trust in the Providence of God, and the ordering of human life according to the principles given by Christ. In 17th century England the term 'Arminian' became a term of abuse against all who resisted the rigid claims of the Calvinists. It is interesting that Grotius was still being used as a basis for theological training when Brunskill went to St Bees in 1848.

After working under Whitwick for nine months he was examined by the Revd J. P. Nicholson curate of Dacre, both in the Gospels and in Grotius in Latin. On giving Brunskill a testimonial for St Bees Clerical College, Nicholson said:

I have recently examined him in the Greek Gospels and Grotius de Veritate, & am of the opinion that his attainments will enable him to fulfil the requisition of your circular.[25]

Armed with three testimonials from Revds Ward, Whitwick and Nicholson Brunskill applied to enter St Bees, and was accepted. His Memorandum book contains these entries:

Augt. 29th 1848. Admitted a student of St Bees.
Decr. abt. 5th. Exd. & placed 10th on the 'Boards' out of 2 [page torn].
May 3rd 1849, Do.
Decr. 4th 1849. Passed!!
Jan. 1st. 1850. Made my *first speech* at a Ragged or Refuge school festival in Whitehaven.[26]

There is some evidence that Brunskill considered applying to the S.P.G.* for employment as a missionary; for he copied out the terms of application and appointment given at a meeting of the Society at Hastings on October 3 1848. A footnote to the report said that the bishop of Madras had said that 'there are 120,000,000 of Idolators or Atheists in India.' Not very complimentary to the old religions![27]

* Society for the Propagation of the Gospel.

NOTES TO CHAPTER ONE

1. *History of Cumberland & Westmorland.* J. Nicolson & R. Burn, 1777. Vol. II p. 443.
   Hist. Gazetteer & Directory of Cumberland. Mannix & Whellan 1847. p. 275.

2. Neither the Mormon Digest of parish Registers (I.G.I.) for Cumberland & Westmorland, nor the parish registers of Kirkland, Milburn nor Brough under Stainmore give Joseph Brunskill's birth in 1755. A John Brunskill was churchwarden of Kirkland in 1625. See *The Ejected of 1662 in Cumberland & Westmorland.* B. Nightingale, Manchester 1911, Vol. I. p. 39.

3. L.M. A leaf torn from a book bears the first 5 of these children of Joseph & Isabella Brunskill; the latter 3 were found in I.G.I.

4. C. & W. Parish Register of Warcop, by Dr John Abercrombie, 1914. p. 127.

5. W.M. MS family tree. The first child John Pearson appears to have been born one month after the wedding!

6. L.M. Letter of 19 Nov. 1814 of Revd John Pearson at Middlegate, Penrith to his 'cousin' announcing the death that day at Penrith of 'your sister' Eliz. Smith. (? Elizabeth Monkhouse who was born 1764.) The back of the letter has the details of Eliz. Smith's estate at Upper Hartsop & Patterdale, taken from the Lowther estate book of 1764 by Geo. Wheatley. The then tenants were W & E Smith.

7. The Queen's College, Oxford. Dr J.R. Magrath, 1921, II, 317, Thomas Monkhouse, 145 Isaac, 319 John, 167 William, 324 John.

8. *Hist. Directory & Gazetteer of Cumberland*. Mannix & Whellan, op. cit. p. 287.

9. L.M. & C.R.O. Kendal. Will of Jane Monkhouse of Newton, 10 Oct. 1859. She died 20 Jan. 1862 aged 83.

10. W.M. MS. Monkhouse, Pearson, Brunskill family trees.
W.M. Typescript Biog. of the Studious Clergyman, the Revd John Pearson.

11. I.G.I. Cumberland. The marr. of John Brunskill to Hannah Leach of Cumwhitton, 28 Mar. 1836. Also the bapt. 31 July 1837 of Hannah the d.o. John & Hannah Brunskill of Newton. According to John Langhorne the dau. Hannah died at Bankfoot 21 Jan. 1877.

12. I.G.I. Parish reg. of Newton Reigny.

13. *Directory of Westmorland*, Parson & White, 1829 under Milburn.
C.R.O Carlisle, Admissions Register of St Bees Clerical College, 1848.

14. W.M. Leaves from a Memorandum book of Joseph Brunskill 1841, p. 24.

15. W.M. Do. pp.24–25.
L.M. Articles of Apprenticeship of Joseph Brunskill to Mr John Ritson of Sunderland, 17 Feb. 1842, but dating from 17 July 1841. Now in C.R.O. Kendal.

16. Information of Mr John Ritson, of 1, North View, Barnard Castle, Co. Durham.

17. C. & W. Parish Registers of Penrith, 1770–1812 by Col. F. Haswell, 1942.
Hist. Direct. & Gazetteer of Cumberland, Mannix & Whellan op. cit. pp. 298, 300.

18. *British History in the 18th C. & after (1782–1919)* G.M. Trevelyan, 1941 ed. pp. 266/7.

19. The speech of the Right Hon. (Henry Grey) Viscount Howick in the House of Commons, 13 Feb. 1843 on moving for a Committee of the Whole House ... to consider the depression of the manufacturing interests of the country. (C.U.L. Lib. LO.28.5^a.) pp 6 & 11.

20. Report in the *Sunderland Echo* by 'Blue Peter' 1981, by courtesy of Mr John Ritson of Barnard Castle.

21. Information from Miss J. M. Wraight, Principal Reference Librarian, Guildhall Library, London. 24 May 1989.
Information by courtesy of Mr John Ritson of Barnard Castle.
W.M. Press cutting of *The Times* 13 Nov. 1931.
Report from the *Sunderland Echo*, ref. 20 above.

22. W.M. The Fleet Papers of Richard Oastler (1841–43). The set incomplete.
    D.N.B. Richard Oastler, 1789–1866.
    The Fleet Papers have recently been republished.

23. The Clergy List 1842.

24. W.M. Leaves from a Memorandum book of Joseph Brunskill pp. 27–32.

25. W.M. Do. pp. 36–37.
    Dict. of Christian Church, F.L. Cross 1957, Grotius and Arminianism.

26. W.M. Do. p. 38.

27. W.M. Do. pp. 42–43.

2

St Bees College
1848–1850

THE ST BEES Clerical College, which Brunskill entered in the Michaelmas term 1848 had operated under difficult conditions. The perpetual curate of the parish was also head of the training college, and his curates were the lecturers. There was a gradual growth in the number of students from 20 in 1817 to over 40 in the 1860s. In the early years Dr William Ainger of St John's College, Cambridge worked alone. In 1826 he was joined by Richard Parkinson of St John's, and in 1827 by John Howard Marsden of St John's. The general tenor of churchmanship during Ainger's reign from 1816 to 1840 was conservative High Church. His successor R. P. Buddicom (1840–1846) was an evangelical of the Clapham sect. His mentor was Isaac Milner dean of Queens', Cambridge. He was followed from 1846 to 1858 by Richard Parkinson, a moderate High Churchman, and canon of Manchester. He had been a lecturer at St Bees until his appointment to Manchester in 1833. He continued to hold his canonry, and was criticised for living at Manchester for his times of residence, while at the same time being perpetual curate and principal at St Bees.

Apart from the lectures which were given in the restored chancel of the parish church, the students lived in lodgings in the parish. Among the 17 students admitted at Michaelmas 1848, Brunskill was placed fourth in the third class (out of 4 classes) at the end of term examinations.[1] He seems to have been a hard-working plodder, acquiring a sound knowledge in divinity and church history, which he expanded as the years went by. One set of his lecture notes survived until about 30 years ago, and have vanished. Only three lectures in church history, given by Mr Middleton, have survived from the autumn of 1849. Brunskill usually wrote them out verbatim. Nothing more is known of his studies, except that he was thoroughly grounded in the Prayer Book view of church history, patristics, and the Scriptures. At his final examination on the 5 of May

15

1850 he passed twelfth out of seventeen. Not brilliant, but passable![2]

In the previous April he inserted the following advertisement in his favourite *English Churchman* for the Trinity Ordination:

> A curacy with title is required by a student of St Bees College. It has always been the earnest endeavour of the advertiser to form his views in literal accordance with the formularies of the Church. In questions of polity he agrees in the main with the *E. Churchman* and *Guardian* newspapers. For references etc. address: George Herbert, P.O. Whitehaven.[3]

He received several offers, and accepted that of Ocker Hill near Tipton in Staffordshire. The whole parish of Tipton had a population of 18,891, and Ocker Hill was a daughter parish. Its vicar was The Revd L. W. Stanton, BA on a stipend of £150.[4] The church was moderate High Church, with the choir in surplices, much to the disgust of the dissenters, and Matins and Evensong being intoned. It was a mining area, tough and working class. Dissenting chapels flourished, and the church had to work hard to establish itself. In those days the Church of England was trying to drag itself from the sloth and squalor into which it had sunk, and come to terms with the needs of the poor in the new industrial areas, as well as the old. In later years Brunskill called it 'The Black Country'. His diary for 1850 has just been uncovered, and this section has been revised to accommodate it. One or two points will be added to fill it in.

It opens with his ordination as deacon in Lichfield Cathedral on the 26 May 1850. He seemed to delight in religious controversy against Papists and Dissenters, and determined to argue his corner as a churchman. His account of the troubles of Mrs Corbett, a widow who had been deprived of the provisions of her husband's Will, and the fate of her son are very moving. He paints the effect of ranting preaching on unstable minds. He makes the acquaintance of a contemporary from St Bees, John Nicklin, who was curate of Coseley, north of Tipton. Nicklin was married, and seemed to 'suffer' under his 'no-Popery' vicar. He was constantly coming over to Brunskill for comfort. In October 1851 he resigned, being unable to stand his vicar any longer. He got a curacy at Oswaldtwistle in 1851, and in 1853 another at Tarleton, near Ormskirk.[5] He was one of a number of underpaid, non-graduate, and poor curates who were at the very bottom of the ladder, and treated like dirt by their vicars, or their vicars' wives.

In November 1850 Brunskill first refers to the great stir in England when Pope Pius IX (Pio Nono) parcelled out England into Catholic Dioceses. There was an immense uproar, led by Lord John Russell; and the church papers are full of little pamphlets written by angry clergymen against Papal Invasion. Brunskill's vicar joined in the hue and cry, and Brunskill was ordered to scrap a sermon he was composing, and join in the attack.

In his early months Brunskill worked hard, constantly visiting, and countering dissenters on his way. He was fertile in suggesting several parish clubs to increase the facilities of the church; he worked hard at his reading to compose thoughtful sermons. He visited the church school, and taught in the Sunday school. His interest in teaching seems to stem from these days. The number of church services was increased, and supported. Those who have worked with a choir will appreciate his comment on the last Sunday of 1850:

'Sunday. 2 Services but did not preach, some unpleasantness with 2 or 3 of the choir'!

DIARY

May 21 1850

Left home for Lichfield; and remained till ...

22. at Hill Top &c, and proceeded in the evening to Lichfield.

23. Bishop's examination commenced.

26. Trinity Sunday, Ordained deacon.

27. Entered upon my duties at Ocker Hill.

28. Heard Dr Hooly preach.

June

4. Attended Ruridecanal meeting.

19. My brother came to stay with me. [John Pearson Brunskill nicknamed 'Pearshaw'.]

August

14. Commenced a regular visitation of the whole parish.

19. My brother left me. Attended a school festival at Hill Top.

20. Signed 'The declaration touching the Royal Supremacy'.

27. Present at an evening party at Mr Stanton's.

30. Mr Rosenthal & I called on Mr Owen at Bilston; returned and found Mr P. Crosthwaite waiting for me.

September

3. Attended a Ruridecanal meeting; subject 'Visitation of the Sick'.

4. In visiting a family of dissenters, am told that in order to be saved a man must have a firm persuasion that he will be so, & yt without this none either was or can be saved. The parties declared that a knowledge of their state was a peculiar privilege only granted to Methodists; & that this belief was very common among them. In the evening called on Mr Cole.

5. While visiting a sick person infected with the above doctrine, a man came in (evidently on purpose) & commenced to discuss the point; but when I requested Scripture proof, it was not forthcoming, &, instead of it I received a volley of low fanatical abuse. The poor creature called me an imposter, false prophet &c. &c. & scarcely uttered a sentence without insinuating I was dishonest, a liar &c. He laid great stress on I John III, but as one of St John's rules for a man being heard, is that he must be possessed of love & charity I remain unconvinced. I have hitherto found the dissenters very courteous & civil, & this is about the first specimen of blackguardism I have experienced; however as

18

it does not affect me in the least, I shall not hesitate to denounce the delusion wherever I find it.

8. **Sunday.** Preached at O.H. in the morning, & dined with Mr Stanton. Mr Davis with me in the evening.

9. Had the service at the funeral of a poor man who had been killed in a pit. There were 3 fatal accidents of this kind in the parish in one week; & a boy drowned in a canal the next.

15. **Sunday.** Had the service in the morning, & preached in the evening. Dined with Dr Underhill but returned to S. School in afternoon.

17. Wrote to Mr Davis respecting house &c.

18. On calling at house No. 211, I found the inmate Elizabeth Corbett to be a poor widow who had been waiting 15 years for a friend to whom she might tell her troubles and from whom she might seek advice. As I spent some time here, & the case is rather remarkable I will devote a few minutes more to record the facts.

E. Corbett had married in … a labourer who represented himself as a single man from somewhere in Shropshire. He was in the habit of leaving her for considerable intervals whenever he got a little money together. This continued for some time till it came out that he had a former wife living to whom he had been married at Shrewsbury 1809. Mrs Corbett saw the first wife & obtained a certificate of the marriage, which I suppose made the second marriage null & void. She was assisted in these enquiries (being herself very poor) by a person named Corbett who was possessed of some property. This person was a few months after publicly married to her & lived with her till his death. The man she had formerly supposed to be her husband was prosecuted & only escaped transportation by their being told that the expense must be borne by Mr Corbett. It is now abt. 15 years since Mr Corbett died, but 4 hours before his death he told his wife in the presence of Dr Scholfield that he had left her sufficient to keep her above want, describing the 2 houses mentioned in his will. This will, a copy of which I have just seen distinctly bequeaths to her these 2 houses, for the term of her nat. life or till she marry again or cohabits &c. or in case she should not have been married to any former husband.

Now in consequence of this last sentence the executors of her husband have never paid her a farthing; & during this long time she has frequently 'even wanted bread'. This conduct of the executors I consider illegal & at all events contrary to reason & com. sense. For Mr Corbett knew perfectly well she had lived with the man, & he could not have considered him to be 'a husband'. Morever if this former match was no bar to her marrying again how is it a bar to prevent her inheriting property? However I have written to Dudley to one of the executors to know why the will has never been proved, and purpose by God's help to know something more about this affair. The rent of the 2 houses is 5/- per week.

Altho' I have written so much, the distressing part is yet to come. For several years this poor woman's chief support has been a son in law who was very kind to her. However, when the cholera was in the neighbourhood, some fanatics held what were called special prayer meetings, & to one of these it appears the poor man went; having been previously denounced as 'abt. to fall into the *jaws of hell*'.

When in 'The Meeting' 2 of these creatures laid their hands upon him & told to go into the vestry & be converted or he was sure to go to Hell! I do not understand that he did this, but his mother says he came home in a dreadfully excited state, being quite unable to do any work. In a few days several of the leaders called & again denounced him in most dreadful language. Unable to endure himself any longer he went to Great Bridge to try to see 'The Preacher'. He did see him but it was only making a hasty retreat over the back premises. Thus disappointed the poor man prayed earnestly on his way home that he might be permitted to see our Saviour on the cross; & he says on looking up he thought he did see him suspended in the air about 10 yards above him, & afterwards close to him. This afforded his fevered brain a glimmer of comfort. But of course he could not remain in this dreadful state long without some change, & as might be expected reason left her seat & he has ever since been a moping idiot!

His poor mother being thus deprived of the staff of her declining years was obliged to apply to the parish. Some of these gentlemen, who represent the 3 Kings of Somerset House (for whom my detestation is every day becoming greater) have as a means of removing him from one parish to another, sent him to a mad-house at Leamington, where he has now been months at an expense of 11/- per week. His mother would gladly have kept him at home had she been able, & having found from her visits to him, that he is being very ill used by his fellows, & also that he suffers from *dirt & hunger*, she starts tomorrow morning on a second pilgrimage to endeavour to effect his liberation.

Oh! the oppression of this hateful new poor law. From my daily experience I am becoming more & more convinced that all the faults of the old one are but perpetuated & exaggerated in the new. And what is to be said of a system of religion producing such fruit as this. The fanatic mentioned in a prev. note was one of those who assisted to drive this man mad. I am given to understand that there are several such cases in this parish, & that the people driven mad by the 'Methodists' cost the parish many hundreds per annum.

19. Received a cheque for my first quarter's stipend. £12.10. which is in a sense 'the first tin I ever earned'. Today was the first time I noticed the leaves to be falling.

21. Festival of St Matthew. Service in the evening.

22. **Sunday.** Preached in the morning. Took the service in the evening, when there was a very large congregation.

23. The day being very fine I have been to Birmingham pr. rail. Wasted 25/- & incurred abt. £3.0.0 more.

24. Mr Nicklin, having arrived at Cosely, called for the first time.

26. Called on Mr N. at Cosely, & returned in time for a lecture on galvanism &c in the school. Afterwards saw Mr Caddick respecting Mr Davis's house.

27. Having advised with Mr Jevon & Mr Stanton I took the house, land &c. fr. Mr D. at £25 pr.an. Mr Jevon having promised to continue tenant of the stables & land at £6.0.0 The E.C. did not arrive today. Mr Nicklin called without seeing me.

28. Spent the evening at Mr Stanton's with Mr Drake one of the secretaries of the Coventry Church Union, consequently Lord Fielding the recent pervert to Romanism was one of our topics.

29. **Sunday** – 'Our Charity', i.e. 3 Services & collections at Church for the Schools. From my experience of this, I trust it is the last 'charity' we shall have for some time. My feelings towards the evening preacher, were either those of disgust or pity.

30. Commenced my sermon, but interrupted by Mr Stanton with whom I had the longest & best conversation I have had yet. In the evening went to tea with Mr N. & hence to Mr Richardson's Philosophical lectures on electricity &c. very good. The night so stormy as to compel me to remain at Cosely all night. Spent the evening very profitably with Mr Richardson.

N. Mr Nicklin returned with me to breakfast & we afterwards walked to Bilston together. In the evening attended Mr R's second lecture, & returned at abt. 10pm.

October

2. Had a long conversation with Mr S. again. Performed the service at the burial of a child fr. T.E. Called on Mrs Corbett respecting whose case I had a week ago seen the Messrs Hunt & Thirsfield, attorneys in Wednesbury. Mr

Wm. Deacon called & invited me to go over in the evening. After visiting about 15 houses of several sects, I went & spent a pleasant evening, except that my controversial habits caused me to be too hard upon a young lady during the supper. But what is to be expected considering the atmosphere in which I am forced to live. The party grossly misrepresented my statements, & in showing her unfairness I forgot that I was *not* surrounded by a group of Ranters or Socinians as usual.

4. Mr Nicklin came to breakfast after which we went to Birmingham. The day was fine & after getting well loaded with old books &c. we returned to tea. Rec'd a letter fr. my sister I(sabella).

5. A private baptism &c. In the afternoon on going for a walk called on my friends Messrs Jones & Hutton, & shortly after Mr White, Incumbent of Darlaston came in. After declaring that he never interfered with any one, he passed to denouncing all *Christian* Churches &c., tombstones as 'Popish', and that the Church of Ocker Hill was kept dark in order to conceal the superstitious practices that were used &c!! When he said Romanism was increasing I ventured to agree with Mr Hutton yt. the Church was increasing fast. This exposed me to a shower of captious questions as to what I did or did not say &c.. Declaring that he only either misunderstood or misrepresented me I turned fr. him. This however wd. not do & after a short tho' most unpleasant & annoying conversation, the only ans. I cd. get to the? What am I to say to those who tell me 'it makes no difference where they go'? was 'teach them the truth'! This I believe was but on my complaining of the prevalent indifferentism being good ground for the papists, which lax notions I attributed to the cant of every man's having a right to put his own interpretation upon the S.S. [? Sacred Scriptures.] This being a doctrine I heard preached by a popular Evan. [?evangelist] on Sunday last. Oh! this horrid religious strife. This was what I vainly hoped wd. have been a pleasant ½ hour consumed in *bitter* wrangling.

6. **Sunday.** Preached in the morning, a funeral in the afternoon, & service at night.

7. Mr Nicklin dined with me, & I afterwards returned with him to Mr R's. lectures at Cosely.

8. Mr Rosenthal called. A funeral at 5: the Choir.

9. Went to the Work house respecting the liberation of Mrs Corbett's son-in-law Price. Spent the afternoon visiting in the neighbourhood of Lea brook without finding a single churchman. There were Welsh Anabaptists, Independants, Ranters & Methodists of all shades. I was frequently told that it made no difference where people went &c. 'That there was Church & chapel & people might follow their own opinion'. All profess to 'like the Church', & in fact there is not 1 in 100 that raises any objection, yet from this old heathenish indifference to truth I can make very little progress.

10. Wrote a long letter to my sister Is. Called at the school where there was confusion worse confounded. Mr Stanton called in the evening & remained some time. Finished my sermon.

11. Rec'd a letter fr. J. Nicholson announcing his intention of entering St Bees &c. Replied to him giving him the desired information, & recommending Durham. Wrote to Mr Davis requesting him to look out for a second hand copy of the Evening Mail for Mr S. & I. – In the evening went down to Dr Underhill's where I met Mr & Mrs Parker & c. & remained till late.

12. Letters fro, Father & Isabella, of a somewhat brighter character than recent ones.

13. **Sunday.** Rode to 'Gaits Hill' & took Mr Nute's duty, 2 full services and a funeral. Returned in time for the night service at Ocker Hill; very tired but afterwards called on Mr Lloyd.

14. Mr Davis arrived & remained all night. Wrote to Father.

15. Out with Mr Richardson to make arrangements for a course of lectures. A private baptism Wm. Holmes. Mr Nicklin, Mr Davis & I went in the evening to a 'Bilston Lecture' & were highly gratified.

16. Rec'd a letter from Miss Rooser [?] & wrote to Isabella.

17. Do. fr. J. Nicholson, who appears to prefer St Bees. [Note: Nicholson did to to St Bees, and became p.c. of Byrness, Co. Durham, 1860 at £75 p.a.].

18. Saw Messrs Hunt & Thirsfield respecting Mrs Corbett; the difficulty now is to get hold of the original will.

19. With Mr S. at the schools, in the evening at Dr Underhill's.

20. **Sunday.** Preached in the morning. Service in evening.

21. Went over to Cosely in the afternoon to comfort & encourage Mr N. In the evening to Mr Rich's lecture. Wrote to I.N. & P.

22. Reading hard all day for my sermon.

23. After reading Greswell, Butler, Stanhope, Porteous &c. commenced writing a sermon on the doctrine of 'The forgiveness of injuries' Matt. XVIII. Spent 4 or 5 hours in the evening discussing parochial affairs; such as the immediate commencement of a Church Club, Evening School, Library, & Choral Society. Also for several additional services to be commenced in Advent next. A private baptism & funeral in the afternoon.

24. In the evening with Dr Underhill to Mr Rich's lecture.

27. **Sunday.** Preached in the morning, a funeral in the afternoon, & took the prayers at night.

28. *Removed* to my *new rooms* with Mr Davis. Service in the evening, it being St Simon & St Jude.

29. My throat very sore, but went in the evening to a 'Bilston Lecture' on the escape of King Charles II, very interesting & returned with Mr N. & Miss Deacon.

30. A funeral in the afternoon. Evening met Dr Hen. & Mrs Parker to tea at Mr Solly's, who afterwards drove us to Wednesbury to Mr Ric's. lecture there.

31. Saw Mr Stanton in the morning. A Romanist funeral in the evening, & noticed that the child's coffin had a beautiful gilt cross on it.

November

1. Still rather poorly, but after reading the *E[nglish] C[hurchman]* which was full of the Papal invasion I went into Birmingham, & returned in the evening to service. Found Mr Nicklin waiting for me, but could not have much time with him. After Service a first & preliminary meeting was held in the School to take into consideration the establishment of a Church Guild. The meeting was adjourned until Monday.

2. A letter from the Librarian at St Bees soliciting subscriptions towards a testimonial to Messers Middleton & Woodhouse. At present do not feel inclined to answer it, but if I do it will be to recommend that it should be confined to their *dissenting* friends who so *exclusively* enjoyed their *patronage*. To have spent your previous life in the propagation of heresy & schism, & to be a cringing obsequious hypocrite, was the only recognised title to the favour of these luminaries. Nevertheless Mr M. is a decent old man pretty orthodox, & a good politician. Woodhouse, poor fellow was very zealous, and his Theology was so dense, & his weakness in being pulled by any sneak so transparent, that I can most easily characterise him by what he was generally known viz. 'a humbug'. Sent for in the evening to baptise the child of a man, prev. believed to be an infidel.

3. **Sunday.** Preached in the morning, Holy Com[munion]. Said prayers in the evening, during which service I stood sponsor for the first time to 2 candidates for glory. Mr Stanton's little boy was named 'Cyprian', Mr Davis' 'Elfric Brunskill'. I hope this new relation may prove (as Mr S.

expressed it) a bond of union between us, after the parting from Ocker Hill.

4. At the school in the morning. Commenced my sermon which I purpose shall be a kind of supplement to Mr S's powerful sermon after the above baptisms. Spent a very satisfactory afternoon in visiting, having received about a dozen promises of children for the school, besides several for the choral society & evening school. In the evening a long meeting of the 'Church Guild' when a committee was appointed. Returned with Dr U. & stayed supper, & met 2 of his sisters for the first time. Remained late endeavouring (& not I believe without success) to impress the Dr with a sense of the Church's wrongs, and also Mrs U. of the truth of Mr S's. late sermon, of which the Dr heartily approved, for he is much better up in his Theology than the average of laymen.

5. Afternoon visiting, evening school, & wrote a letter to Isa.

6. In the morning continued my sermon, but afterwards saw Mr Stanton who wished me again to take the morning Sermon, as he wished in the evening to preach on the late Papal Bull. He thought considering the noise our neighbours at Tipton are making it wd. be as well if I also touched the subject. [Note: Pope Pius IX by his Letters Apostolic 29 Sept. 1850 established the R.C. Church in England & Wales with one archbishop and twelve suffragans, all with territorial titles. The wording of the Brief referred to the Church of England as 'the Anglican Schism'. A furious storm was provoked, led by Lord John Russell, which culminated in the Ecclesiastical Titles Act 1851.]

7. Commenced another Sermon, having for its object to show that the recent act of the Pope in parcelling out this country into new Dioceses is a schismatical act without precedent. A letter from Is. to which I replied.

8. & also wrote to Pearson. Finished my Sermon, having drawn my arguments from Wordsworth's Philosophicus Anglicanus.

9. Mr Davis & I walked over to Cosely, but did not see Mr Nicklin.

10. Preached in the morning, but made so much noise that Mr D. could not hear me! Now that I know of this fault I will endeavour to remedy it. The S. School was very much more orderly, but Mr Woolridge after manifesting a bad spirit of opposition resigned the Superintendancy, on the ground of interference from Mr Davis. May his resignation be accepted. Mr S. preached an hour in the even. but was rather flat.

11. Sermon, visiting, & meeting of C. Guild.

12. A great Meeting of the Clergy of this Archdeaconry, but unable to attend. Regret this much because I have since learned that an attack was made upon Mr Gresley by the Puritans, which however only served to display their weakness, for without me Mr Gresley was most enthusiastically received.

13. At the school in the morning. Finished my sermon. Met Mr Richardson at Dr Underhill's to dinner, afterwards to lecture.

14. *The Guardian* [note: the church paper] of today full of the quarrel between Pope Lord John Russell, & Pope Pius IX whether shall give bishops to the English Church. The Presbyterian Pope has published a hypocritical letter, in which he advocates an exterminating policy against us poor Churchmen. After the great meeting at St Martin's Hall our cause was somewhat popular, since which however the a/cs have been darker & darker. 'Well, come weal, come woe, we'll gather & go, & do or die for freedom'.

15. From the *English Churchman* of today I learn that Wiseman is busy preparing to prove his & the Pope's assertion, that the English Government were favourable to the scheme. Above all reptiles that crawl I detest a man so unscrupulously mean & unprincipled as Lord J. Russell & therefore trust that before this agitation ceases he may get

his deserts. After giving all the encouragement in his power to the Romish sect, who but he would have endeavoured to throw the blame upon, & raise the popular odium against a few defenceless Clergymen whose only crime is an honest adherence to the Prayer Book.

17. **Sunday.** Service in the morning. Funeral in the afternoon & preached at night. Pleased by the receipt of a letter from *Simey* at Durham, who is anxious to renew the correspondence. Grieved by an unkind letter from Father, who amongst other disagreeables declared our principles to be at a discount there, i.e. the would be 'Village politician' of Newton Mr Isaac Carr, reads *The Times*, & not being able to resist its sophistry & inconsistency, believes its statements on *the* subject of the day. & forthwith finds no difficulty in laughing 'The Priest' & Father out of their principles. This however is no more than I expected, nor do I think it a fair criterion of the state of affairs generally.

18. Commenced my Sermon. Called on Mr Blakemore. Evening school & a long meeting of the 'Church Guild', some better prospect having modified the declarations.

19. Called upon Mr Stanton & Mr Sokket [?]. Working at my sermon all the evening.

21. At Birmingham with Mr Nicklin. Called at 'the George' 5 minutes after Mr Garner's departure. From the *Guardian* of today I gather no encouragement, but rather the reverse in consequence of the unfortunate turn the Anti-popery agitation has taken. Discussed the above subject & stayed supper with the Deacon's.

22. A letter fr. Lord. The E.C. somewhat encouraging especially the fact of Mr Baylee's having Lord Fielding in hand. Choir practice at night.

23. Out with Mr Stanton making arrangements & subscriptions for the clothing club. A tough discussion at Mr Hickman's on our grievances. Finished the night at Dr Underhill's with a large party & a *warm* debate of abt. 3

hours. With the exception of *W.U.* who behaved like a *Protestant*, the state of feeling in the company gave me great encouragement. Noticed Dr. T.U. using arguments which *I* had a few weeks before drilled into him.

24. Sunday. Very stormy. Preached in the morning. The rain having penetrated the school we had no S.S. in the afternoon.

25. Looking up subscriptions to the Sunday School clothing club. In the evening a meeting of the teachers, when Mr Davis was appointed Superintendent.

26. Visiting, & at the Bilston Lecture.

27. A letter fr. my dear friend Steabler, informing me that he was ordained last Trinity, & is now Curate & Military Chaplain, at Bloem Fontein, the most northern town of Natal. Visiting in the afternoon. Mr S. took tea with me, after which I spent the evening in replying to the above letter. It has filled my mind with many thoughts of auld lang syne, & of the mysterious future. It is not yet 4 years since we parted but 'when shall we 3 meet again'.

[Note: William Anderson Steabler was ordained deacon in 1850 at Capetown, and priest at Graham's Town in 1855. From 1850 to 52 he was curate and acting chaplain to the forces in Bloemfontein. On his being made priest in 1855 he became rector of St James Graaf Reinet, in the Graham's Town diocese. His name recurs in Brunskill's diary of November 1854. As this friendship went back to 1847, before Brunskill went to St Bees, it is possible that the acquaintance derived from Sunderland where there was a family of *Stabler*, photographers, who photographed some members of the Ritson family.]

28. Busy with my sermon.

29. Still some encouragement fr. the *E*[*nglish*] *C*[*hurchman*].

30. Feast of St Andrew. Service in the evening.

December

1. **Advent Sunday.** Service in the morning *& afternoon*, & preached at night.

2. Walked over to Cosely for dinner, but returned before dark, & got a good amount of work done previous to attending a meeting for the admission of members into the Ocker Hill Church Guild. I paid my 10/- & became a Vice-President. We made a good start with 30.

3. Finished my letter to Steabler, & to Bilston.

4. Service with Sermon this evening, being the commencement of a regular weekly service. Mr S. afterwards delivered the first lesson to the Choral Society. There was a good attendance, but this is only a preliminary to a regular society, with a professional teacher.

5. *The Guardian* as *gloomy* as ever; but at least 2 or 3 have ventured to speak out, amid the general din. Visiting & evening school.

6. Startled by intelligence in the E.C. of Lord Ashley being at the head of a movement for assimilating the Prayer Book to dissent. At first, owing to the present state of opinions, this was rather alarming, but upon the whole there was so much *practical* information in the E.C. that it somewhat cheered me. Took tea with Mr Stanton & returned with him 'to practice'.

8. **Sunday.** Preached in the Morning. Funeral. The S. School in much better order.

10. Attended a meeting of this Rural Deanery at Handsworth, which was to have been better than its predecessors, Mr Stanton having to prepare a paper on the subject of the day, *viz.* 'How can we best deal with dissenters'. The paper however was not attended to, each member delivering himself of any am[oun]t of twaddle & stale truisms he chose, so that after a long meeting I found my stock of knowledge increased by nil. These chapters must fail in their object, if not better managed.

Spent the evening with Mr Solly senr, & on leaving his door, owing to the darkness & fog, I ran my head against some hard substance with considerable damage to my left eye! However by the aid of hot water I managed to keep it open until the next night when I had to preach.

14. Letters fr. Hayton & my sister I. replied to both & also wrote to Father.

15. **Sunday.** Preached in the morning. A very wet day, but this was counterbalanced by the great satisfaction I felt after my work at the S. School, where I had a splendid class.

18. Thornton called with the latest intelligence fr. St Bees & remained to service in the even.

20. After digesting the news of the week, went down to Wednesbury to see Messers Hutton & Jones.

21. A letter fr. Father informing me that he had forwarded some 'eadables' for which I had written.

22. **Sunday.** Service in the morning. A good day at the schools, & preached in the evening. Miss D. Wynn & the Messers Thornton at Church. Feel in good spirits, for altho' excessively exhausted, I believe my sermon was much more intelligible than usual.

23. Mr Stanton & Wynn called in the morning, the latter remained to dinner, & accompanied Mr D & I to Cosely. I partly went to complete arrangements for relieving Mr Nicklin a Sunday as he wanted to go north on a *particular* business.

However to my *great satisfaction* I found that while his Incumbent entertained a high respect for Mr S & I, he could not think of permitting our sentiments to be disseminated from his pulpits!!! This poor man has never seen or heard Mr Stanton, & only exchanged a few words with me on the subject of 'Cottage Lectures', therefore as we have neither of us published anything, his opinion of us serves to confirm mine that the fatalist party are ready at any time to assist the Erastian in expelling us from our cures.

24. Some hams &c. arrived from home. Busy preparing for a supper to which we (ie. the Incumbent, Curate, & Schoolmaster) invited the Choir & other friends to the number of about 40. The feast went very well, after which we perambulated the parish singing Christmas Carols. Wrote to I. to prevent her having a dull instead of a merry Christmas.

25. **Christmas Day.** A letter fr. I. with the same good intention to myself. Preached in the morning. Dined & spent the day (excepting my return to evening service) with the Messers Deacon. I enjoyed myself exceedingly, & believe that I conveyed more information on the Ecclesiastical questions of the day, than in any one company I ever remember. They appear a happy *united* family, & a great contrast to the prevailing ignorance & blind prejudice.

Obtained a pastoral address issued today by the Incumbent of Cosely addressed to his parishioners of all classes & *denominations* (the parish is mainly composed of *anabaptists* & other wild sects) as 'Beloved in the Lord, called to be *Saints* &c' begging them on the grounds of their *common* 'Christianity & his good character to give him their voluntary aid in the due maintenance of public worship &c'; 6 schools &c; especially 'as the pure faith of our Protestant Church is in more than ordinary peril, fr. foes without, & false or mistaken friends within'!!

Now I am not a little comforted to think that my Christianity is not so intensely 'Common' as to include me among Mr Vance's friends, altho' he says 'the essential doctrines of our common Xianity, those to which the trembling spirit clings as her *last* hope are few, & level with a child's comprehension'.

Service with sermon every day this week, with a congregation = to between 30 & 40. The weather is delightfully mild, too warm to walk with an overcoat. I observe the Sun does not rise till [blank] & sets abt. 3.00 pm here.

29. **Sunday.** 2 Services but did not preach, some unpleasantness with 2 or 3 of the choir.

31. Wrote to P. & a long letter to Isabella. A letter from Simey. Went to service at 11 pm.

NOTES TO CHAPTER TWO

1. L.M. Printed Lists of exam. results. Christmas 1848.
   Notes in: St Bees College, 1816–1895 by Canon Trevor Park, vicar of Natland, Kendal. With thanks for permission to quote.
2. L.M. MS. in C.R.O. Kendal.
3. L.M. Press Cutting.
4. Clergy List. 1851.
5. Clergy Lists of 1851, 52, 53.

Ocker Hill
1851

BRUNSKILL'S DIARY for 1851 begins to reveal a condition which led eventually to his dismissal. He felt faint at the Communion on New Year's Day. Then there is a recurring sore throat, and repeated tiredness. There is no doubt that he worked hard, was a keen controversialist, and did not spare himself. Did he know how to project his voice in public as well as in private? Had he learned how to preserve his health against the strain of work? Did he and Mr Davis, with whom he shared rooms, have proper domestic help? Until his ordination as priest on Trinity Sunday his work continued fairly evenly, interspersed with regular calls from Mr Nicklin bemoaning his fate at Coseley. In January he refers to the Revd W. J. E. Bennett MA vicar of St Paul's, Knightsbridge, London who had fallen foul of the bishop of London over the daughter church of St Barnabas, Pimlico. Bennett had been vicar of St Paul's since 1843 on the princely stipend of £1,000 a year.[1] He had contributed handsomely to the building and furnishing of St Barnabas from his own pocket. The bishop objected to certain ritualistic practices at St Barnabas, and Bennett resigned. There was the usual uproar in the church press, to which Brunskill refers.[2] Bennett was not long without a parish, and in the same year the Marquess of Bath gave him the living of Frome Selwood, Somerset, at a stipend of £762 with house. Bennett was a prolific writer of books and pamphlets which occupy nearly three quarters of a column in Crockford.[3]

In addition to the conditions of poverty in Brunskill's mining parish, the religious atmosphere was antagonistic. Until 1852 there were no public burial grounds except churchyards controlled by the clergy. In that year an Act was passed enabling corporations to provide municipal cemeteries. This did not remove the grievance of dissenters whose ministers were not allowed to conduct dissenting funerals in churchyards. Only the clergy of the Established Church could officiate on consecrated ground. As we see from the diary of 31 October 1850 Brunskill had to take a Romanist funeral under this rule. Not till the Burials Act of 1880 was relief given to other denominations to conduct their own burials in churchyards.

This perhaps, helps to explain the dismissive language used by him. It was not just the cheap scorn of the theological college student or tutor. In part it remained for all of Brunskill's life, and was part of the adversarial tone of the times. On the 20 January 1851 he refers to a Roman Catholic chapel as a Romanist Meeting house. On the following day he refers to an intelligent miner who had 'apostasised' to the 'Catholic' church; he talked himself hoarse trying to persuade the miner that he had left the Catholic Church of England for the Romish Schism! He almost revels in the attacks of 'dissenters' of all shades as proof that 'these aggressive attacks cheer me, as proofs that we are stirring the dry bones.'[4] In another place he refers to dissenters as anabaptists and other wild sects. Though Brunskill never adopted the ritual extremes of the Puseyites, he did accept the view of the Oxford movement that the Church is a sacred mystery, a holy fellowship, with the solemnity of its worship and sacramental ordinances.[5]

For the first six months of 1851 Brunskill's ministry at Ocker Hill followed a regular course. Among John Langhorne's papers is a delightful reminder of Brunskill's application to the bishop of Lichfield for priest's orders. There is a small envelope inscribed in a child's hand 'To Uncle Brunny', containing the bishop's reply:

39 Harley Street,
London.
26 May 1851

My Dear Sir,
     Your letter has not reached me till this morning. I shall be glad to receive you as a candidate for Priest's Orders at the approaching Ordination on Trinity Sunday next.
     From the statement which you have made to me, I cannot but think that your time has been well employed, in discharging the proper duties of a Parochial Minister, & especially in visiting the people 'from house to house'.

I could have wished indeed that you could have had more time to prepare yourself for your examination. But the spirit manifested in your letter leads me to hope that you will be found very *sufficiently* prepared. Nothing at least could better entitle you to favourable consideration than the plea which you have put in.

I remain, my dear Sir,
yrs. very faithfully,
J. Lichfield

The Revd Joseph Brunskill.[6]

The ordination took place at Lichfield on the 15 June, and immediately after he and a friend took a short holiday near Rugely. On the 23 June he went by train to London, and there follows the most interesting and graphic part of the diary; and until the 5 of July he has a hectic holiday, sometimes in the company of the Revd J. T. Ward, vicar of Askham, and the Revd Dr Wm. Jackson rector of Lowther, and their ladies. He attends the Great Exhibition, the House of Commons, sees the Duke of Wellington at early service at the Chapel Royal, and, to cap it all, sees Queen Victoria with the King of the Belgians and other royalty driving in her carriage in Rotten Row. He attends the consecration of the famous Anglo-Catholic church of St Matthew, Westminster, and says: 'The Service was a most painful piece of *Mumbling*. tho' a choir was in attendance, the very canticles were preached. To what extent will not blind prejudice drive men!'[7] He concluded the day sensibly by going to the Adelphi Theatre to see Paul Pry, and was much pleased with the acting of Miss Woolgar. He rushed all over Town, and returned to Staffordshire on the 5 July quite exhausted; only to find that his vicar had left for London, leaving him to take all the Sunday services!

After three weeks' grind his spirits begin to flag, and his health to fail with a relaxed throat. In September he takes a week's holiday in Warwickshire, enjoying the country scenery. He takes another four days off in early October, and by the 16 decides to look for another curacy, it becoming clear that his vicar had had enough. Mr Stanton gave him notice to leave on the 31 December, and paid him off. The diary ceases from October till December.

There is another side to the story of his departure which Brunskill gave many years later when from 1893 he was rector of Ormside. In a letter to the *Church Times* he said that the £40 grant from the Curates' Aid Society towards his salary at Ocker Hill had been stopped due to the 'sayings and doings' of James Prince Lee, then bishop of Manchester. He had persuaded a number of lordly subscribers to the Society (including the Duke of Newcastle & Mr Gladstone) to withdraw their donations and to apply them direct to those parishes of the bishop's approving. The Society became insolvent, and Brunskill was not fully paid for the last months of his curacy.[8] It may be that the vicar had no money after the 31 December.

He had now to look for another job. The market was not encouraging. The church papers of the day, *The Guardian*, and the *Ecclesiastical Gazette* are very instructive of the state of the market for unemployed curates. Bearing in mind that the Curates' Act of 1813 had laid it down that £80 should be the basic wage, there were some startling differences.

The Guardian:

22 Oct. 1851
***

A second curate is wanted for a manufacturing district in the diocese of Ripon. A title will be given; stipend about £60. Apply stating views fully to Revd H. S. c/o Mr Hicks, Bookseller, Wakefield.

5th Nov. 1851 A curacy for a deacon offered in agricultural parish near York. £50. Alne Vicarage, Easingwold.

Ecclesiastical Gazette:

Oct. 1851.
***

A curate wanted of sound Church of England principles for manufacturing district in Leeds. Daily prayer. Comfortable home offered as remuneration. M.N.R. Post Office, Leeds.

Oct. 1851.

Curacy wanted by married clergyman; Views anti-Tractarian, etc.

"   "

Curacy offered with Title at the Bishop of Ely's next ordination. No gentleman of Evangelical views need apply. Revd W. Airy, Keysoe, Kimbolton.

"   "

A clergyman with independent means, who after fourteen years hard work in the Church, having met with much disappointment and discouragement from frequent removals from several spheres of duty, owing to the death of some of his employers, and coming into residence of others, is anxious to find some sphere of other permanent employment, and in some place where there is a good school, to educate his son. His testimonials are of the highest character. R.B.C., c/o Messers Carpenter & Woolams, 16 Old Burlington St, Regent Street.

Dec. 1851.
"   "   Incumbent wanted for a small chapelry in the Lake District; a Clergyman of independent means & moderate church opinions. Apply (prepaid) to Revd S.T. Clarke, Colton, Milnthorpe.

"   "   The Governors of the Wellington Union (Somerset & Devon) are looking for a Chaplain from January 1852 as the previous chaplain has resigned through ill health. Salary £50 per annum.

Jan. 1852.   A curacy was offered in a populous London parish at £120 a year.

Jan. 1853.   To patrons of small livings. A married clergyman without family, near forty, and of moderate private means, would be willing to devote himself to the amelioration of a small agricultural parish of which he might be appointed incumbent, or would not object to a Curacy with sole charge. A.B. Post Office, Swaffham, Norfolk.

The general system was that the bishops inserted notices in the church papers that they would be holding ordinations at certain times. Candidates were to apply by a certain date to sit the bishop's examination for two or three days before the ordination. Candidates presented themselves for examination. If they passed, the bishop ordained them, and they departed to their parishes. The bishop seemed to have little control over training, or terms of employment. From then on the curate was in the market, and a non-graduate, such as Brunskill after two years at St Bees, had less hope of employment than a young graduate after three at the university. The clerical advertisements are dominated by graduates, immature and untrained in pastoral work. A bishop might never have seen a candidate until he presented himself for examination a few days before an ordination. It was left to the curate to find a post; the bishop does not seem to have been consulted. Brunskill appears to have sent this notice to *The Guardian* of 26 November 1851:

> A curacy wanted about Christmas by priest, unmarried. He has had experience in a populous district, and been accustomed to intone the service. Address: O.H. Post Office, Tipton.

The letters O.H. suggest Ocker Hill.

DIARY

January 1851

1. Commenced the 2nd half of the 19th cent: & a new year by receiving the Holy Communion. Obliged to leave the Church for a time from faintness, for wh. I cd. not account.

2. During the day I endeavoured to improve my 'condition' by a longer walk than common. Spent the evening very pleasantly at Mr S's. Very wet, & prevented going to Birmingham. From the *Guardian* I learn that the Bp of London is behaving in a most arbitrary manner with poor Mr Bennett. [Note: The Revd W. J. E. Bennett, MA, vicar of St Paul's, Knightsbridge, & St Barnabas, Pimlico]. The Bp declares it to be the most painful case he has experienced for 26 years, & so it ought to be if he has any feeling.

3. Went into Birmingham & paid my tailor & bookseller abt. £5. Did not see Thornton, & returned at 3. Called to visit a poor young man (said to be dying) that I attended in a fever abt. 2 months ago. In the first instance I was not informed of his illness until he was insensible, & now again after he had been ailing some weeks, I only arrive to find him in his last agonies. Having had some hopes of his profiting under his former sickness which when out he had appeared to disappoint. I did not feel surprised at his absence fr. Church. However, he is now gone, & all he cd. tell me was that he had been better since his former illness.

4. A desultory visitation, called at Mr Stanton's, & in the evening at Dr Underhill's.

5. **Sunday.** Preached in the morning.

10. At Birmingham & answered a letter fr. Is. in re Hove.

12. **Sunday.** Service in the morning; preached in the evening. My throat too sore to take my class in S. School.

18. Feeling very tired in the evening, I was just contemplating spending an hour or 2 with Dr U. when I was agreeably surprised by Is[abella] walking in with her luggage, having left N[ewton] in the morning, a week sooner than I expected.

19. **Sunday.** Is. accompanied me to West Coseley where I took the service for Mr Nicklin. Said prayers at O.H. in the evening.

20. In order to meet the first train to London I drove Is. into Bir[mingham] by 8 am and thus ended our short opportunity for gossip, which however we had made the best of. Went to see the Romanist meeting house & got into controversy with (I believe) the Sacristan which lasted for 1½ hours, & tho' I am the reporter, he was completely silenced by my Catholic line of argument! Returned to dinner & wrote to Aunt & Father.

21. Schools in the morning, & in the aft. while visiting over ground which has been the scene of the zealous labours of 'Father Ignatius' then F. Spencer.

[Note: Fr Ignatius: Revd Joseph Leycester Lyne (1837–1908), mission preacher, ordained deacon 1860, and priest 1898, had great gifts of oratory, and held missions in many cities. Attempted to revive the Benedictine order in the Church of England; bought Capel-y-ffin in 1869, four miles from Llanthony. On his death it passed to the Benedictines of Caldey.]

I found an intelligent miner, who had many years ago apostatised to what *he* called the *Catholic* Church. I talked my throat sore in my endeavours to prove that he had left the Catholic Church of England for the Romish schism, &

parted on good terms, promising to supply him with books &c.

22. Fulfilled the above promise, but prevented by my throat from prosecuting my visiting.

24. A pit accident by which 3 men are precipitated 40 yds. down the shaft.

25. Received a box of eatables fr. Father containing honey & Elder Syrup for my throat. Learned from Dr U. that one of the above men was a parishioner of ours, & that he died yesterday. Con[version] of St Paul. Even Service.

26. **Sunday.** Preached in the morning, unable to teach, but took the service in Even.

28. Mr Nicklin called, & I accompanied him to Brettle Lane.

30. Martyrdom of King Charles I. Read *The Guardian*, schools, & walked over to Cosely to dinner. Very much pleased with Dr Pusey's reply to Mr Dodsworth & the Bp of London. From the speeches of *The Manchester Men* & *The Guardian*, I am inclined to be more hopeful as regards the threatened onslaught upon the Church through her Prayer Book.

February

2. **Sunday.** Preached in the morning. Holy Communion. Said prayers afternoon & even. Mr S. in the even. explained the operation &c. of the S.P.G. & A.C.A.S.* – but 2 collections only produced £2.2.0., (a) ¼ of which was fr. 'ourselves'.

3. Commenced writing the first of a course of lectures on the 'Figurative language of S[acred] S[cripture]' from 'Jones of Nayland', wh. I purpose continuing every alternate Wednesday evening.

[Note: William Jones 'of Nayland' (1726–1800) Anglican divine, endeavoured to keep alive the High Church traditions of the Nonjurors.]

* Now Additional Curates Society.

4. Finished above, & went to Wednesbury in re Mrs Corbett. In the course of my afternoon's visiting I arrived at a Good new house quite an oasis in the desert of squalor & dirt & where moreover I had reason to expect the inmates were Church people. – Well, when at last the door was opened I found myself in the presence of a well dressed person who might have been mistaken for a lady. But no sooner had I introduced myself as 1 of the Ministers of the Parish, than the person (who was holding the door as if afraid of my entrance) cried we were all Puseyites, & that she went to another Church! & wanted nothing with me. Altho' very anxious to have a rest & discuss the subject, explanation was impossible, & after learning a particular or 2, I was obliged to decamp grumbling yt civility was anybody's due. – Since this I have called on a dissenter, who was as kind as Miss Morris was insulting having offered me money to those I find in need. The above adventure has been magnified (as I anticipated it would) into a rough shaking & summary ejectment!

9. **Sunday.** Said prayers in the morning & preached in the evening &c.

11. Another funeral fr. a pit accident.

12. Called to enquire after Messers Wynn & Rosenthall, who are both very ill.

16. **Sunday.** Owing to a bad cold &c. very much dissatisfied with my preaching. Said prayers in the evening.

17. Kept to my rooms endeavouring to nurse myself. My fowls 'all right'.

22. Altho' my Natal day, & being my 25th, I had hoped to 'turn over a new leaf' I was later up than ever. Found a letter fr. Is. congratulating me, & enclosing fr. Mrs Ward [Note: the wife of the vicar of Askham], & also a very beautiful 'Keeper' [? a ring].

21. [sic] Mr Wynn still very poorly, but I sat a short time with R. who is better.

23. **Sunday.** Said prayers in the morning. Schools &c., & preached in the evening.

24. Fest. of St Matthias. Said prayers in the even. Spent the afternoon in a 2nd. long discussion with a man who 17 years ago joined the Roman schism. My books he did not appear to have read, & persisted in his old assertion that he had turned to the Catholic Church &c, that the 'Protestant' Church commenced at the Reformation, & is now only supported by civil law. His Irish wife appears to have perverted him, & was in great trepidation lest I should shake down the groundless structure she had built up.

    A premature resignation of the Russell ministry has passed over without materially altering the position of Ecclesiastical affairs.

March

4. Attended a Ruridecanal chapter, rather an improvement on the last, & afterwards went into Birmingham.

5. **Ash Wednesday.** 2 full services.

6. Morning prayer to be continued during Lent.

7. Mr & Mrs Nicklin had tea with me; an additional Sermon in the even. to be continued during Lent.

9. **Sunday.** Rose early & said prayers in the morning, & preached in the even. 2 funerals in the afternoon, one of the parties had been killed in a pit, making the 4th. such that I have buried, besides others that have been buried elsewhere.

23. **Sunday.** 4 funerals.

28. A boy 4 years old burnt to death at school, during the time allowed for dinner.

29. Wrote to Hayton, & J[ohn] P[earson] Brunskill.

30. **Sunday.** Preached in morn. Service in even.

31. Delivered at 8 pm the 3rd of a course of famil. lectures preparatory to Holy Communion.

April

2. Attended the inquest upon the boy, who had died the same even. Verdict 'accidental death'.

3. The *dreaded* 'manifesto' from the Bp's. appeared today, & as it is as harmless as can well be imagined, we may now breathe more freely.

10. Saw Mr Garner at Birmingham.

13. **Sunday.** Preached in the morning, said prayers in the evening, after which I learned with extreme sorrow that some rich tyrannical dissenters are bent in having the surplices off the choir boys.

14. Wrote to Isa. & saw Mr Wynn for the first time since his sickness.

15. Wrote to P. [? Pearson his brother].

17. The wind got out of the East.

20. **Easter Day.** The weather delightful. Preached in the morning &c.

21. Service in the even.

22. Do.

23. No Evening service as hitherto.

26. Wind N.E. & again intensely cold.

29. Just on the point of starting for Rugely when I rec'd a note fr. P. to stop me.

May

1. St Philip & St James. Service in Even.

3. The dissenters have recently circulated some handbills against a State Church, & Rates, & today a virulent thing (that is just being distributed) was brought to me, entitled '15 reasons why I am not a Churchman'. It is by far the most false & abusive of anything I have seen.

When I consider the almost complete indifference into which the people of this neighbourhood are fast lapsing, these 'aggressive attacks' cheer me, as proofs that we are *stirring* the dry bones.

4. **Sunday.** 'Our Charity'. Three services & as many collections towards diminishing the deficit in the Building fund of the Church. Amt. collected £14. &c. Mr S[tanton] preached in the morning, a Mr Rooker in the afternoon when he shouted as much heresy in half an hour as contradicted all our teaching for years. 'Prebendary Gray' preached in the even; a good unwritten sermon, & flatly contradicting the afternoon preacher.

   Returning to my rooms fr. Mr S. at night I was overtaken by a man who, after remarking upon the weather, passed to infidel objections to the S.S. [? Sacred Scriptures]. By a little direct questioning I found he had been originally a Methodist, but was now a *Mormonite* Preacher. After a long talk the only proof I rec'd that [? Jse – ? Joseph Smith the Mormon visionary] was a true prophet was that this poor young man imagined him to be so, or as he expressed it, 'he *felt* it.' The apostacy of this man is a fearful commentary upon that most dangerous tenet held by the Methodists, which they pretend to ground on I St John 2. viz. That if anything be firmly believed it will be true for that very reason.

7. The Mormonite called according to appointment, when after a long talk I lent him 'Jones on the Trinity'. [Note: pub. 1756.]

8. After giving notice to abt. 200 I met the catechumens for confirmation, & purpose doing so 3 times a week till June 3.

11. Preached in the morning. Mr S *replying* to Mr Rooker in the evening.

13. Went into Birmingham & saw Thornton.

21. Left home a year today. Wrote to Palmer.

22. 12 months today since I first saw Ocker Hill. Wrote to Aunt Jane (Monkhouse) & [?] Batho.

June

12. Went up to Lichfield for Priest's Orders. Met Lord, Shaw &c. at the Swan. After dinner an animated discussion on Church matters in general, the views propounded being almost universally sound.

Palmer came, & we arranged he should drive us home with him on Sunday even.

14. Again I enjoyed myself greatly in an after dinner discussion on Convocation, the Bps of Exeter [H. Phillpotts] & Manchester [Prince Lee]. My opponent this time lost his temper which did not help his *cause*. I humbly hope that the ventilation of these subjects, will cause increased enquiry into the true principles of the Church.

15. Trinity Sunday.
On this day I was admitted to the awfully responsible office of a Priest of Christ's Church. May God assist me, now that I must give a/c for the souls of others as well as my own.

I thought of Keble's 'list ye pure white robed souls &c.' as the numerous candidates filed out of the choir.

We next repaired to the Palace & rec'd our Letters of Orders, & also had an interview with the Bp I believe my place was the 11th out of abt. 21. Lord was second below me, & Shaw below that; but this last I cannot a/c for.

Found Palmer waiting for me at the Swan, with whom after luncheon Lord & I drove home to Rugely abt. 8 miles. Here there was no evening service, which was disappointing. The vicar we understood preaches against Puseyism! but his new born zeal has not prevented the Romanists fr. building a splendid new Meeting.

16. Out for a drive to Beaudesert, which I enjoyed highly. The country here is very beautiful, & the Deer & brechins* in the park strongly reminded me of my native hills. In the

* Dialect for brackens.

evening a long walk to Armitage. The Church here has been recently & well restored. To bed *very* tired, with promises of drives in various directions.

17. A walk to Etching Hill &c. The Palmers beyond the comprehension of Lord & I.

18. To Colton where the Church is being repaired. Saw some old frescoes.

19. Dined with Mr George Palmer; but returned to service.

20. Left Rugely by an early train & parted with Lord at Lichfield. Stopped there to service, & then came on to Ocker Hill.

21. Busy preparing for Sunday.

22. **First Sunday after Trinity.** All the services, Mr S. being at Wolverhampton.

23. Left my rooms at 6 am for London. Took the Government train fr. Birmingham wh. gave me time to examine the country, with wh. I was generally disappointed except in Northamptonshire it appeared lightly wooded & too flat & barren. Did not see a 'Gee ho' team the whole distance. Noticed 4 or 5 horses in one plough on even the light chalk of Beds. I think the only place where any commencement had been made with the hay harvest, was in 2 fields between Birm. & Coventry; tho' I was informed further up that much had been carried.

 After many stoppages I arrived at Euston Sqr. abt. 3 pm & proceeded immediately to 132 N[ew] Bond St where on arrival I was rather at fault in finding it to be apparently a shop, forgetting that there was as the shopman said 'a private door'. Found Isabel & Miss Ann waiting for me, & greetings over, the former commenced to remonstrate with me for my sickly appearance. After tea &c. out thro' Hyde Park to Rotten Row, where for abt. an hour we admired the company and their beautiful steeds, during wh. time without any announcement & quite unexpectedly the *Queen* drove past in an open carriage, accomp. by the King of the Belgians, the Prince of Wales & Princess Royal. Her Majesty was fuller in the face than I expected fr. her portraits. There was no demonstration, beyond a few of the horsemen backing to one side.

Returning I called on I. Westmorland, & on my way to the Polytechnic signed a petition fr. the Pharmaceutical Society. Much pleased with the Institution, & heard a lecture on the Pendulum experiment to demonstrate the Rotation of the earth. The experiment I consider 'bosh', but the lecture was useful as I had not previously had time to attend to the matter. Returned home & chatted until late.

24. Out with Isa. at 9 am & called on Mr & Mrs Ward, Emma [Note: from Askham vicarage.], & Dr & Miss Jackson [Note: prob. Dr Jackson, rector of Lowther]. Found them at breakfast, but all very cordial. Borrowed a synopsis of the Great Exhibition in preference to the ½ lb. of paper containing the catalogue, & started thence for the Crystal Palace. We entered the South Transept at 11 am & found everything quite = to the glowing descriptions we had read. We were particularly struck on entering at the open & apparently unoccupied appearance, which notwithstanding its contents, the vast structure has. To give a description of the various sights would be to rewrite the synopsis wh. we found exceedingly useful. By following its directions we were enabled to take a regular tho' hasty view of the Western half in abt. 6 hours of very hard working. We then had some slight refreshment which we thought reasonable, & the additional luxury of a wash &c. for the sum of 1d.

Thence to Kensington Gardens to hear the band play, & see the ride &c. with which we were much pleased. At home at 8 pm, & after a short *rest* a long & tiresome walk to the Lowther Arcade &c, returning to supper at abt. 10. And while I write the watchman is crying 'past twelve', ergo if I am to hold out under this sort of thing I must — retire!!

25. Wednesday. To the Morning Service 8 am at St James Church wh. I thought the best preached service I had yet heard. Returned to breakfast & afterwards with Isa. called at Sackville Street, whence Emma [Ward] accompanied us to Westminster. In time for the service, which I thought the *worst* choral service I had heard. Noticed some of the monuments especially the Poets' corner. Thence by an order fr. the office of the Lord Chamberlain to view the new house of Lords. A porter on leaving this took us through *Westminster Hall* to the Court of Exchequer where the judges Alderson, Park, Platt, & Martin appeared to be trying a Patent case. In going down Parliament Street I rode on the box of the omnibus, & the 'civil driver' pointed out the spot where Mr Drummond was shot [Edward Drummond, private secretary to Sir Robert Peel, and shot 1843 in mistake for Peel], the horse guards, the escutcheon on the house where Sir Robert Peel died, Whitehall, Downing Street &c.

After leaving the Exchequer, we took a steam boat to London Bridge. Going ashore there we made our way to the Royal Exchange. Here 'Cassells London Conductor' became serviceable. Some City business prevented our seeing through the Mansion House. Emma was very much amused at the sight of the money in the Bank of England where they happened to be counting the shillings fr. the Exhibition. We now had some luncheon, & then proceeded west via. Cheapside to *the* Post Office. Back to St Paul's, where after examining the principal monuments we attended evensong. The service was much better than I expected. The Royal children of Belgium had also been there, & got into a carriage as we were at the gate. From here we walked down Ludgate, Fleet Street, (past the office of the E[nglish] C[hurchman] through Temple Bar & took an omnibus in the Strand to Sackville Street, where we arranged to go to Madame Tussauds. We were a large party, Ann B. & Edward W. accompanying us. I was exceedingly gratified here & much that I saw will help me to idealise many great men that I can never see. The rooms were crowded & the heat may have contributed to make my spirits as exuberant as they were. In returning we concluded this 'full' day, by all packing ourselves into an odd sawdusted little place (wh. however had the advantage of being private) where we tried to quench our thirst with 2 pots of stout.

26. Thursday. Started with Emma & Isa, but joined by Mr & Mrs Ward, when we proceeded to the National Gallery. Thence walked to Westminster & took a boat to Kew. Here we merely took a little refreshment & then on by a cab to Richmond, where we took an omnibus via Pope's Villa, Twickenham &c. to Hampton Court. Having arrived abt. 4 pm we were obliged rather to hurry, but the Palace being clear of visitors, we made good progress. The views from the windows were most charming, & the collection of paintings far surpassed anything I had previously seen.

On emerging fr. the palace we decided upon leisurely taking some refreshment, but hearing a bell announcing the departure of a steamboat, our party hurried on board, while I procured what biscuits &c. I could conveniently take after them. It was a glorious midsummer evening & the first 3 out of the 4 hours required for the passage were exceedingly pleasant. The boat was crowded chiefly with foreigners, & as the banks of the river are covered by a succession of villas whose inhabitants generally turned out to hear our band, the scenes were almost enchanting. On passing Richmond I was seated on the paddle box in conversation with an intelligent German gentleman, who on seeing the view here rapturously exclaimed that it was 'fine, very fine'. He said they had heard many things about England, but it had far surpassed all their imaginations. He contrasted our happy state with the miseries the recent wars on the continent had inflicted. He himself had lost thus abt. £1000. He said they were a large party & purposed going through England.

27. Friday. Isa. & I went down to Greenwich, but finding no conveyance to Kent, aft. viewing the park, hospital &c. we returned to London Bridge & made for the Tower, meeting Curley on the way. After some waiting we fell to the lot of

a very intelligent Warder & were highly pleased. Thence per omnibus to Wells Street. Rather late for service, & either from the *excessive* heat or exhaustion I was about used up. In the evening, however, we again strolled out with Miss A. & Mr Russell thro' Leicester Square & I was kept up too late for going to Covent Garden before 6 am in the morning.

28. To morning prayer at St Andrew's. Strolled alone fr. Wells St to Leicester Sqr. Thence to Wellington St for a *Guardian* returning thro' Covent G[arden] market to enjoy my paper over the best of mutton chops, at a 'stout' house in L[eicester] Sq[uare]. Still returning called to see Mr Ward, when Capt. Lowther coming in I was introduced, & we arranged abt. going to the House of Commons. In the even. we walked out to Rotten Row.

29. **Sunday.** At 8 am to service (accom. by Isa) at the Chapel Royal, St James, when I saw the greatest sight in London, 'the most notable man in Christendom', the iron Duke himself! He is a stouter man than I expected, & also looked much fresher than even the usual a/cs. led me to hope for. I of course took the best of looks at the great hero to whom we are so much indebted for the peace we are now making so much of. I have long been anxious to visit London, lest the 'iron' should be again converted into clay, ere my eyes enjoyed the feast they now took to the ...

Returned to breakfast & thence to Xt. Church, Hoxton, where Mr Scott himself preached an able sermon on the character of St Peter. I think it was the best *congregational* service I have yet known. Dined with Elizab. B. where I met Mr & Mrs W[ard]. In the even. we started for St Barnabas, but turned into St Stephen's Westminster. Greatly cheered on entering to hear the familiar strains of an Anthem. The church was well filled with a really poor congregation. The sermon was clear & practical & well delivered. The Church I cannot describe, but it delighted me beyond measure. The whole effect of Church & service far surpassed anything I had ever seen, & to come unexpectedly upon such an oasis, cheered me exceedingly. On returning I notice that a new Church to be dedicated to St Matt. was to be consecrated next morning by the Bp of London. [Note: this is a famous Anglo-Catholic church]. Grieved to find that E. & Mr I. had been employing their time at their A/cs.

30. Isabella being tired! & wishing for a rest I repaired alone to the consecration. Met Horegood at the door, & afterwards talked over old scenes. The Service was a most painful piece of *mumbling*, tho' a choir was in attendance, the very canticles were preached. To what extent will not blind prejudice drive men! Notwithstanding the intense heat H. & I walked down to Leicester Sq. where we parted. Being disappointed in my expectation of getting to the House of Commons I repaired alone to the Adelphi to see Paul Pry, & was very much pleased with the acting of Miss Woolgar.

July

1. Tuesday. Called at Sackville St & thence with Is. & Emma to the Exhibition. This was our only wet day & for our employment; it was rather an advantage than otherwise, tending to cool the palace. After some difficulty we procured an omnibus from the Burlington Arcade, but so completely blocked up was the road, that after riding a little way past Apsley House (the rain having ceased) we got down & walked thro' the park. Just before entering the E. end we observed a large branch wh. had just fallen upon a boy & killed him. We now proceeded to inspect the eastern half (of the Crystal Palace), this time taking the Galleries first, as being less crowded. After abt. a five hours' walk we repaired to our old qrs. & had some refreshment, with a wash &c. the latter for 1d.! Thence we hastened home, as I wished to accompany Mr W[ard] and Dr Jackson to the House. This I had regarded as my next best treat to seeing 'the Duke'. When near the house we saw King Hudson [Note: George Hudson (1800–1871) 'railway king', builder & decorator of several railways] riding home to

dinner, & presently afterwards we met W.N. Hodgson MP for Carlisle, who informed Mr Ward that Lord Blandford was just then speaking on the 'Church question'. Tho' I immediately congratulated myself upon our good luck, I was unable (fr[om] having been for the last week or 2 rather out of the. [centre] of policies) to say what this Ch. question was! I soon however found that it was a formal motion to H.M. for Ch. extension. The strangers' gallery being full Dr J[ackson] repaired to Mr Baily who soon had us ushered into the G[allery]. Here we sat until midnight seeing & hearing many notable men.

I had long been anxious to hear the spirit in which 'the House' discussed church questions, & was highly gratified at the improvement in tone. Messers Hume & Co. were by no means sparing in compliments as to the increased efficiency of the establishment. I was particularly pleased with W. B. Hope, & Sydney Herbert. The lay bishop of Marylebone repeated his slanders agst. the Lord Bp of St David's. Towards the close of the debate & near midnight Mr Horsman made a savage onslaught upon the Bp of Bristol. [Edward Horseman (1807–1876) whig politician, MP for Cockermouth 1836–52; junior minister; Chief Sec. for Ireland 1855; attacked Ecclesiastical Commissioners 1847, and the bishops 1850. Against the Reform Bill of 1866.] I was surprised to see the Radicals &c. allow themselves to be so much carried away by an ex parte statement as they were, for as expressed to Mr Ward at the time, there was surely another side to so black a story. And so it proved, for Horsman failed to *prove any* of his charges, & was very severely handled by Mr Gladstone, Sir Jas. Graham [of Netherby, Cumberland] & others afterwards.

When we got into the streets it was a few minutes past twelve, & raining fast. However after some difficulty we found a house open where we obtained a glass of stout each, over the counter! surrounded by draymen &c., & then plunged thro' the dirty street to our rooms, highly delighted with the evening's work.

2. Wednesday. Accompanied Mr Ward to the British Museum. In the afternoon went with Isabella to the Brighton station, '& saw her off'; returned by 'the Monument'.

3. Accompanied by the Miss Bs. we all went down to the docks & had the pleasure of using a 'tasting order' at St Catherine's. Parting with my friends on Tower Hill I took a boat for Chiswick. In going up narrowly missed a regatta. Saw Mr Bowerbank, but got nothing beyond promises, & professions of readiness to deliver up the [? glass]. From here I made haste down, & obtained another order fr. Mr Baily for the House of Commons. On this occasion the committee was being appointed for Chancery reform. I heard Lord John Russell speak, & consider his powers as an orator surpass those attributed to him. I left the House early in order to meet Mr Russell with whom I was to get to the Haymarket, where we expected Henry VIII wd. be the after piece. In this I was disappointed, Mr R. failed to come, & I suppose I strolled towards Bond Street.

4. Friday. Started fr. Bond St across Hyde Park with the intention of reaching St Barnabas' Pimlico [a famous Anglo-Catholic church], in time for the service at 8 am. However I kept too much to the west, passing close past the Crystal Palace & so into Brompton, wh. caused me to arrive late, & only heard the conclusion of the service. Still I had seen St Bs. & that was something for my pains. After the descriptions I had heard of the church I was somewhat disappointed in its size & general effect, especially after having seen St Stephen's, wh. I think is by far the best & finest Ch. I have yet seen.

Fr. hence I rode to the end of Piccadilly & thence walked fr. Regent St & right across to Tottenham Court Road (where I had my boots cleaned for 1d. in the street) & so on to Fitzroy Sqr. Here I saw Mr Smith on the matter of elocution & regret this was my only visit. After walking a little I again took an omnibus to the end of Bond St, & had my dinner at home for the first time. Again setting out, I *walked* to Regents Park & to the Zoological Gardens. Here I wandered about for some time, much pleased with all I saw; but feeling strangely alone in a crowd, and particularly struck with the preponderance of foreigners over natives. The Hippopotamus was laying out in the sun, & was much what I expected. I also saw a young Ourang out-ang, and a poor seal. Emerging at the West gate, I made my way to Lords cricket ground, St John's Wood, & saw the conclusion of the Oxford & Camb. match. Another short walk & another 6d. ride to Bond St again.

This might have been thought sufficient for one day; but it was now Miss A's turn, and she *must* keep an engagement at Mile End, where she was to go & see the people returning from Epping Forest Fair. So, after a change of boots, we walked down the Charing Cross & thence rode to the City, where we parted, I to call upon Mr Russell at Beards in ... & she to walk on to her destination. In due course Mr R. & I followed, & found it a distance of at least 2 miles, & this through a very low & crowded neighbourhood. Well, as the even wore on, vehicles of all descriptions began to arrive, & made their way as best they cd. thro' the vast crowds & fire works. We had plenty of refreshment, & at somewhat past eleven pm we started back again. It was too late for more than a ride of abt. 1 mile out of the 3 or 4, & we patiently trudged on, Mr Russell going home with me.

5. Saturday. Awoke early in order to return to Staffordshire, feeling excessively tired. After a hasty breakfast, Mr R. & we started for the Euston Sqr station, &, as for a considerable distance we were unable to find a cab, Mr R. volunteered to carry my bag, or else I verily think I might have remained in L. so completely jaded & footsore was I. The station was densely crowded; but after some manoeuvring I obtained a place, & in 8 hours had safely accomplished about 100 miles into Birmingham, arriving at my own rooms abt. 4 pm.

Here I found Mr Nicklin waiting for me, full of trouble fr. the bad & tyrannical behaviour of his Incumbent; & before he left me at 9 pm we had arranged that he shd. forthwith take steps to resign his curacy. [Note: the Revd J. Nicklin eventually obtained the curacy of Tarleton, Ormskirk, Lancs. in 1851.] I had now to think of the work for the following day, & as Mr S. was in town, the whole duty, with the additional afternoon catechising, as well Holy Co[mmunion]. However I had had 2 sermons in L. with me & notwithstanding the hardness of the work, was so much benefitted by the change of air that I felt less tired at 9 pm on the Sunday than I had generally done at 11 am.

This improvement in my health however did not continue long & in abt. 3 weeks finding myself falling away again, I resolved to try the air of Warwickshire for a few days & that producing a change, then to resign my curacy, for I feared lest my throat shd. become permanently relaxed, & that I shd. be altogether disabled. However, it was not until

September

23. that I started for Warwickshire, & the change of air produced very perceptible effects upon [me], before I had gone many yards fr. the station at Dockers Gate, found Mr Garner just returning fr. shepherding in his gig. He was cautious, said he had despaired of my ever coming over &c., & proceeded gradually to relate his troubles. I walked over to Kenilworth in the afternoon & saw Jones, returning to B.S. at night.

24. In the morning rode round the fields with Mr G. & in the after[noon] walked to Temple Balsal & back. Lovely weather & more lovely scenery. The views not extensive; but the country very thickly covered with the Warwickshire weed. Mr G's house I consider very pretty. We now understand each other, & I believe it to be my duty to show that all Brunskills are not Atkinsons; & in order to ally his anxiety I undertake a mission to Abbey Dore.

25. Walk over to Kenilworth again, having appointed to dine with Jones. It is here rather a stormy day; but was dreadfully so on the coast.

26. Went to Coventry, tho' morning very cold & wet. Much pleased with the Churches of Coventry. Dined & remained all night with Mr Knight.

27. Returned to B.S. in the morning & thence to Ocker Hill, somewhat improved by my excursion.

October

8. Attended the great meeting at Derby for the revival of Di[ocesan] Synods. Very much pleased with Arch[deacon] Denison & Canon Trevor. [G.A. Denison, archdeacon of Taunton from 1851; rigid defender of High Church principles. Between 1854–1858 was prosecuted in the civil courts for teaching the doctrine of the Real Presence.] Met Lord here, & went home with him to Peniston.

9. Raining all day, so that I cd. not leave the house. The Queen at Liverpool this day; & also the day app. for the great wrestling match between Jackson & Atkinson for £300. at Ulverston.

12. Assisted Lord in his sunday school. The Ch. the most poverty stricken I have yet seen, & Mr Wm's sermon the worst I have yet heard.

13. Returned to Ocker Hill, in order that I might be in time for the meeting of the Grt Br. Me. Inst. [?] for wh. I had prepared a speech. Mr S. not being there &c. caused me not to deliver it.

16. At Birmingham, returning from whence I borrowed the *Ecc[lesiastical] Gaz[ette]* & determined to make a personal app[eal] for a curacy at Bridgenorth therein mentioned.

17. Hired a horse at Dudley & rode over abt. 17 miles, & fd. Mr Wasey fr. home!
    About the beginning of this month I became aware that I was yet to have my share of hard usage fr. Mr Stanton [his

vicar]. My rupture with him caused some who wd. not before, to speak freely agt. him to me. Endeavours to convince him of his injustice, I found to be only a waste of strength, & therefore resolved to get away, & being obliged to take something, closed with Mr Sharpe. I had purposed not to go home till summer, but Mr Stanton called on [me] & paid my stipend up to that day (Decr. 31.), wh. I supposed & afterwards found correctly was a notice to quit at once.

NOTES TO CHAPTER THREE

1. C.L. 1851
   Crockford 1865.

2. *Guardian* Jan. 1851.

3. *Crockford* 1865.

4. 3 May 1851.

5. *The Church in the Age of Revolution*, Alec R. Vidler. Pelican Hist. of the Church vol. 5. 1961, p. 158.

6. L.M. The bishop of Lichfield (Lonsdale) to Revd J. Brunskill 26 May 1851.

7. W.M. Diary 30 June 1851.

8. L.M. Letter to *Church Times* 26 Feb. (no year given) when Brunskill was rector of Ormside.

NB:
The Revd John Nicklin was curate of Coseley, Staffs under the Revd W. F. Vance, BA, T.C.D. 1819, and vicar of Coseley 1850, and author of *Verses from the Mines & Furnaces* and sermons 1829.
Nicklin (a St Bees student) held the following posts:
Curate of Coseley 1851; Tarleton, Ormskirk, Lancs 1852; Hesketh with Becconsall, Chorley, Lancs 1855; Oswaldtwistle, Whalley, Lancs 1865; St John's, Blackburn 1866; and finally vicar of Salesbury, Blackburn 1868–1873, gross income £120, population 1292.

The samples of clerical advertisements at the end of the introduction to the diary have two marked with ***, suggesting the posts which interested Brunskill.

4

Three Curacies
1852–1853

THE YEAR 1852 opened with Brunskill returning to Newton for a short and much needed rest, but finding his father in a surly mood. Had it occurred to his father that his son was too abrasive to find a suitable parish? On the 30 of January Brunskill makes his way to the parish of Horbury, a daughter parish of the mother church of Wakefield.[1] The vicar was the Revd John Sharp, MA (Cambridge), and vicar since 1834, on a stipend of £230, with a population of 2683. He had been ordained deacon in 1833, and immediately on being made a priest in 1834 he had been appointed vicar.[2] He was one of the favoured ones! The church was High Church, with daily services, reservation, choral services, and a musical curate Richard Bussell to do the work. The curate (who was soon to leave) examined Brunskill in music, and does not seem to have been impressed. Brunskill found daily services exhausting, and was told to go at the end of two months' engagement. He arrived at St Mary's, Leeds on the 10 of March. This is probably one of the occasions when his father had to help him with money.

St Mary's, Leeds was one of those parishes which had been established on the initiative of the famous Dr W. F. Hook, vicar of Leeds. In 1801 the population of the town was 53,162; by 1831 the total was 123,393. When Dr Hook was elected to Leeds in 1837 there were 8 churches in the town, and 9 in the suburbs, with 18 clergy. The parish church was rebuilt and opened in 1841 to accommodate nearly 4,000 people. By an Act of Parliament of 1844 these district churches were converted into parish churches, and their curates into perpetual curates. When Dr Hook left for the deanery of Chichester in 1859 he left Leeds with 36 churches; the three schools had increased to 30, and the churches had 29 parsonages. St Mary's was part of that expansion, and was very much a working class industrial area.[3]

Brunskill's salary was £80, with £60 deducted for lodging at the vicarage. The vicar was the Revd John Bickerdike, MA

(Cambridge), appointed by Dr Hook in 1848. His stipend was £300, and the population 12,048.[4] Brunskill only remained nine months, and later said that he was worn down by the unhealthiness of the place and shortage of money. Even these few months were formative; he attended the lectures of Dr Hook and wrote them into his memorandum book, since lost. This book covered the period at Leeds, Mansergh, and the first few months at Mallerstang. Dr Hook in his letter to the bishop of St David's (Connop Thirlwall) in 1846 proposed that (1) all children ought to receive elementary education; (2) that the state alone can enforce this education; (3) that religion is an essential part of education, (but as in England no one religion is common to the whole people); (4) therefore let the state establish rate-paid schools in which all children may receive elementary secular education; and (5) let classrooms be attached to these schools in which at stated times the clergy and ministers of the several denominations may give religious instruction.[5] In addition to Dr Hook's educational and charitable work, the standard of worship at the parish church, his learned preaching and teaching, and above all the excellence of its choir set standards for city and market town churches all over the country.

Up till then the public services in many churches were dull and slovenly, and far from attractive to the poor who formed a large part of the population in working-class parishes. Despite his short stay in Leeds, there is no doubt that Dr Hook left his mark on Brunskill, who was convinced that services in church should be cheerful and well sung; that teaching in school and church should be of a high standard, and freely available to the poor; that the poor should have free and unhindered access to the ordinances of the Church, without hindrance by the rich and powerful. But Brunskill did not accept Hook's view of state education, which materialised in the Education Act of 1870. We can only regret that Brunskill had not been one of Dr Hook's curates; they had so much in common.

When in a few years Brunskill became curate of Askham he bought a book which summed up this view of the church. It was *Milford Malvoisin, or Pews and Pewholders* by the Revd F. E. Paget, rector of Elford near Lichfield. Alan Webster still has this book. Paget is better known for the book, *The Owlet of Owlstone Edge*. The dedication of the Milford book gives an excellent summary of Brunskill's views.

To one
whose glorious privilege it has been
to be the sole
FOUNDRESS OF A CHURCH
for the use and benefit of a poor and neglected
population; and who,
in the arrangement of that church,
did not forget
that where rich and poor meet together
before God
the maker of them all,
there it is fitting that the distinctions
of worldly rank
should be laid aside.

One of Brunskill's endearing qualities was his searching mind. As we see from his visit to the Great Exhibition, he did not confine his interests to the church.

Among the Webster papers is this short reading list from the Leeds days:

A Series of Sermons on the Epistle & Gospel for each day etc., by Isaac Williams. 2 vols. 11/- Rivingtons.
Work & Wages, by Vere Foster, Messers Clark, London.
The Law of the Love of God in the first four Commandments, by Dr Moberly, 3/6. D. Nutt, 270 Strand, London.
Introductory Lessons on the British Constitution, J. W. Parker, pp. 72.
Chapters for School Reading & Home Thoughts. Hope & Co.
Sermons on National Subjects, by Charles Kingsley, second series, R. Griffin & Co. pp. 339.
Why the Clergy advocate Homeopathy, by Dr Griffiths Jones. Leath.
The Clergy List for 1854. 9/- Charles Cox. 12, King Wm. Street, Strand.
Church Dictionary by Dr Hook, 7th ed. John Murray, London.
An Act for the more effectually to prevent profane cursing and swearing, 19. Geo. III, cap. 24.[6]

It is clear that by September Brunskill was looking again for another curacy. It is fascinating to look at *The Guardian* and *Ecclesiastical Gazette* to study the market. The extremes of worldliness, wealth, and poverty are there to be seen.

Guardian, 6 Oct. 1852. A clergyman will be much obliged to anyone who will recommend him a thoroughly good servant to act as Ladies' Maid and Waiting Maid. She must be a good Churchwoman, be highly recommended and perfectly understanding her business. Address to Rev Lewis Bagot, Leigh Rectory, Cheadle, Stafford.

Ecclesiastical Gazette. Nov. 1852. To Patrons & Incumbents. A married Clergyman of independent fortune, who will shortly be disengaged, is desirous to obtain the INCUMBENCY or CURACY of a parish where there is a good house, containing four sitting, five best, and five servants' rooms, stabling for four horses, double coach-house, and convenient out-buildings. The advertiser is willing to devote both his time and means to the moral and physical improvement of those committed to his charge. He holds no extreme views, and would not object to take land in lieu of stipend. A prospect of permanency indispensible. References unexceptionable. Address (prepaid) A.W. care of C. Govette Esq., 10, Lincoln's Inn Fields, London.

Ecclesiastical Gazette, Nov. 1852. A title for orders of £25 per annum with small parochial duty (one service on Sunday) and the probability of finding occupation in Tuition is offered in the diocese of Winchester etc. etc.

The one which attracted Brunskill's attention is in the *Guardian* of 22 Sept. 1852:

Wanted, a curate in priest's orders for a well situated Perpetual Curacy in the County of Westmorland. The population does not exceed 250. Address (prepaid) A.B. Mr E. Branthwaite, Bookseller, Kendal.[7]

The parish was that of Mansergh, near Kirkby Lonsdale in the Lune Valley. The incumbent was Revd J. Rowlandson, a literate, who had been ordained deacon in 1818, and priest in 1819 by the bishop of Chester. The vicar of Kirkby Lonsdale had appointed him to the perpetual-curacy in 1830 at a stipend of £85, and a population of 232. Brunskill applied and was accepted, and entered upon his new duties on the 12 December

1852. Three curacies in one year was an ominous start in the ministry. The parish was a few miles from Kendal, with excellent fishing in the river Lune, with fine views of the Casterton, Barbon and Middleton fells. It is a lovely district.

Looking at the perpetual curacies which were served by men living on little more money than curates, and with minute populations, one wonders how the clergy filled their time. They were, of course, still close communities, with the squire, parson and schoolmaster at the top of the ladder, with the 'Big House' and its servants in command. When my Grandfather the Revd W. H. Breay was appointed by the vicar of Kirkby Lonsdale to the perpetual curacy of Middleton, next to Mansergh in 1894, he received this instruction from Dr J. Llewelyn Davies on his interview at Kirkby Lonsdale vicarage: 'Breay, when you are vicar of Middleton, it will be your duty to resist the influence of the big house' (naming the family)! It was not flippant advice. When my grandfather introduced *Hymns Ancient & Modern* into the church, the lady of the manor was so affronted, that he had presumed to introduce the offending books without permission, that she sent her maid down to church on Monday morning to remove the books! There was a fearful row; but the books were returned, and used. Fortunately my grandmother had a private income, which enabled them to keep a cook and odd-job gardener, and maintain some independence.

Mansergh was similarly placed, with the squire, Edward Wilson, Esq. of Rigmaden occupying 'a pleasant mansion in this township'. The chapel (church) was described in 1849 as a 'neat building, repaired a few years since by the late Christopher Wilson Esq. father of Edward Wilson Esq. of Rigmaden.'[8] The perpetual curate Revd John Rowlandson had been at Mansergh since 1830, and supposing he was 21 when ordained deacon in 1818, he would have been about 55 when he engaged Brunskill as his curate. He was still as Mansergh in 1860. He had 70 acres of glebe, and an income of £92 gross.[9] On Brunskill's arrival he retired to a house in Sedbergh, hoping perhaps that his curate would do the work, and the bishop of Chester remained in ignorance of his absence. The private arrangement was that Brunskill should not be a licenced curate; no-one need know!

As far as the burden of work was concerned, Brunskill should have had a quiet time, pottering gently round the parish, getting to know the farmers and villagers, and having plenty of time for reading. He was anxious to get out of an industrial parish; Rowlandson wanted an unlicenced curate. But it placed Brunskill one further step down the ecclesiastical ladder; he had no security of tenure.

He began his work on the 12 December 1852, and very soon was busy visiting all the houses in the parish, enquiring who was ready for confirmation, who was sick, and so forth. Never had the inhabitants seen such energy! The arrangement of the chapel came under his scrutiny, and the squire's new pew did not meet with his approval. It was one of those spacious 'loose boxes' with a door, and seats on all sides, one with its back to the Holy Table. This activity came to the ears of the incumbent who became suspicious, and anxious lest his rest should be disturbed, and perhaps the bishop ask questions.

On the first quarter-day, when the curate's salary fell due, Rowlandson wrote from Sedbergh raising several points. After giving details of the payment of his salary at the bank at Kirkby Lonsdale, he stated that on no account was Brunskill to ask the bishop of Chester for an extra confirmation. This might be construed as a reflection on the bishop's non-performance of his duties, 'which I think no discreet clergyman would prematurely or rashly hazard'. Brunskill had recently written to the bishop of Chester for a licence, without first seeking Rowlandson's advice. This was too much! 'A little more experience and knowledge of the mode of managing clerical matters in this diocese would have induced greater moderation and order, which would be no disadvantage to you'. He then advised Brunskill that he expected him to work with quietness and moderation, with a mutual forbearance and courtesy.

He also raised the matter of a Mrs Lewthwaite to whom Brunskill had recently given the Sacrament. She had not only neglected public worship, 'but gloried in her neglect'. She had only recently come out of her delirium and madness, which needed special consideration. He requested that there should be some sign of repentance before she was given the Sacrament. He concluded with the remark that he had so expressed himself to point to the quiet way in which he wished the Chapelry to be attended to. Brunskill replied that he offered Mrs Lewthwaite the Sacrament because he believed she was dying. As to the licence, he had understood that he might remain without a licence, and 'I declared myself quite satisfied, and repeat the same assurance now.' [10] Brunskill had changed his tune; the time would come when he would realise that bishops are best kept at a safe distance, and in ignorance! Why stir up trouble with too much activity?

Two episodes were to cause his downfall. According to Alan Webster, Brunskill altered the family pew belonging to the squire, which had one of its seats with its back to the Holy Table which he thought disrespectful to the Sacrament. The second is referred to in the public dispute between the bishop of Peterborough and the Revd Thomas Hugo, rector of West Hackney which figures in the *Church Times* of June/July 1874. The bishop complained of the lawlessness of some of the clergy in ritual matters. Brunskill intervened in a letter of the 6 July giving his own experiences. Referring to his time as curate of Askham (and 'filling in' for the vicar of Penrith) 'I had given out a hymn after the third collect, and I was summarily threatened with inhibition by bishop Waldegrave, unless I followed what had been to me the unknown custom of the absent incumbent. And in an earlier curacy [Mansergh] being delated to Bishop Graham of Chester by the Squire for NOT interpolating prayers between the Creed and Sermon, as he said my predecessor had done, the Bishop threw me out of a valued sole charge. The aggrieved parishioner has chiefly thriven by official patronage and episcopal theories of lawlessness. And the same causes are stopping the supply of clergy and ruining the Establishment. J.B.' [11] I am afraid it must be said that Brunskill followed his own line, did not wear the black gown, stuck to the Prayer Book, did not consult, and was aggrieved when anyone questioned his departure from the custom of the parish which he ignored; he was his own bishop!

The matter of the squire's pew was heard in the Consistory Court of the bishop of Chester sitting in the old vicarage at

Kendal, and Brunskill lost, and was dismissed from his curacy by Rowlandson without right of appeal because he had no bishop's licence. But the missing diary did say that the bishop of Chester agreed to sign a testimonial for Brunskill when he applied for another post; and that is an indication that Rowlandson had taken leave without permission.

The people of Mansergh were not unmindful of the genuineness of Brunskill's hard work. In September 1853 they drew up a Memorial, thanking him for 'the kind manner in which he has instructed the youth, visited the sick, and encouraged the aged in the right path towards a happy end'. A subscription was taken of over 40 inhabitants, amounting to £2.17.0. James Lewthwaite gave 2/6d, and Mary Lewthwaite 6d. Neither the parson nor the squire subscribed.[12] His dismissal probably dates from September, and he had to look for other work. He applied to the bishop of Carlisle, and was offered and accepted the curacy of Mallerstang, near Kirkby Stephen, where the perpetual curate, the Revd R. Robinson BA, had been suspended for two years for intemperance. This time he was licenced.

DIARY

(Ocker Hill)

January 1852

4. I went as usual to the Sunday School, but Stanton came in without noticing me, & being too late to go anywhere else I took my place in the nave of the church. The service being ended I went into the vestry & asked him if I might preach on the Sunday evening next, wh. after some equivocation he granted. In the evening I went to Moxley & heard Hutton preach. He did not nearly = what his popularity had led me to expect. Went home with him to supper where I met the 2 Bagnals, & found Stanton had been slandering me to them.

5. Went to Birmingham, but did not see Thornton. Walked on to Solihul, to obtain some information from Hatherly on

music. In the evening a long conversation with the Romish Priest, wh. necessitated my remaining all night. In the morning I walked on another 7 miles to Balsal street, to say good bye to Mr & Mrs Garner.

11. Preached my farewell sermon to a somewhat larger congregation, having said the Service in the morning, & bid adieu to a weeping Sunday School in the afternoon.

12. Left O[cker] H[ill] on my way north. I felt very weak, & Mr Davis carried my bag to Wednesbury, where I had a glass of brandy while waiting for the Omnibus. Mr D. accompanied me to Wolverhampton, & I next stopped at Chester.

    At Chester I remained a few hours, & was much pleased with the fine old place. The view fr. the walls & the remembrance that fr. thence was witnessed the fatal flight at Rowston Moor [Note: Battle of Rowton Heath, 1645] was interesting. The cathedral appeared neglected, & the choir was weak. Passing on fr. thence I arrived safely at my brother's rooms in Liverpool, where after some time he joined me. He was looking better than I had ever seen him, & greeted me by exclaiming that 'I should be an auld fellow before him yet'. I was too much exhausted to do justice to his excellent supper.

13. After a long sleep we proceeded to look around the town with wh. I was much pleased. In the afternoon I went on to Penrith where I remained all night.

14. Walked over to Newton, & met Father in a surly mood near the house. He only invited me in on condition that I wd. be civil &c. in wh. I promised reciprocity. I now found myself lower in 'condition' than I had supposed; but I had been much harassed & without rest for a long time. A fortnight's good nursing however saw me much refreshed.

18. Preached at Newton, & left after experiencing much kindness.

30. Arrived at Horbury. Immediately after tea Mr Burril began to sift my musical abilities.

31. Occasion to feel in bad spirits, from suspicion that I was to have no rest here.

February

1. Mr Sharp sung the service, & I preached 2 sermons.

4. Do.

8. 2 Do.

9. Previous suspicion of Mr Sharp being in treaty with another confirmed, & have notice to roll on!

11. Went into Leeds, & called on Mr Bickerdike, who offered me his curacy, with some *compliments*.

13. A letter from Mr B. wishing me to mention the time when I could go to St Mary's.

15. **Sunday.** Preached 2 sermons &c. & feel very much tired.

22. Do.

23. A letter fr. Isabel[la] congratulating me on my 26th birthday.

24. Went into Leeds again by invitation to preach & remain over Shrove Tuesday. Present at a tea party, to the members of a children's sick club. Almost suffocated by the fumes fr. some neighbouring vitriol works. Much talk with Mr Greenwell, the now S[enior] Curate, who advises me to take it, i.e. the curacy. Mention made of some things being disagreeable. Did not preach & left undecided.

28. After corresponding with friends, wrote to Mr Bickerdike, & accept the senior curacy of St Mary's. The best terms I am able to make, being at the rate of £80 pr.an. with £60 deducted for lodging &c. at the Parsonage.

29. Throat very sore; but take part of the service in the morning & preach. At a funeral in the afternoon, my throat so painful as to cause me to perspire.

March

1. From partial rest yester-even, my throat more cool, but in reading a lesson this morning, feel my very [sic] chest sore. Smythe left for Cambridge.

2. Letter fr. Mr Bick[erdike]. Wrote to the Bp of Ripon.

3. Walked with Mr Burril to Stanley, & having a pair of new, tho' easy shoes, was enabled to stop his boasting respecting his pedestrian powers. Returned just in time for even. prayer.

4. Letter fr. the Bp of Ripon requiring testimonials, for wh. I wrote to Mr Davis.

5. Walked into Wakefield market. Altogether it does not = Penrith. eggs 18 pr. 1/-, fowls 1/6. &c.

6. Accompanied Mr Norris to Normanton. The Church has been pretty carefully restored, & a neat new school built. Returned by a pleasant walk, to Kirkthorpe, wh. Ch. was only being restored, but promised well. Walked on through Heath, the 'West End' of Wakefield, fr. whence we took rail back to Horbury.

9. Started my goods.

10. Followed them to St Mary's, Leeds, after having been at Horbury about 6 weeks. I had availed myself as much as I could of the open country, & excepting my throat had improved my health, wh. made me partly regret the change to the smoke & bustle of Leeds.

   However, my disappointment having worn off, I had several other reasons for being thankful for it. First I found the Daily Service &c. beyond my powers, not to mention my deficiency in music. Secondly Mr Sharpe practices & recommends 'Reserve' [? 'reservation', or priestly hauteur] or Sacerdotalism. I saw that it greatly impaired his usefulness, & felt it so contrary to my nature, that to attempt it was a grievous burden. Thirdly, I had had an opportunity of mixing with the Society of a rich Yorkshire village, & in this time had learned as much as I probably ever should have done at Horbury. The school was in a very efficient state; & my daily catechisings were consequently more pleasant; but here again I had probably gained as much experience as I should have done by a longer stay.

Our conversations at Table were often very interesting, both Mr Sharp & Mr Norris, being good company. Mr Burril was as silly, & talked little beyond small gossip. I had accepted the Curacy for 3 months at the rate of £80 & to live in the Parsonage at £1 per week; yet Mr Sharp refused to pay me more than £5!! I told him I should not have taken the curacy on any such terms. Being *willing* & able to fulfil my part of the contract, Mr S. was bound to fulfil his. He however met his reward, for just before leaving I began to know that he was very like falling between 2 stools, which so happened. The daily services were obliged to be stopped, & after advertising in *The Guardian* & *Gazette* even he was some months in obtaining help.

NOTES TO CHAPTER FOUR

1. It will be remembered that from 1864 to 1867 the Revd Sabine Baring-Gould was curate of Horbury, his vicar being the Revd John Sharp. It was the vicar who gave Baring-Gould the charge of the lower part of the town at Horbury Brig. There he did much for the poor, composed the hymn 'Onward Christian Soldiers', and in May 1868 married Grace Taylor of Horbury. See: *Crockford* 1896 for his many writings, and *Onward Christian Soldiers* by William Purcell, 1957.

2. *Crockford* 1865.

3. D.N.B. Dr W. F. Hook, (1798–1875).
   Life of Dr W. F. Hook, by his son-in-law W.R.W. Stephens, 1878, 2vv.

4. C.L. 1852.

5. D.N.B. Dr W. F. Hook.
   Alan Webster has pointed out that Hook's view of elementary education was in contrast to that of Joshua Watson (1771–1855) the philanthropist of the old High Church tradition; who held that the church should be sufficient to undertake national education according to the tenets of the National Society. In educational matters Brunskill took the Watson view. (See *Joshua Watson* by A. B. Webster, 1954)

6. W.M.

7. Press cuttings are taken from the original papers in C.U.L.

8. Hist. Topography & Directory, of Westmorland, Lonsdale & Lancashire north of the Sands. P.J. Mannix, 1849, p. 356.

9. C.L. 1852
   Crockford 1860.
   Crockford 1896 for W. H. Breay of Middleton.

10. L.M. MS letter of Revd John Rowlandson at Sedbergh to Revd J. Brunskill 16th Feb. 1853.
    L.M. MS draft reply in pencil from Brunskill to Rowlandson, scarcely legible.

11. W.M. Folder of press cuttings. Brunskill's letter to *Church Times* 6 July 1874.
    Bishop Waldegrave was bishop of Carlisle from 1860.

12. L.M. & C.R.O. Kendal. WDX/848/10. The testimonial of the parishioners of Mansergh to the Revd J. Brunskill. Also in his hand is an unsigned testimonial to the Bishop of Chester certifying Brunskill's pastoral diligence at Mansergh.

NB:

The second of Brunskill's diary/memorandum books is missing. It covered his days at Leeds, Horbury and Mansergh, with a few early months at Mallerstang. It was formerly in the possession of Mrs I. M. Langhorne of New Hutton, Kendal, where I saw it thirty years ago. Latterly it was with Alan Webster, and cannot be found. The principal events in the diary have been recalled by both of us and with the exception of the letter to the bishop of Carlisle, which I copied, the remaining memories are from Brunskill's letters to the press.

5

Mallerstang
1853–1855

JOSEPH BRUNSKILL was appointed curate of Mallerstang in November 1853. The Revd Robert Robinson the perpetual curate had been suspended by the Bishop of Carlisle for intemperance; he found a curacy near Thirsk for the two year period.[1] Robinson was the son of a considerable scholar, the Revd Dr Robinson DD who for many years was the head of Ravenstonedale grammar school, and at the same time taking in a small number of men training for Orders. Latterly he was rector of Clifton near Penrith. The son was BA of Trinity College, Dublin, and had been curate of Clifton 1825–30, of Tong, Salop, and lecturer at Wolverhampton collegiate church 1830–44, and finally came to Mallerstang in 1844. It was then a remote and self-sufficient dale, with a road running its length on the way from Kirkby Stephen to Hawes; the railway did not come till 1876. The weekly Monday market at Kirkby Stephen was the hub of that world. The annual routine of the small grazing farms was lambing time, clipping and sheep washing, haytime, mowing bedding, and cutting peat and 'flawes' (turves) for fuel. The routine was enlivened by four annual events, the first being Outhgill fair; the second the passing of the Scots drovers of sheep and cattle on their way to Yorkshire fairs; the third was Brough Hill Fair, when a miscellaneous assortment of men and things defiled through the dale; and the fourth was the autumn Luke Fair at Kirkby Stephen when cattle and sheep were sold, mainly to pay the rents. Haverbread and blue-milk cheese were the staple diet, fustian and clogs their working attire, rushlights and farthing candles their lights. Their doctor was a long way off, so that much faith was placed in 'yerbs' and country remedies.[2] The only two educated men in the dale were the schoolmaster and the parson.

The condition of these remote schools and parochial chapelries was far from satisfactory, with little to stimulate the minds of their rulers. There is a graphic account of one of these lonely charges in the life of Richard Kearton the eminent naturalist from Swaledale, who was born in the middle of the last century in upper Swaledale, in the chapelry of Muker.

> In my time the popularity of the Established church was at its lowest ebb. This was no doubt due to the poor type of incumbent prepared to accept the poor stipend and soul-corroding loneliness. If we ever enjoyed the uncertain services of a really able parson, our good fortune was almost certain to be due to some kink which had sent the poor man (to us). I remember one whose brilliant scholarship might have won him a bishoprick ... but alas, his habits ruled any kind of promotion impossible.[3]

Mallerstang church was once a chapel-of-ease in the Forest of Mallerstang; and the earliest record of the dalesmen subscribing to the schoolmaster-priest is from 1543. In 1660, Lady Anne Clifford, countess of Pembroke (Thomas Carlyle's 'antique She-Clifford of those Northern parts') endowed it with a farm in Cautley with a yearly rent of £11 to supplement these meagre subscriptions. In the early eighteenth century this, with the aid of Queen Anne's Bounty, was increased with two small farms in Garsdale and Sedbergh, and it was established as a perpetual-curacy with the double duty of teaching and preaching. By 1810 the living was worth £94, and in 1867 £157. But there was no parsonage. Some of the clergy paid a schoolmaster to do their duty. During the late eighteenth and early nineteenth centuries, when the Revds John and William Bird of Crosby Garrett held the living in plurality they paid John Garthwaite about £25 a year to teach in the chapel school.[4] As the chapelry was within the old parish of Kirkby Stephen the vicar took half the surplice fees, and all the mortuary fee of 8s. 6d. on the death of every landowner. The Revd John Fawcett was perpetual-curate from 1819, living first at Shorgill; he later bought the Deepgill estate, and improved The Thrang. He did his own teaching, and was the first to try and raise a subscription to build a new schoolroom.

For three hundred years the children were taught in a small upper room, approached by a flight of stone steps, at the back of the chapel. The church part was furnished in the old ways, with pews lengthwise along the building like a college chapel, with the three-decker pulpit in the centre of the north side, and the holy table behind its rails at the east end. A dingy surplice was thrown over the back of a pew, ready to be donned on Sunday, while the weekly loaves of Middleton's Charity were laid on a window sill. James Middleton the clerk occupied the lower portion of the three-decker, giving out a psalm from Tate & Brady, and pitching the note with a preliminary tootle on a flute, while the clergyman took that and other opportunities of recruiting his energies with a pinch of snuff. Men like Garthwaite and Fawcett did their best in primitive conditions; but the schoolroom could only accommodate about half the children of the dale.[5]

The Revd Robert Robinson was appointed to Mallerstang in 1844, paying Thomas Whitehead the schoolmaster £30 a year, increased to £50 by subscription. He had of course to find his own accommodation. Remembering these two expenses, his small income would still be above the £80 minimum laid down in the Stipendiary Curates Act 1813.[6] He may have had some private means; for early in his tenure he reslated half the church roof, and rebuilt the east end at his own charge. He also paid for the replacement of the commemorative stone put by the countess of Pembroke above the door, which had fallen and broken.[7] Robinson had started well, but within ten years he had lost heart and taken to the bottle; loneliness had broken him. When he died in 1878 his funeral sermon was preached by the Revd William Thompson MA, a native of Outhgill who said this, that: 'He was as much at home in the company of the humblest labourer as of the rich and learned, and was equally the favourite of all classes. His talents in the pulpit were of no mean order. He was the eager patron of youthful promise, and by his ready help in learning more than one Mallerstangian have been stimulated to persevere and succeed.'[8] It is easy to be censorious about gifted men broken by loneliness, the lack of promotion for poor men, the failure of the church to provide for sickness and old age, and above all the crippling liability for dilapidations which consumed savings, and prevented acceptance of promotion. The system was wrong.

This was the dale and church to which Brunskill was sent,

which for the first ten months was covered by the missing diary. It is the writer's recollection that Brunskill was a vigorous visitor, had a jolly social life in and around Kirkby Stephen interspersed by visits to his sister Isabella at Hackthorpe, and his father and stepmother at Newton. His first months were addressed to the appalling condition of the school in the loft at the back of the church. In the course of a letter to the Bishop of Carlisle he wrote:

> The chapel is a very plain oblong building having about one fourth of its space to the westward walled off. The ground floor of this division is used as an entrance to the chapel, and also to the miserable loft above, which serves for a schoolroom. This apartment is too small for 20 children, yet there are at least 41 children in the dale who ought to attend. Moreover, as regards light, warmth, ventilation and arrangement, the room is worse adapted for a school than any other I have yet seen. And all this in addition to the great evil that the children must desecrate the Church and graveyard around.

Brunskill suggested the building of a 'neat school' at the south-east corner of the graveyard, facing the turnpike road. The bishop of Carlisle rejected the idea.[9]

The surviving diary opens in November 1854. A few points can here be made. The minor clergy serving in the whole parish of Kirkby Stephen were dined once a year by Mr King, the vicar of Kirkby Stephen. The mention (5 November 1854) of Mr Wyvil late curate of Kirkby Stephen, then at Lunds, underlines the precarious position of the minor clergy, who when the term of their appointment came to an end had to take what they could find on the open market; the less fortunate took the dregs. Wyvil took the perpetual curacy of Lunds at £76 a year with a population of 60, in the remote part of upper Wensleydale called Abbotside. The remote chapel is still standing, but now inaccessible.[11] On 30 November Brunskill did some teaching in the chapel school. On 6 December he mentions the new schoolmaster who 'admits his ignorance of the art of teaching'. On the 26 December he takes coach and train to Sunderland, staying mostly with his old master Mr John Ritson. One strong impression from the diary is the severity of winters in those days. Mr Robinson returned to Mallerstang in March 1855, and the relations between him and Brunskill were uneasy. Brunskill wrote a few letters to the bishop of Carlisle reporting the return of the incumbent, and Brunskill's painful position. He concluded with the tactless remark: 'enough is known to give an unfavourable impression of the Discipline of the Church, especially to estranged members who are in a large majority here'. No bishop likes to be told he is not doing his duty, and relations with the bishop became cool. Brunskill rode over to Askham Hall to see Dr Wm Jackson rector of Lowther and Chancellor of Carlisle for his advice, and was told he was entitled to six weeks' notice as from a new incumbent. Brunskill went to live with his father at Newton. There was some talk of him taking the chapelry of Lunds as Wyvil found it uncongenial. He did not return to Mallerstang, and he claimed that he was not paid for the last part of his duty there; nor did he receive proper notice.

On April 23 he was engaged by the churchwarden of Barton near Penrith to take charge of the parish on the death of the vicar, at 30s. a week, which he happily served from Newton. This had one interesting sequel. In 1871 he published a pamphlet under the aegis of English Church Union. It was called Letters of Commendation, and was a paper delivered to the Union at Penrith in 1867. The writer urged the need for the clergy, when their young people left home to seek work elsewhere, to give each a letter of commendation to the vicar of the parish where they were going, so that they could be befriended by the local church.

> I remember that about the year 1852, when I was Curate in charge of a parish in Lunesdale, a 'term hiring' occurred shortly before a Confirmation, and my catechumens were scattered, some of them probably missing their confirmation altogether, and of those who came in as strangers there was probably some whom I did not find, even as literally was the case, upon the highway. The same bad effect also happened to a large class I had with difficulty gathered when temporarily Curate of Barton: and I knew a case in West Cumberland, where their Clergy were diligently preparing their candidates for Confirmation, when suddenly sixty were absent – a 'term hiring' had scattered the flock.[11]

He went on to mention a similar experience when he worked in Leeds, and with the cooperation of the clergy, bishop Longley of Ripon altered his arrangements.

One thing emerges from this account, that Brunskill was a keen and hard working pastor. Perhaps, having no degree, he was at pains to prove himself equal to any who were more fortunate, and this may account for his determination to see that the poor were properly cared for. He would brook no obstruction.

His duty at Barton came to an end on the 8 July 1855.

DIARY

1853–1855

[The diarist is resident curate of Mallerstang, nr. Kirkby Stephen]

November

5. **Sunday.** Did not use the occasional Service for the day.

6. Not at market [at Kirkby Stephen]. About dusk, while feeling very anxious for war news, a slip fr. the *Leeds Mercury* of Saturday was brought me fr. Kirkby, with very exciting intelligence of a Russian attack upon Balaclava, and that the Light Cavalry had been almost anihilated.

7. Having to dine at the Vicarage [at Kirkby Stephen] I walked into Kirkby somewhat early in order to get up the papers at the 'King's Arms'. The position of the Allies seems very critical. Spent a pleasanter even than last year at this time, Messers Jackson, Mason, Edger.

14. Rode down to Eden Place & found Reginald B. off in Durham. In *The Times* read an article describing the fatal charge of the Light Cavalry at the Battle of Balaclava. It made a deep impression; saw also Gen. Canrobert's Dispatch; & afterwards met Mr Milner with whom I repaired to Blades' surgery. B. said that the *Express* of last even. contradicted *The Times* a/c. but reported another great

battle to have been fought on the 5th inst. Ret'd to wait till Thursday.

15. A stormy day with sleet & rain. Mr Wyvil late Curate of Kirkby & now Inc. [incumbent] of Lunds called.

16. Not feeling very strong. I did not venture out for the *Guardian* (the High Church paper) but it arrived by 'darkning'. It was rich in war news & I was impatient. There was all that could be gathered respecting the 5th before Sebastopol & full a/c of Balaclava. Thus before we have particulars of one battle we hear of another murderous slaughter. The G. gave the letter of *The Times* own corr[respondent], who on a fine bright morning saw the whole battle of Balaclava with its Cavalry Charges fr. an adjoining height. It was the most affecting, graphic & exciting a/c it has yet been my fortune to read. Having no-one with whom I cd. talk myself cool, it was late in the morning before I slept, and then only to dream of that fearful struggle of devoted men. Poor Capt. Nolan in whose career I felt a deep interest was the first soldier shot, and it seems striking that the first of Light Horsemen kept his seat some distance even after death.

17. The *E[nglish] Churchman* also contained Mr Russell's letter [William Howard Russell of *The Times*] and was a better no. than usual. It speaks out strongly of at once declaring Poland to be independant & to look for the worst fr. Austria. It cont[ains] Lord Raglan's dispatch of 5th – 5 gen'rs wounded.

18. Mr Wyvil in returning called & had dinner; he brought me 6 Papers fr. Miss Powley, wh. makes the no. of Newspapers I have read this week 18! I had a Graaf Reinett Herald fr. Steabler directed to Mansergh [near Kirkby Lonsdale where Brunskill had been before serving Mallerstang] wh. came straight to me here. It announced 'Birth on August 3rd at G.R. [Gr. Reinett, S. Africa) to the wife of the Revd W.A. Steabler, Acting Chaplain, of a Daughter'! So the world goes on.

19. **Sunday.** C. proposed that we should drive down to Kirkby Church in the even. although on arrival he went 'To Meeting'! Learned at Mr Jackson's that besides the 5 Generals wounded on the 5th General Sir G[eorge] Cathgart had been killed.

20. Rode to Kirkby on C's pony, & thence on to call on Mr Collinson, who had returned. Found the old man still hearty, but weaker. At the 'King's Arms' found *The Times* of Saturday full of news fr. the Crimea. Read it through & learned with deep regret that besides Gen. Cathgart, Gens. Strangways & Goldie were slain. From this one can only conclude that the British have been greatly outnumbered & been awfully exposed. The siege progresses, tho' slowly.

22. Rec'd my half year's Stipend £40.0.0 A good covering of snow fell today.

23. Rode into Kirkby for news, amid some snow showers. Lent £5. to Isa. etc. *The Guardian* had just got Lord Raglan's Dispatch published yesterday. I have often remarked that I considered a new *Guardian* undisturbed over a good fire a great luxury. And after a good tea I enjoyed this, & heard the wintry blasts howl past my closed shutters; I could not but think of the brave men exposed on the bleak hill tops of the Crimea, or protected only by canvass! Every effort ought to be & is being made for their comfort.

    As I expected the Battle was fought in the valley of Inkerman & for all future time will be called by that name.

    The Queen's address to the Army after the battle of Alma has returned & just been published. It is an admirable document, well written and deeply affecting.

    Even at the end of the Battle of Inkerman the Allies only numbered 14,000, yet out of the 60,000 Russians opposed to them they have killed, wounded or taken 15,000!! Up to the 8th they had more than maintained their ground.

24. The E.C. today contains part of Mr Russell's letter. The morning was dark & wet so that he could not see much of the battle.

26. **Sunday.** The snow wh. fell on Wednesday etc still lays thick wh. may a/c for the very small congregation I had.

30. St Andrew's Day. At school in morning & had a more satisfactory class. [The school was held in an upper room at the back of Mallerstang chapel.] Afterwards to Kirkby. The position of the Allied armies seems improving. Reinforcements pour in. Learnt from *The Times* yt. Parliament meets on the 12th.

   The Guardian's eloquent article on the battle of Inkerman & fund of war news could not prevent my laying it down with a sickening feeling that the bitterness of ecclesiastical partisanship must be obtruded upon us at even such times as these, e.g. The Bp of Manchester attends a mixed meeting of various dissenters – to denounce his brethren. [James Prince Lee, bp 1847].

December

2. The E.C. wh. I read today contains a pleasing letter on the improved estimation of the English with the French since Inkerman.

3. **Sunday.** Heavy showers, & very stormy towards even. A collection for the stove 10.4½. Introduced prayers for the sick & wounded of the Allied Armies.

6. At school appearances under the new Master were rather more encouraging. Mr Hird called & spent even. with me. He rather improves on acquaintance, & now admits his ignorance of the art of Teaching & appears willing to read suggestions of Sullivan etc.

7. At Kirkby arranged with R.B. [R.R. Bradley, MA curate of Crosby Garrett] to go North next week. In *The Guardian* I got a full account of the fearful storm in the Black Sea on the 14th: 1000 men & £2,000,000 lost. A gigantic calamity. But the exertions making at home for the succour & comfort of the Army is very encouraging. A Treaty with Austria has been signed, but its contents still only conjectural. Some sound remarks on 'Protestant agitation' now.

8. In the E.C. I gather that the new Alliance is prob. favourable to the Allies. The *Daily News* of yester – even. has news fr. Bucharest of the 6th that Omer Pacha has marched for the Crimea!

15. As more is known of the Treaty it seems more favourable. The Parliament met on the 12th, and as I expected the Ministers made a good defence of their proceedings. In Cumberland this week I was half surprised to find some of my friends even more rabid agt. Gover't than I expected.

16. From Hackthorpe rode back to Mall[erstang].

20. Sun rose at 10.15 am & set at 2.30 pm.

21. Arranged with the Bradleys to go to Sunderland next week.

24. Sunday. Nice congregations. The Church being simply decorated with evergreen, and well warmed with a neat stove, besides having had some repairs done, afforded a pleasant contrast to its state last year at this time.

25. Christmas Day. congr. 18 Com[munican]ts 5. A quiet day, wh. left me time to think of the state of the Crimean army etc. Weather wild with heavy hail showers.

26. Went into Kirkby in order to start for Sunderland tomorrow. While spending the even. at Mr Flowers, I rec'd a note from Mr Wyvil saying he was too ill to take my duty! However after some suspense R.B. proposed to remain & relieve me. At Eden Place all night. Not very well in the morning. The Miss Sleddales came before light in Kilvington's carriage [Thomas Kilvington of the Castle Inn, Brough], & 'picked up' Miss E.B. for Tebay. However before we had gone ½ doz. miles I became so giddy etc, as to be obliged to get up outside, even in the snow on Ashfell. After a cold journey we arrived safely in Sunderland by 7 pm. Left Miss E. to go to Bainbridge Holme in a cab, & made the best of my way to Mr Ritson's in Villiers Street. The door was ans'd by Harry, who I c'd not recognise in the least. Found a cordial welcome. Mr R. very little changed, and the rest much the same.

27. Altho' still too unwell to enjoy myself as I cd. have wished,
I went down with Mr R. to business, and thence after a few
minutes to the News Room. Mr Seymour one of the MPs
for the Borough, having accepted the recorderership of
Newcastle, has resigned his seat for re-election, & it seems
likely there will be a contest.

The Times has lately been condemning Lord Raglan
strongly, & therefore I am fortunate in having access to so
many other papers to get up the answers. Called on Tom
Law & had a long walk with him over the new Docks etc.
To my great annoyance he says it is commonly reported
here that I am engaged to E. & have come on purpose to
be married. I guess the B.s themselves have started this.
With Charley R. called at Bainbridge Holme & on returning dropped in at the Atheneum where Mr Seymour was
addressing a large meeting. He shouts too much; but there
was some good speaking.

29. Went by coach to Rainton where my friend Lord was ill of
Rheumatic fever & his Rector an old friend of my Grandfather's was also an invalid. Lord was mostly confined to
his bed; but we had lots of talk, & notwithstanding my
need of a rest I was obliged to take all the duty.

January 1855

1. In a Gale of wind I took coach again for Sunderland, and
arrived in time for the Nomination. Also for Mr R.'s
family party, wh. was rather 'slow'. After dinner, J.G., W.
& I walked down to the Pier; it still blew very hard; but the
moonlight on the waters was very fine. The storm at this
time was doing great mischief at the other side of the
Channel – flooding Hamburgh etc.

3. At 9 pm left Sund. for Newcastle.

4. At 6 am left N. arriving at Tarn Lodge abt. 11 am.

5. Newton in the evening.

6. A pleasant day for my return to Mal[lerstang].

14. **Sunday.** Regularly 'broke down' during evensong. Fainted & very sick, but enabled to walk home, & after keeping quiet & warm for a day or two with careful diet I recovered my strength again without medicine. I now think that symptoms wh. I attributed to my Throat, & want of rest etc, for years, are those of a stomach complaint, & have begun a restoration by discarding tea etc for breakfast, and being careful not to eat unless really hungry.

February

24. After six weeks or more of Frost & Snow the cold being on the average 12 dr. lower than usual, a gentle thaw today.

25. **Sunday.** Very small congregation, the snow upon the ground being alleged as an excuse for neglecting Worship, also extra work in 'fothering' [i.e. feeding sheep etc].

26. More snow again, wh. about 10 am. was drifted so as to block up the roads again. When first cut the snow was in some places 5 ft. deep.

March

2. During the past 2 months there has been much angry discussion on the management of the war. *The People* have proved very impatient of drawbacks. However today I have news of the Army at Aupatoria having won a great battle over the Russians on the 17th ult.

3. The thaw has continued until today; but there was snow in the morning & it is freezing tonight.

4. **Sunday.** Omitted the Evensong at Mallerstang in order to take R.B.'s duty at Crosby Garrett. The day was cold but bright & I had a pleasant ride. The Church seems at a very low ebb at Crosby.

5. Started at abt. 7 am in the rain for Tebay, where I first heard that the Emperor Nicholas had died on Thursday last.

6. Fr. Hackthorpe walked over to Grt Strickland to see Mr Jowett. He is uncomfortable in consequence of the interference of some of the Trustees. A bright warm day. In the evn. went down to Clifton.

7. Another fine day, & P. having said Fa. wd. bring me a pony up in order that I might go to the coursing, I returned with Is. to H. Waited until about 12 am. & then walked up to Knipe Scar, where I got P's horse, & rode some five hours.

8. Went down to Newton & fd. all well. For the first time for 7 weeks some attempts were made this afternoon to plough, although the sun scarcely thaws the previous night's frost.

9. Colder with frost.

10. Started to return to Mal[lerstang] at 7.30 am. Snowing fast & the ground well covered. Not so much snow at Tebay, & scarcely any in the Dale. To the S.E. of Ravenstonedale I was surprised to see ploughing.

11. **Sunday.** Snowing slightly all day. A middling congr. in the morn.

12. Very thin covering of snow soon melted, but all looks very white in the country.

17. Snow & Rain during the morning but in the even. a good covering of snow.

18. **Sunday.** The snow upon the ground & heavy rain thinned the congregation. Preached on God's dealing with the Nation of Israel preparatory to the observance of a National fast etc. on Wednesday next. Sun set at 5.30 pm.

19. A bright morning, so I purpose going to market for almost the first time this year.

21. **Wednesday.** Weather very cold & stormy, yet I was able to have two services, 7 in the morn. & 2 ev.cong.

22. A strong cold wind with snow hindered my keeping an appointment with Reg. to go to Brough.

23. Still snowing, yet I ventured out, & at the Toll learned that Mr Robinson [the perpetual curate of Mallerstang] had arrived! Thus fulfilling the worst rumours of his intention. I have yet heard nothing fr. the Bishop & am in an unpleasant position. Called upon Mr King [the vicar of Kirkby Stephen] who told me that Mr Mounsey had written to say that Mr R's testimonials had been accepted. Having also rec'd a letter fr. Mr Serjentson about his curacy nr. Thirsk, I went on to see Mr Jefferson [the vicar] at Brough. I had refused the curacy because of not knowing when I would be at Liberty. Mr J. recom. me to write again now. Remained to tea at Eden Place.

24. As I expect Reg. this afternoon, I have called upon Mr Robinson & found him much what I expected & apparently little changed. He has no Licence, nor had he heard of the acceptance of his Testimonials, but on hearing this last he banished all his doubts & told me he would preach tomorrow. He also said he had discovered he had no Parochial Charge & wd. make Mr King look after that. He appears to be a disagreeable man. Under these circumstances I have thought it best to write to the Bp as follows:

> My Lord,
> Having been informed that Mr Robinson had returned yesterday, I considered it my duty to call upon him this morning, when he told me that he purposes Preaching tomorrow. He admits that he has no Licence from yr. Ldship, but expects one. Under these circumstances wd. Your Lordship kindly inform me how I ought to act or what is my position.

Bradlay & his nephew came up this afternoon; as I am placed his company was acceptable.

25. **Sunday.** & with the finest weather of any this year. Dreading that Mr Robinson wd. be taking forcible possession I went to Church 20 minutes before the time; but to my astonishment he was in the Desk & going rapidly thro' the Psalms. There were a few of his partizans assembled; but the cong. was not large for the day. He read the Com[munion] service fr. the Desk & Preached fr. II Sam.

16–11 & 12. placing himself in the place of David as a persecuted innocent man & the victim of malice etc.

In the afternoon he was present, but he allowed me to take the service. I delivered a lecture as usual on the 2nd. Lesson. In the morning I took my seat in the Chancel. I fear the discussions on the affair have tended to mar what wd. have been a pleasant Sunday.

As supplementary to what I wrote on Saturday, I purpose writing again to the Bishop, but will first perhaps show it to Mr King.

> My Lord,
>   I addressed your Lordship shortly on Saturday & now beg to add some a/c of our proceedings yesterday. In accordance to the advice of Mr King I had resolved to allow Mr Robinson to take his course under protest. I had requested the Clerk not to ring the Bell before the normal time; but I suppose he was in some doubt whom to obey, and when I reached the Church some 20 minutes before that time (10.30) I found Mr Robinson in the Desk reading the Psalms. Having gone prepared to take any part of or all the service I went to the seat as usual within the Com[munion] rails; but Mr Robinson proceeded with the service to the end, reading the Com[munion] service from the Prayer Desk instead of standing at the North side of the Table. I mention this last mainly because he claims your Lordship's sanction for the usage.
>   In the afternoon he was there, but allowed me to take the service, & although I have had an average attendance of 20 out of the 210 [population] or less to this Evening Prayer with Lecture, he states it as his intention to discontinue all but the Prayers during the summer months. I fear, my Lord, that notwithstanding my endeavours to [act] in what is to be a painful position, enough is known to give an unfavourable impression of the Discipline of the Church, especially to estranged members who are in a large majority here.
>   I am, etc.
> P.S. It appears, My Lord, that I may say of course I have not considered my ministry closed here without the usual notice.

After sending the above I had 2 or 3 letters fr. his Lordship fr. wh. I guessed that Mr Robinson was to remain & therefore that I had better go north & so avoid him.

30. Went down to Hackthorpe, & fr. thence called upon the Chancellor to whom I explained my case. He said I was entitled to a six weeks' notice as fr. a new Incumbent, & gave me encouragement to hope for some preferment fr. the Bishop.

31. Went down to Newton with Isa. per rail in the morning & met Father at Pen(rith) station.

April

1. **Sunday.** Worshipped at Newton, but took no part of the service, not being very well.

6. **Good Friday.** Assisted in the Com[munion] service.

7. **Easter Eve.** Preached at Xst Church Penrith.

8. **Easter Sunday.** Assisted & preached [probably at Newton].

11. With Isa. went to stay at Askham for a day or 2.

12. While sitting after supper, a servant suddenly announced that Mr T. Gibson Vicar of Barton was dead. He had just been found so in the garden.

14. At Mr W[ard]'s suggestion I wrote to Col. Lowther calling his attention mildly to my claims to preferment at Lord L[onsdale]'s hands. Mr W. said also that he wd. get me the occasional duty at Barton. I then left for Crosby Garrett, Mes. B. having gone, & Mr Newby [the rector] not having returned.

15. **Sunday.** I took the services & preached twice at Crosby Garrett, & then walked by Kirkby to Musgrave Rectory where I remained all night.

16. Went back to Mallerstang.

19. Rode with Cleasby [prob. Thomas Cleasby of Ing Hill] to [? Flokrigg] & then returned to Kirkby. I had prev. heard fr. Lodge & Mr Wyvil abt. the Inc[umbency] of Lunds [a chapelry in Abbotside, Wensleydale] & Mr Balderson talked of resigning to me; but all came to nought. Being

locum tenens at Kirkby fr. the week & Mr King unable to entertain me, I put up at the King's Arms tonight.

21. Saw Mr Newby who had just returned to Crosby Garrett; but no fee for last Sunday. Spent the even. with the Jacksons.

22. **Sunday.** Rather nervous and weak for my work at Kirkby S.

23. At about 4 am. started with Cleasby & Parkin Blades for Penrith Fair & Newton. Found Mr Elwood Ch. warden at Barton, waiting to arrange with me to take the charge of that parish, wh. I did at 30/- per week.

29. **Sunday.** Rode to Mr Elwood's at Thorp, where I left my bag & dined during the whole time I was at Barton. During the 11 weeks I was there I had to prepare the catechumens for Confirmation, this being the fourth 'set' I have sent up in 5 years. The church somewhat awkward; but liked the people. All this time I lived at Newton wh. I enjoyed very much.

July

8. This being my last Sunday at Barton I dined at Dalemain.

NOTES TO CHAPTER FIVE

1. Diary 22 Nov. 1854. His half year's salary £40.
   Diary 23 Mar. 1855.

2. *History & Traditions of Mallerstang Forest & Pendragon Castle*, Revd W. Nicholls, 1883, p. 115 et seq. Reminiscences of Revd Wm. Thompson MA a native of Outhgill, MA Queen's Coll. Oxford. For one year temp. headmaster at Sedbergh Grammar School, married an heiress, lived at Guildrey Lodge, Sedbergh, became a magistrate. Memorial in Sedbergh church. Author of *Sedbergh, Garsdale & Dent*, 1910.

3. *A Naturalists Pilgrimage*, Richard Kearton, 1926, p. 12.

4. *Hist. of Mallerstang*, op.cit. pp. 35, 36/7, 39, 42.

5. Ibid. p. 119.

6. *The Church in an age of negligence*, Peter Virgin, 1989, p. 229.

7. *Hist. of Mallerstang*, op.cit. p. 34.

8. Press Cutting, N.D. in possession of author.

9. L.M. Copied by author from original diary c. 1947. Printed in: *Maller-stang, a Westmorland dale*, Mary M. Thompson, 1965, p. 50.

10. Yorkshire Arch. Soc. Record Series, vol. CXXX, 1967. *Abstracts of Abbotside Wills* (1552–1688) for refs. to Lunds.

11. Letters of Commendation. A Paper read at a Meeting of the English Church Union, Sept. 1867 by Revd J. Brunskill, Curate of Swindale, Headmaster of the Free Grammar School at Lowther, 1871, p. 14.

NB.
The diary of the Revd Joseph Brunskill dates from Nov. 1854 to Dec. 1860 with many gaps. It has been put into sections to facilitate a commentary.

6

All Hallows
1855–57

THE BISHOP who sent Brunskill to All Hallows was the Hon.
Hugh Percy DD who was bishop of Carlisle from 1827 to 1856.
He was an aristocrat, not too familiar with the clergy, always
punctual, and efficient in undertaking several reforms, especially after the Reform Act 1832, and the Report on Ecclesiastical
Revenues of 1835. In the old diocese of Carlisle (excluding the
Chester deaneries) there were 4 benefices with under £50 a year,
23 between £50 and £75, 25 between £75 and £100,and 25
between £100 and £150 out of a total of 127 benefices. The
richest had between £900 and £1,000 a year.[1]

It was still an age of pluralities; the bishop himself had
£3,000 a year, but also held the chancellorship of Salisbury
Cathedral from 1811, and a prebendal stall at St Paul's from
1816.[2] The chancellor of the diocese of Carlisle was the Revd
Wm. Jackson DD from 1846; he was a fellow of Queen's College, Oxford, rector of Lowther from 1828 (£283 p.a.) and rector of Cliburn from 1840 (£188 p.a.). In 1855 he resigned the
chancellorship in favour of the archdeaconry of Carlisle (£200
p.a.). Dr Jackson later became provost of Queen's College,
while still holding his northern preferments, and living in gentle
comfort at Askham Hall.[3] He was succeeded as chancellor of
Carlisle in 1855 by Charles James Burton who had from 1821
been rector of Lydd in Kent on a stipend of £1,247 a year.[4] On
his appointment he left two curates to do his work, while he
retired to Stanwix, and held an occasional consistory court.

At the other end of this scale of profit and power was the rector of Asby inhabiting the coldest rectory in the diocese on the
princely stipend of £54 a year;[5] while the rector of the adjacent
parish of Ormside (£166) also held the perpetual curacy of
Hensingham, Cumberland (£126) with the chaplaincy of
Chatham dockyard.[6] The perpetual curates of All Hallows and
Newton Reigny received £80 a year, the stipend of a statutory
curate under the 1813 Act.

There were also those who dropped out of the system; E.C. Wyvil whom Brunskill met as curate of Kirkby Stephen, was BA of Jesus College, Cambridge, was curate of Lunds for two years on £75 a year with 64 remote fellside parishioners, lost heart, gave it up, and went to live in Hawes, and eventually died in about 1874 in the house of a clerical relative in Bedale.[7] The system was rotten and broke men's hearts. Brunskill was virtually at the bottom of the ladder. His later career cannot be understood, nor his determination not to be put down by the system and those who fattened on it, unless we appreciate the twilight world of ill paid curates and lower incumbents. He was a fighter.

The chapelry of All Hallows (of 250 inhabitants) in the old parish of Aspatria had been served since 1812 by T. Thompson on a stipend of £80 a year. He was now too old for work, and bishop Percy sent Brunskill as curate, Thompson paying £15 towards the £80 wage, while the bishop found the rest, probably through Queen Anne's Bounty, which received an annual Parliamentary grant of £100,000 towards relieving the lot of the poorer clergy.[8] One of the first matters to come to his notice was the condition of village education.

It is difficult at this distance in time to appreciate the appalling condition of village schools graphically illustrated in the life of George Moore the philanthropist (1806–1876) who was born at Mealsgate in the nearby parish of Bolton. Village schools were very bad; most of the schoolmasters were men who could not succeed in any other occupation. 'They were for the most part disabled by accident or demoralised by drink.' 'The country-folks were asleep. They were droning on in the old way. Everything was in a state of stagnation. While the world outside was undergoing rapid movement, the world in this little bit of England was standing stock-still. The schools were there, but nobody looked after them – neither gentry, clergy, statesmen [the old estatesmen farmers], nor the rate-payers.'[9]

George Moore determined to try to improve the school conditions by securing the erection of a new school at Bolton, supplanting that of Boltongate where he received his first schooling at the hands of 'Blackbird' Wilson, who was notable for his imitation of bird songs. The parish of Bolton contained 1,100 inhabitants. There were three schools; two of the masters were addicted to drink. They had no books, and had no proper means of teaching. The third was a poor fellow, a collier, who had fallen down a coal-pit. His leg was so badly broken that it had to be cut off. This accident was his only qualification for the office of schoolmaster. When he saw what Mr Moore was trying to do for schools he said 'Mr Moore, I know I am not fit to be a schoolmaster, but how am I to live?' Moore replied 'If you will come to London I will get you a situation; and if you do your best, I promise you I will never let you want'. He trusted him, went to London, and by industry became a clerk on the Great Western Railway. Mr John Moorby, the new head of Bolton new school was chosen by Mr Moore from National Society's Training School. He fixed the fees at about half the rate of the old schools, and relied upon annual subscriptions to make up the deficiency. Mr Moore also took an interest in the Grammar School at Uldale, and the Free School at Bothel in the parish of Torpenhow. In 1853 he was appointed a trustee of Plumbland school, and in the following year persuaded the trustees to have a public examination which was conducted by the Revd William Mandell Gunson MA, fellow and tutor of Christ's College, Cambridge, who officiated as inspector.

This was a singular request, for Mr Gunson had also been born in Bolton parish, though he was sixteen years younger than Mr Moore. He also had been taught in the old school at Bolton before going to Sedbergh, and then to Christ's College. In 1847 he was 28th Wrangler, and 4th Classic in the Tripos examinations. He was fellow from 1847 to 1881, and tutor from 1851 to 1870. He was ordained in 1849. He was remarkable in the history of the college for, during his time as tutor the number of men gaining high places in the Tripos examinations improved greatly. It was he who suggested to Mr Moore that another school was required for All Hallows. He began to solicit subscriptions from the farmers and landowners with little success. There were many objectors: they said that they would never get thirty children to the school, 'and how can we pay the master?' When Mr Gunson mentioned the scheme to

Mr Moore he responded warmly, and between them they paid in equal shares four fifths of the new school. The new headmaster Mr John Green was a certified teacher, and appears in the early pages of Brunskill's diary. Within a year Mr Green was married. This is how Mr Moore's biographer describes the improvement: 'When All Hallows school was opened it soon filled with children. John Green ... proved an excellent schoolmaster. His wife, to the astonishment of the parish, taught the girls sewing. Such a thing had never been known in the neighbourhood. The number of pupils grew to between sixty and seventy, for the excellence of the teaching drew scholars from the neighbouring parishes.' The school was placed in two acres of land which was laid out in plots, and gardened by the children. This pioneer work was effected fifteen years before the Education Act of 1870. The new school was nearly completed when Brunskill arrived in July 1855. Mr Green was warmly supported by him; he stood in at the school when Green was absent. But something went wrong. At the Committee Meeting held in August 1856 the committee condemned Brunskill's arrangements with Mr Green, and Mr Gunson (no doubt on holiday at Aspatria at his father's) was very abusive on parish matters. Had Brunskill interfered with Mr Gunson's arrangements? Or, had he tried to channel the school towards the National Society, of which Brunskill had just been made organising secretary in the diocese? Whatever the cause, Mr Gunson seems to have written to Mr Moore, and he in turn to the new bishop of Carlisle, who summoned the unfortunate curate to Carlisle in November. The stormy interview can be read in the diary. It is probable that as Mr Moore, and no doubt Mr Gunson as well as the bishop, were strict evangelicals, they took strong exception to Brunskill's high church leanings. That sealed his fate, and he soon had to look for another job. In fairness it must be said that the work which Mr Moore and later Mr Gunson did for education in a very backward part of Cumberland was enlightened, and Brunskill should have been more sensitive to pioneer work, and not so dogmatic over church control of local education.[9]

The new bishop who interviewed Brunskill was H.M.

Villiers, a narrow evangelical of the Clapham sect, and an able extempore preacher. He was a strong disciplinarian, and within a year of his arrival in 1856 suspended a number of clergy for drunkenness. It is possible that the trouble at All Hallows school was the occasion of Mr Moore and the bishop becoming acquainted. They became friends, and not long after Brunskill's removal Mr Moore stayed at Rose Castle, and warmed to the evangelical piety of the bishop's house. The bishop warmly supported Mr Moore's work for schools and travelling libraries; and when the bishop died Mr Moore founded an educational trust in his memory. Through the pioneer work of these men 'the clergy were forced to take an interest in the schools, and the sleepy farmers were at length compelled to look after the education of their own children. Not only were the schools properly built and inspected, but Sunday schools were established in all the parishes. Sunday schools had never existed there before. The attendance at church was greatly increased, and a new life was infused into the district.'[9] Mr Moore's invitation to bishop Villiers to visit Bolton and All Hallows churches will be given after the next section of the diary.

As the bishop was patron of All Hallows any hope that Brunskill would succeed to the parish was vain, and the year 1856 closed with Brunskill at Newton expecting his dismissal, though he continued to do duty there. The chance death of Mr Rayson the curate of Askham in January 1857 raised his hopes. As he had relatives at Askham and Clifton, and his sister Isabella at Hackthorpe he would be on home ground, and he gladly accepted the offer; and, after some difficulty with the bishop over notice, it was agreed that he should stay at All Hallows till Easter and then go to Askham as curate.

On the 19 February 1857 Brunskill wrote to his half-sister Hannah at Newton and mentioned his sharp correspondence with the bishop over his length of notice, but eventually the bishop was forced to concede his leaving at Easter. He also added: 'Last night I learned that the Curate of Wigton is being worse treated than I am.' He added that he would be in Carlisle for assize week, and would travel to Newton by the midnight train.[10]

Reference has been made to the fact that shortly after his arrival at All Hallows, Brunskill had been made organising secretary to the National Society for Education, which was the Church of England counterpart to the non-conformist organisation of British Schools. His salary was to be £50 a year, to include travelling expenses. The work was heartbreaking; the clergy rarely gave notice of his preaching in their churches, and the collections were so pitifully small that they never met the cost of his salary. In addition he had to pay a deputy to do his duty. His new vicar of Askham kindly allowed him to preach away from home, but as the receipts remained low the post was terminated on the 19 November 1859.[11]

DIARY

1855–1857

July 1855

14. Arrived at All Hallows.

15. **Sunday.** Preached my 'Inaugural Discourse'. The Church is very small but has been decently restored. No Evensong as yet.

16. Decided to remain here over this week, having obtained very nice lodgings. Walked to the New School (2 miles) which I found nearly completed. The Shell of the Building is better than the fittings. It is calculated to accommodate abt. 90; but it is badly placed for a large attendance.

21. Went into Carlisle to see Mr Mechi, & hear his Lecture on the present state of farming. Found Carlisle in a state of bustling preparation for the meeting of the Royal Agricultural Show, wh. is in fact now being held. I liked Mr Mechi's appearance better even than I expected, & enjoyed the Lecture, taking especial pains that he should be well cheered.

23. Returned by Carlisle to Newton.

26. The Show Day. Weather finer than expected; exhibition very good. [There are a number of breaks in the diary; this resumes in 1856.] From this time till 25 April 1856 there was little change at All Hallows. The failure of the Schoolmaster, who had been engaged by Mr Geo. Moore previous to my arrival, was a continual source of trouble & anxiety. After having had notice to leave for 6 months he ceased work today, without having another situation to go to. Returning from Newton here I had been over Penrith Fair I met Mr Green the new Master, & we arrived safely at All Hallows. My confident hopes in Mr Green's success, & the aid he would be to me in the Parish, naturally raised my spirits; but amid the pile of papers etc. wh. had accumulated during my week's absence, I found a letter wh. gave fresh cause for thankfulness. The letter conveyed my appointment as organising Secretary in this Diocese to the National Society for Education – my stipend of £50 per an. is to include all travelling expenses, wh. may be considerable, but still I hope enough will remain to raise me above the harassing embarrassment of the poverty which has followed me somewhat strangely at least all the 6 years I have now been in Holy Orders.

When I went to Ocker Hill my stipend was to have been £90. The Curates Aid Soc. however was unable to pay its Quota of £40 owing to the evil effects produced by the conduct of the Bishop of Manchester [James Prince Lee]. My removal from Horbury led to expense, & in Leeds I had to pay £60 per an. for Lodgings. Worn down there, I retired to Mansergh on a stipend of £70, whence I had to remove on the return of the Incumbent in less than a year. The Bishop of Carlisle then sent me to Mallerstang, wh. being very much 'out of the way' was expensive; but my 'affairs' were improving, when I had to remove again, this time without an hour's notice. And what is worse the Sequestrators gave me no compensation & up to this time I have not been paid for even the 'work done' in Mallerstang.

April

28. Mr McDonough not having left the school house, Mr Green stayed with me, & today after an early breakfast, I went with him to school where I remained all day.

May

18. Trinity Sunday.

19. It is six years today since I first 'took rooms' as a curate.

25. Sunday. A good school & full Church.

26. Started for London, going to Newton for the night. On my way met Mr Deakin coming here. Not very well.

27. Left Penrith at 9 am. Travelled through by a 'Third' comfortably with good company.

28. Spent the morning making calls, very tired. In the even. nevertheless endured 5 hours partial suffocation at the Princesses theatre, in order to see Mr Chas. Kean's revival of the Winters Tale.

29. Awoke at my lodgings in Surrey St, Strand by the joyous ringing of many bells. This being the Queen's Birthday, & also the day of rejoicing for the restoration of peace. Being now lame from the excessive walking of yesterday &c. I did not turn out early & then strolled up to Bond St. I there learned that Mr Byers had gone to the Review or inspection of the Household troops at the Horse Guards. I immediately took a cab thence, but had missed the principal part. In the afternoon went to see the gaity occasioned by the Queen's Drawing Room. In nearly the last carriage we saw Sir Harry Smith. His breast was covered with stars & medals. [N.B. He had served with Wellington in Spain and at Waterloo; served in India, and particularly S. Africa. Died 1860] The day was a full holiday. Returned at about 1am. fr. the illuminations. During the visit I saw through the Arsenal at Woolwich, the Crystal Palace, Regents Park Zoological gardens by day. During evenings, was at Albert Smith's & Gordon Cummings' lectures etc at The Polytechnic.

On Sunday although ill & tired (very) I got to the Temple Church, thence to a Luncheon at Bond St being unable to make my way to Notting Hill where I ought to have dined. In the afternoon crossed the Park to 15 Kensington Palace Gardens & waited till a 5pm dinner with Mr Moore. Met the Levesons etc. Thence, having learnt that Notting Hill was near I called on Miss Jackson who returned with me North on Friday.

Tuesday & Wednesday were occupied with the business of the National Society. On Thursday saw Mr Moore at 5 Bow Ch. Yd., thence by the Sanctuary to the House of Commons. Here I had much enjoyment; heard Lord Palmerston announce that our Ambassador in America had received his passports. Heard Admiral Sir Chas. Napier, Berkeley, Col. [? Dunne], Sir E.B. Lytton, Disraeli, Housman etc. But was especially fortunate in again hearing Mr S[idney] Herbert [who d. 1861). The speech was on army education splendidly delivered to a full and most attentive house.

June

11. Notwithstanding feeling very much exhausted from the effects of my late journey & being in considerable pain, I attended the laying of the foundation stone at the new Church at West Newton by Dr Montague Villiers our new Bishop. His Lordship was all bows & smiles; but made an indiscreet & invidious speech contrasting his doings in London with the clergyman who merely wears a black coat etc. ...

After hearing his Lordship at Wigton, Maryport etc, & meeting him sometimes, I am only confirmed in my first impression that the appointment of so narrow a partizan is peculiarly unfortunate. We were soon able to reckon that he had filled the first 5 vacancies by strangers. [I] found him impracticable & unwilling to cooperate in the promotion of an educational Exhibition, wh. I had first proposed in Feb'y & met with the approbation of the Diocesan Education Board & especially Dean Tait [later Archbishop of Canterbury, d.1882]. All this time amidst much difficulty we kept struggling on with the School. During the autumn we almost despaired of drawing scholars to such a desolate spot. The Committee at the General Meeting in Aug'st condemned all my arrangements with Mr Green etc, & highly approved of our apparent success; but I had no thanks fr. them as a body. Mr Gunson was *very abusive* at this meeting on Parish matters.

November

12. Some time in Nov'r I had a letter fr. the Bp & saw him next day at his office in Carlisle. Mr Moore not satisfied with several refusals of a grant fr. the so called Ch. of E. Education Soc. had begged his Lordship's interference on behalf of Bolton & All Hallows. To *him* the Secretary stated that having made enquiries he had been told that 'Mr Sherwen & I were not their sort of men', and that *therefore* they had refused a grant. This the Bishop himself told me, beginning by saying that I had only myself to blame for the loss of the grant etc, and that he had comforted the Secretary by promising that when the Living was vacant an 'efficient' man should succeed.

As the Bishop made this cool announcement that all my labours, standing and & Privations were to be disregarded & that I should not even have the poor little living wh. had been promised me on condition wh. I had fulfilled to my sore costs, he stood with his back to the fire while I sat looking him hard in the face. I continued staring, carefully avoiding showing any consciousness of criminality, & allowed him to finish without my speaking.

This mode of pleading 'not guilty', possibly caused him to realise our relative positions & he might remember that as Bishop of Carlisle he had now other duties than executing upon poor curates the behests of a Society wh. he acknowledged to have assisted in forming for the promotion of 'particular' views.

He hesitated & somewhat retracted, & I remarked on the injustice of these secret reports & hoped that our work wd. surely stand ag'st them. In the talk wd. followed he recommended me to read a tract called 'The Sinner's Friend', & spoke to me of being still uncoverted! On parting he talked of doing what he could for me!! I also learned at this interview that Mr Thompson [the incumbent] had besought the Bp to withdraw my Licence, so that he might save the £15 per an. wh. he pays towards my stipend. Thus after finding my fears had not pictured my position to be as bad as its reality, I returned to Newton somewhat wearied in spirit. In consultation it now appeared evident to all of us that no more sacrifices must be made for All Hallows.

1857
Spent the close of the old year & beginning of new at Newton.

January
6. A letter fr. Mr Ward [J.T. Ward, vicar of Askham fr. 1832] announcing the death of poor Mr Rayson yesterday & offering me the Curacy of Askham. Wrote to thank Mr W. & to the Bp to enquire if *I was* really to be removed from All Hallows & mentioning this offer.

20. Ans. fr. the Bp saying 'you are quite right to accept the curacy' etc., but wishing me to remain until Trinity Sunday. Gave Mr Thompson formal notice, & wrote to Mr W. accepting.

27. Saw Mr Ward at Askham, & found him very anxious for my early arrival. Pleased with the prospect of more school work.

February
3. A disappointing letter fr. the Bp telling me that I ought to have given him a formal notice, and that until I did so my 3 months wd. not reckon. Wrote to him that I had supposed his consent & notice to Inc[umbent] was all that the law required. Requested that the letter of the law might not be enforced ag'd me considering that I had so repeatedly

waived its advantages. E.g. my having had no notice on leaving Mallerstang, coming here at once, at a loss, & for a smaller stipend than the Law awarded.

7. Went into Carlisle according to engagement to read a paper to the Diocesan Schoolmasters Assoc. My subject was 'The Bible & its safeguards'. A fair attendance. Afterwards saw Mr Mounsey [the deputy-registrar]. He had not had any communication from the Bishop; but confirmed my impression that the law did not require me to give him a notice.

8. **Sunday.** About an average congregation; but greatly encouraged by the attendance & devout behaviour of the 'little ones'. The Service was altogether as good as I could have wished.

9. Wrote again to the Bishop.

14. Another cross letter fr. his Lordship. Ans'd.

15. **Sunday.** Weather fine, M[orning] cong. good.

17. Wrote to Mr Ward & Mr Whiteside. [Revd Stephen Whiteside BA, PC of Thrimby, 1858]

20. A letter fr. Isa. confirming my impression at my last visit of Father's declining health. This decides me to go to Newton fr. Carlisle next week.

22. **Sunday.** Very windy. Cong. small. My 31 birthday. Time – Eternity.

23. Went to Carlisle but fo'd the Educational Meeting was not till tomorrow. However the Judges having arrived for the Assizes there was much to see. Attended Service at the Cathedral. Spent the night at Upperby. Much conversation with Mr C. on our Soc.s & the Bishop.

24. St Matthias. Shrove Tuesday. Walked in fr. Upperby to the Cathedral Service at 11 am. Afterwards to the Court House for the Trial. At 4 pm went to the Town Hall to the meeting of the Dioc. Educat. Soc. Besides abt. a doz. members of the Com[mittee] including the Bp, Dean, Archdeacons,

Messers Morewood, Brown, Olivant etc who had apparently concluded the business at some preliminary meeting, there was only abt. 6 more individuals present! W. Marshall Esq. MP coming in proceeded to propose that a second organising Master should be employed wh. led to some slight debate, the Bp promising to provide Diocesan Inspection. This over, the Dean read fr. a printed paper the names of the new committee (wh. ought at this meeting to have been elected) & Geo. Dixon Esq. having closed the meeting by a vote of thanks to the Bp we immediately separated. Of course I shall neither subscribe nor go to the expense of attending again till there be some reform upon this fashion.

At 8 pm heard a lecture fr. Mr Thackeray, and at 12 left Carlisle for Newton.

25. Awoke by 'Pearshaw' [his elder brother John Pearson Brunskill, b.1824] who contributed much to my enjoying a few very pleasant days.

27. Went to Askham. Read & explained to Mr Ward my correspondence with the Bishop. Mr W. expressed himself quite satisfied& said he wd. write to the Bp expressing his regret that I cd. not come to him before Easter. He is however willing to wait & accompanied me to take my rooms. Returned by Hackthorpe with Isabella.

March

8. **Sunday.** Very cold & snowing, wh. might seem unfortunate, for I was to preach at Uldale & Ireby on behalf of the Nat. Soc. Mr Clarke coming to All Hallows. Both the congregations & collections were disgracefully small, ill repaying my labour & expense.

9. After a restless night awoke to find myself well 'knocked up' most prob. from yesterday.

10. Still unequal to my work. Had a call fr. a person who said he had been sent by the Bp to see the curacy &c. The whole style of himself & wife were unprepossessing, but

after a long conversation I found him so 'unsound' that I told him with all earnestness I was very sorry he was coming.

15. **Sunday.** Pooh. The most stormy Sunday I have experienced in Allerdale.

19. Wrote to Mr Lonsdale.

22. **Sunday.** Again very cold. High wind with snow.

25. Saw Jane Nanson of Blennerhasset, about whom I had heard shocking a/cs. of her being beaten & starved &c. by Geo. Wilson & Wife with whom she lives. She seemed almost covered with sores & bruises. Wrote to her Father, Jos. Nanson, Foundry Inn, Adelaide at Bradford.

26. Recd a cheque for a qrs stipend fr. the N. Soc. Heard fr. Mr Barwise that he is willing to take my duty at All H. on Sunday morn, wh. will enable me to preach for N. Soc. at Aspatria.

27. **Friday.** Newspapers interesting fr. the General Election. Nomination at Carlisle yesterday. But the event wh. is most noticeable is the Judgement (on final appeal) respecting the Knightsbridge Church ornaments. I am most deeply thankful that so much of the last decision has been reversed. Waterton after dragging his Minister through 3 Courts, only obtains the removal of a small + [cross] fr. the communion Table, & is ordered to pay his own costs!

In the evening heard a rumour that the conservative candidate for Carlisle had been returned at the head of the Poll. This is also thankworthy, for the defeated candidate yesterday asked for votes on the strength of his supporting Lord Palmerston who had sent us a Bishop who fraternises with all denominations!

28. Heard fr. Nanson of Bradford offering to send money for the conveyance of his poor daughter home, if I wd. make arrangements. At Plumbland learnt that the contest for West Cumberland was likely to be close. The 'Yellows' [Note: the Lowther interest] are careless.

29. Preached at Aspatria for N. Soc. All H[allows] even.

21. 'The Nomination' at Cockermouth, whither I went. My first visit to C. Enjoyed much. After the Hustings &c. rode forward to Bassenthwaite. Saw the Revd Sherlock at Scarness & obtained his services as Local Treasurer to N[ational] S[ociety]. The House at Scarness was built by my Great Grandfather [Mr Wane] cir. 1703, 'a fine old E[nglish] G[entleman]' who lived at a bountiful rate, & kept hounds.

April

1. Returned by 'Marshals',Uldale, Ireby &c.

3. Started the poor girl Nanson to Bradford. 'The Polling Day'! I walked on to Aspatria, & remained till evening, when we heard that the 'Yellows' were victorious. Found it very pleasant, as not being so much 'a stranger in a crowd', as I have too often been. Mr Whiteside called [the Revd Stephen Whiteside, BA 1858 PC of Thrimby, and later vicar of Shap] as the 'gentleman' with whom the Arch[deacon] had arranged for the interregnum between my leaving and Trinity.

10. **Good Friday.** Cong. very small. Some old snow drifts abt. Skiddaw.

12. **Easter Day.** Again a thin cong, 4 Com[municants], but the weather was very cold – hail.

13. Stormy with hail & snow. However in the afternoon I went to Hayton School Festival. The Fells very white.

14. At school wh. I am to look after for Mr Green, who is absent, & wd. be married in Cheshire yesterday.

   However the attendance being small, I yielded to urgent requests to go to Newton for a wedding on Thursday next.

16. A bright morning & gay marriage.

19. My last Sunday at All Hallows. Crowded congregations for my farewell.

20. Busy packing up my goods.

22. My 'notice' having expired yesterday, I left poor All Hallows by first train.

This being the day fixed for the election of Proctors, on arriving in Carlisle I was pleased to see several Clergymen astir. After Service in the Cathedral at wh. more than 20 clergymen were present, there was an interval of some half hour, during wh. the number increased to about 30. It being evident that the 'natives' could carry any candidates they chose to propose, after some ventilation, I was gratified by hearing the 2 names proposed, that I had suggested viz. The Revd Messers Porteus [Edenhall] & Thwates [Caldbeck]. The Revd L. Hodgeon recently appointed Dioc[esan] Inspector by the Bp was proposed & secd. but only abt. 3 or 4 votes.

Had dinner with Mr Tireman, who talks of coming to visit me. There seems a good prospect of our obtaining a committee for the Depository. [Note: For National Society books.]

[The diarist leaves for Newton.]

Not long after Brunskill's departure from All Hallows, Mr Moore invited bishop Villiers to preach at Bolton church. As a bishop had never been seen in the parish within living memory his arrival caused a great stir, and the church was packed. At a later date, when Mr Moore was staying at Rose Castle, the bishop drove by horse and carriage to All Hallows to preach. As they bowled along the bishop asked him if there were any particular difficulties Mr Moore would like him to mention in his sermon. He mentioned a few, and to his astonishment the bishop raised them in his address, but in tactful form. The service was in aid of the Church of England Education Society, an evengelical trust of which the bishop was a member. This is how Mr Moore described the visit: 'The church is perhaps the smallest in the County, and so great was the crowd that both the church and churchyard were crammed. There were eight to nine hundred people there.' The church was abandoned, and a table and chair were provided for the bishop in the churchyard. 'I think it was the grandest sight I ever saw. The bishop preached a powerful extempore sermon and made a deep impression on

106

the people.' Mr Moore continued: 'The bishop is a giant at work. He never tires of working and doing good. God grant that he may be spared for many years to bless and benefit my benighted and beloved county.'

The effect of Mr Moore's pioneer work, and the encouragement of bishop Villiers in forming the Diocesan Education Society, was to raise men's hopes for the enlargement and improvement of schools in Cumberland.

NOTES ON CHAPTER SIX

1. *Prelates & People of the Lake Counties.* C.M.L. Bouch, 1948. pp. 379/80 for bishop Percy; p. 380 for benefice incomes.

2. Clergy Lists 1827 & 1855.

3. Clergy List 1855.

4. Clergy Lists 1821 & 1856. Burton was also chaplain to the bishop of Carlisle, and was probably one of his evangelical friends. W.M. Press cutting of 24.4.1877, probably by Brunskill on the death of chancellor Burton.

5. Clergy List 1856. Not all the stipends noted are correct;e.g. Mallerstang is given as £60. Whereas the terrier of 1810 made it £95, taxes included. See *Hist. of Mallerstang* op.cit. 380.

6. *Prelates & People* op.cit. 380.

7. Clergy Lists 1855, 1856.
   Crockford 1860 & 1874. The relative was C.E. Wyvill on a family living at Bedale.

8. W.M. Diary 12 Nov. 1855.
   The Church in an Age of Negligence, Peter Virgin, op. cit. pp. 20, 226.

9. D.N.B. George Moore 1806–1876.
   George Moore, Merchant & Philanthropist. Samuel Smiles, 1878, 146–164.
   Alumni Cantab: J.A. Venn, 1947 part II, 1752–1900, for William Mandell Gunson, MA 1822–1881.
   Crockford 1865, for W.M. Gunson.
   Prelates & People, op. cit. p. 421 for Moore's admiration of the bishop.

10. L.M. Letter 19 Feb. 1857. Brunskill to his sister Hannah. That it was Hannah & not Isabella is proved by the ref. to Isa at the end of the letter.

11. Diary 26 June 1855 & 19 Nov. 1859.

NB:
When Brunskill died in 1903 one tribute in the press mentioned that when he was at All Hallows a Mr Christie of Carlisle attacked him and Mr Green for

introducing a Scripture book to the school which contained two hymns of a Romish tendency. Christie was a Protestant fanatic who pursued both men with great vigour. Brunskill made a brisk reply in the press which even persuaded the bishop that no Romish infiltration was intended. The editor of the Carlisle paper rebuked Christie for making much out of very little. This appears to have been the first of the dozens of letters which Brunskill wrote to the press. (W.M. Press cutting dated 10 March 1903.)

7

Askham
1857–1860

THE PARISH of Askham, to which Brunskill was now licenced, was part of the immense Lowther estates. The parish churches of Lowther and Askham are about a quarter of a mile apart, divided by the river Lowther. Askham vicarage is next to the church; the school is in the centre of the village on the green. In addition there are the hamlets of Helton one mile to the south, and Low Close (where Brunskill lodged) to the north.

Until the late seventeenth century Lowther church was next to a village of seventeen properties. In 1682 Sir John Lowther removed the village and rectory, leaving the church alone in the park, dominated by the then Lowther Hall. The rector was accommodated elsewhere. Following the demolition, Lowther Newtown was built to house the principal estate officers. At a later period Lowther village was built, between Lowther Newton and Hackthorpe to take estate workmen. The old village of Hackthorpe is on the old highroad between Kendal and Penrith. To the east is the hamlet of Melkinthorpe, and to the south-west the small hamlet of Whale. In Brunskill's time the Lowther endowed Grammar School for boys was at Hackthorpe, more or less in the centre of the parish.

By the beginning of the nineteenth century the Lowther family derived vast wealth from mines of coal and minerals, from about 100,000 acres of land, and many properties. Before 1832 they controlled nine members of Parliament, and had the advowson of 32 parish churches. At the time of Brunskill's appointment to Askham, William Lowther second earl of Lonsdale (1787–1872) owned the new Lowther Castle, and had been a government minister in several Tory administrations.[1] The yellow 'favours' of the Lowther political interest dominated Cumbrian elections for years.

Every employee and tenant on the estate had his or her allotted place, with the maids and servants at the Castle, and the ploughmen and shepherds on the land at the bottom of the pyramid, while at the apex was his lordship's Principal Agent, Mr Benn, exercising immense power over tenants and employees, all in 'his Lordship's' name. Placing in church on Good Friday reflected the rigid social structure. The earl and countess occupied special red upholstered seats in the chancel, between the choir and the holy table. The housekeeper at the Castle had her maids under her wing in one aisle; while the male employees of castle and estate, with their families, could sit (if they were church goers) in the other aisle. Farmers and gentlefolk occupied the nave, while other members of the Lowther family and their guests sat in the gallery. It is said that at one time servants were not paid if they did not attend church on Good Friday. Until this century social precedence was observed in going up to receive the Sacrament; though it is reported that the Duke of Wellington once said to one giving him place 'No, no, my man. We are all equal here.' In the parish of Greystoke under the Howards the rector's wife came third in the procession.

'God bless our squire and his relations,
And keep us in our proper stations.'

Thus a curate in lodgings was a very lowly creature in that world of power, money and rigid class distinctions, a hundred and forty years ago. 'His Lordship's wishes' were paramount both at Lowther and Askham. Within these constraints a large number of men and women found employment and security.

The Revd J. T. Ward had been vicar of Askham since 1832; and had formerly been headmaster of the Lowther Grammar School. The parish church was entirely rebuilt by the earl of Lonsdale in 1832–3. William Brown was the old schoolmaster, and the Revd Thos. Rayson the late curate. The stipend of the vicar was £180 a year[2], out of which he paid the curate. The church was arranged in the old way, with the principal residents and farmers having their proprietory pews with doors in the main part of the building. Lord Lonsdale's, in right of the lay rectory, was by the communion rail; the vicar's came next, both with doors. Then came the two decker pulpit. The church clerk sat at the door by the back. The last church clerk to hold the freehold was Harry Bateman, the village carpenter and wheelwright. The writer remembers him well from his curacy there in 1942–44.

One old custom has nearly died out. At a village wedding the youths would tie the church gate so that the bride and bridegroom could not leave the churchyard without scattering pennies and half-pennies to the crowd. During the scramble the gate would be untied, and the couple make their escape. But the trick was for a member of the family to take a shovel, cover it with coins, and heat it on the vestry fire. By the time the service was over the coins were pretty hot. When the couple came to the gate, the coins were thrown over, and following the confusion from shrieks and burnt fingers, the couple made their escape.

Apart from diligent visiting, Brunskill's first care was the state of village education, which was abysmal. Mr Brown, the headmaster had been at Askham school for 53 years, and was down to six boys; he was too old to teach, and did not want more.[3] It is curious that it was left to the curate, rather than the vicar, to take the initiative. Perhaps it was that the vicar did not wish to hurt the old man's feelings by removing him. The school endowment was only £12.10s. a year. Mr Brown was pensioned off with £10, leaving the school with £2.10s. Apart from any grant from Lord Lonsdale, and weekly pence brought in by the children, there was little for fuel, books and repairs.

There was also the small dame school at Helton taught by Ann Clark, with a master who had failed on his farm in Martindale, and thought that teaching was easier.[4]

There were plenty of clergy about. The Archdeacon Dr Jackson was at Askham Hall, while his curate Revd Henry Robson lodged in Lowther village. The Headmaster of Lowther Grammar School at Hackthorpe, the Revd Robert Johnson was ill and soon to resign. The Revd J. T Ward was at Askham vicarage opposite Askham Hall, with Brunskill his curate lodging at Low Close. Brunskill worked hard trying to raise enthusiasm for a new school building at Askham with little success. By Christmas 1858 a probationary schoolmaster James Ainsworth had been found, and by the following September had gathered 30 pupils.[5] He was paid £20 a year, probably with help from

Lord Lonsdale, who refused to increase the salary to £25 until a new school had been built. Poor Ainsworth was soon in dire straits for want of money.

The vicar seems to have been sympathetic to Brunskill's duty to preach elsewhere for the National Society and allowed him to go.

After evensong on Sunday 6 November 1859 Brunskill was approached by the Revd Robert Townson, BA of Queen's College, Oxford, and lately a master at Rossall School.[6] He appears to have filled in as head of Lowther school during the sickness of the Revd R. Johnson. He asked Brunskill whether he would consider exchanging jobs. Townson seems to have been incapable of keeping order and was anxious to escape. By the 12 of December Ainsworth at Askham School was in despair for want of money, and on the point of resigning. On the 15 December Brunskill went to the archdeacon and sounded him out about the headship of Lowther school. The trustees accepted the resignation of the Revd Robert Johnson on the ground of ill health on the 23 December, and at the same meeting dismissed the under master Mr John Atkinson for drunkenness.[7] After much negotiation between the archdeacon, Mr Joseph Benn (Lord Lonsdale's principal agent), the trustees of Lowther school and Brunskill, it was eventually agreed that Brunskill should be the head of Lowther school, with the hope that the under master should be a trained teacher. After much parleying the trustees accepted the suggestion of Brunskill that James Ainsworth should be his under master. By the 24 January 1860 Brunskill was headmaster of Lowther Grammar School;[8] he and Ainsworth remained there for the next 22 years. His salary was £80 a year, and Ainsworth's £60. There were three other schools in Lowther parish; the mistress of the girls' school at Hackthorpe was to receive £30 a year, and the Dames at the little schools at Whale and Melkinthorpe 12 guineas a year.[9] The trustees paid for the fuel at all four schools. Brunskill and Ainsworth had to find their own lodgings.

Brunskill and Mr Ward the vicar of Askham agreed, in view of the hostility of the bishop of Carlisle towards Brunskill, that he should not resign his curacy of Askham, but not be paid or do duty there. In return Mr Townson was to serve for a time as paid assistant at Askham church, and so fill the gap. Mr Townson did not stay long; within the year he was appointed perpetual curate of the lonely parish of Grayrigg in the gift of the vicar of Kendal, where he stayed six years.[10] The work of Brunskill and Ainsworth seems to have been well received, for on the 15 August 1862 the Trustees agreed to the following additions to all the teachers' salaries: Brunskill £80, Ainsworth £20, Miss Griffin [at the girls' school] £20, Miss Cowan [? at Whale] £4, and Mrs Crowden [? at Melkinthorpe] £2. The Trustees also agreed to ask Lord Lonsdale for a house for the headmaster in the village.[11] Thus by 1862 Brunskill's salary was £160 a year, which was quite respectable for the lower clergy, let alone teachers.

His early days were not trouble free. In June 1857, when he was trying to obtain support for enlarging Askham school by taking in part of the village green with the consent of Lord Lonsdale, he approached Mr James Mawson an architect who lived at Lowther Newtown[12] for help with the estimates; Mawson refused. Now that Brunskill was installed at Lowther school Mawson did what he could to undermine the position of the new teachers by alleging that they were not competent to teach the Latin required by the school statutes. Mawson had been talking to Whitwick the perpetual curate of Newton [Brunskill's home village], and J. Bland the new curate of Lowther, trying to find out from the chatter of curates whether Brunskill was really competent to teach. Brunskill decided to face his persecutors, and after roll call in school on 13 March at which Mawson's son was present he accused the son of his unfair and persecuting system against him and his predecessor. He warned him of the consequences, and the injury to the school. The following day he learned that Mawson had defamed Brunskill to Mr Ainsworth, and that evening Mawson determined to storm Brunskill in his lodgings. His landlady Mrs Scott asked Brunskill whether he wished to see him, and he refused. After the boarding party had been repulsed, the landlady and sister condemned Mawson's conduct. Brunskill wrote in this diary, 'it was a case of kill or be killed'. His early years in Hackthorpe were dogged by an underground opposition, to which Dr Jackson the rector listened from time to time, and against which Brunskill had to fight.

Lowther Grammar School was founded in 1635 by Sir John Lowther, his uncle Richard, and John Teasdale rector of Lowther with 317 acres of land and tithes in the parish of Haile in Cumberland, worth then about £100 a year. The first school was built in 1640. It was closed in 1740, when Lord Lonsdale planned to turn it into a carpet factory. How long it remained thus is not clear; but it came before Chancery and is referred to in a Scheme of 10 February 1831, and it was under its provisions that Brunskill was appointed, and the trustees elected. At some earlier date a new school building was erected at Hackthorpe. The trustees were local gentlemen, and at the time of Brunskill's appointment they were: H. Lowther Esq. Sir George Musgrave of Edenhall, E. W. Hasell Esq. of Dalemain, and Dr Wm Jackson the rector. In 1849 when Mannex compiled his Directory of Westmorland John Atkinson was schoolmaster and superintendent registrar. If it was he who was dismissed in December 1859, he seems to have been supplanted by a new head and made undermaster. There was the girls' school at Hackthorpe taught by Mary Thompson in 1849, and a dame school at Whale founded in 1739, and a second one at Melkinthorpe; and all were under the wing of the Lowther foundation. Thus in the recent years before Brunskill's arrival the grammar school had an unhappy history.[13]

The diary refers 24 September 1859 to a visit Brunskill paid to his aunt Miss Jane Monkhouse of Newton when she informed him that she intended to include him in her Will. It was signed on the 10 October 1859, and its main provision was that she left her dwelling house at Newton with land and peat mosses to her niece Sarah Sowerby, and on Sarah's death to be divided between her nephew Thomas Sowerby, and Joseph and Isabella Brunskill the children of her niece Mary Ann Brunskill. Miss Monkhouse died in 1862.[13] Through this Will some of the Monkhouse books from Oxford descended to the Brunskill family.

As Brunskill's position was now more certain at Lowther, he

Joseph Brunskill

Wild Boar Fell,
Mallerstang
(Dr John
Hamilton of
The Thrang)

Mallerstang Church before 1909
(Courtesy: Mr Giles Thompson & Mrs Jill Butterworth)

was married on the 4 April 1861 at St Thomas Church, Sunderland to Lydia the daughter by his second marriage of John Ritson his old master. She came to live with Joseph at Hackthorpe.[15] Their early days in lodgings cannot have been easy. Their first child John Ritson Brunskill was not born till 11 May 1865.

Hackthorpe,
11 May 1875

Mr dear Mamma,
    I am 'very proud and happy' to be able to inform you that Baby arrived safely this morning. He is considered a very fine Boy. Both are doing very well. With united kindest regards

Yrs. aff.
Jos.[16]

NOTES TO CHAPTER SEVEN

1. **Askham Church**
   A Sketch of the Church of Askham and some account of the early Parish Registers. Mary E. Noble. C & W Trans. N.S. vol. 4. 1903
   Askham Parish Registers. Mary E. Noble. 1904.
   Lowther church
   Hist. & Antiquities of Cumberland & Westmorland, J. Nicolson & R. Burn, 1777. vol. I. p. 440.
   The Parish Registers of Lowther 1540–1812, ed. Col. J.F. Haswell, 1933.
   Introduction by Revd J.F. Prince, rector of Lowther in 1932.
   The Lowther Family & Estates.
   The Yellow Earl; the Life of Hugh Lowther, 5th Earl of Lonsdale. Douglas Sutherland, 4th ed. 1969, p. 7–16.
   D.N.B. William Lowther, 2nd Earl of Lonsdale 1787–1872.
   Clergy List 1860 for Lowther patronage.

2. Clergy List 1855.
   Hist. & Topog. of Westmorland & North Lonsdale, P.J. Mannex, 1849, p. 200.

3. Diary 4 May 1857 & 15 May 1857.

4. *Hist. & Topog. of Westmorland* op. cit. p. 200.
   Diary 6 May 1857.

5. Diary 20 Sept. 1858.

6. Diary 6 Nov. 1859.
   Crockford 1862.

7. Minutes of Trustees of Lowther Charity Schools 23 Dec. 1859, by courtesy of Lowther Estate Office.

8. Diary 24 Jan. 1860.

9. Minutes of Trustees of Lowther Charity Schools etc. 10 Nov. 1832. The rate does not seem to have been raised in 1860.

10. *Crockford* 1866.

11. Minutes of Trustees of Lowther Charity Schools 15 Aug. 1862, & 8 Aug. 1863.

12. *Hist. & Topog. of Westmorland* op.cit. p. 230.
    Diary 5 June 1857.

13. *Hist. & Topog. of Westmorland* op.cit. p. 230.
    The Parish Registers of Lowther 1540–1812, ed. Col. J.F. Haswell, 1933. Introduction by the Revd J.F. Prince rector of Lowther 1832. The date of the Chancery Scheme 10 Feb. 1831 is taken from the newspaper advertisement 16 Feb. 1882 by the Education Department notifying the public of the New Scheme for the management of the Lowther Schools. (L.M.)

14. L.M. & C.R.O. Kendal. Will of Miss Jane Monkhouse of Newton 10th Oct. 1859.

15. W.M. Typed 'family register'.

16. L.M. 11 May 1865.

8

Sermons and Lexicons

DIARY

1857–1860

[The diarist, having left All Hallows, on the 22 April 1857, proceeds to Newton for the night].

April 1857

23. Although the 'boy' was at Newton I went towards Askham.

24. Fr[om] Hackthorpe by A[skham] to the R[ailway] station [prob. at Clifton]; but still no luggage. Got a sermon out of my desk, wh[ich] I had brought with me. My bag with the sermon intended for Sunday etc. having been carried off fr. the R[ailway] Station at Carlisle. Fr. H[ackthorpe] went down to Penrith & found my luggage 'shunted' in consequence of the pressure caused by P[enrith] Fair. Had the luggage put into the Passenger Train & got it safely to Askham by 6 pm. I now find that the keys for my 3 boxes have gone in the carpet bag. My new rooms felt cold, & not being very well did not unpack much.

26. **Sunday.** I now miss my hood and stole, wh[ich] were also in the bag; but in good heart with the substituted sermon. After the service cordially complimented by the Vicar [The Revd J.T. Ward]. More pleased with the church than I had expected. No sermon in the afternoon. Snowing.

27. The Vicar called early.

28. Much to my relief the bag arrived. Unable to arrange my books – no case.

31. Walked over to Hack[thorpe] in even. rem. all night. Mr Wood called today.

May

1. Drove the Ws. [Wards] to Clifton to tea.

117

2. Visited sick at Helton.

3. **Sunday.** Gave notice that on S. next that even serv. wd. be at 6pm. After serm. walked to Clifton. Not tired.

4. Administered H.C. to 3 invalids at Helton. Having some days ago been to Widewath with Mr W. on some errand, very much pleased with the scenery in that direction. On visiting what should be our central school at Askham, I found only some half dozen poor little fellows present. The Master an old man, said he did not wish for any more pupils. I hope to arrange for his being pensioned. When I attempted to give a lesson, I found that the poor scholars had been less or worse taught than any I had yet known.

5. To Hack. in the even.

6. Visited School etc. at Helton, & began 'House to House'. There is both a Master & Matron [Ann Clark, in 1849] here where there is only room for a Matron. The Master is a plain man who, unequal to working a small property he owns in Martindale, has taken to teaching as easier. He spoke of being aware of his deficiencies, & I think may be improved. Had him a long time in the even.

7. Gave a lesson at A. Schl. & called at the Vicarage having resolved to walk over to Newton where 'the boy' still remains. I had already made several proposals abt. reviving the School; & not willing to be too forward had concluded that it wd. be best to wait till Mr W. mentioned the matter. Having found the Ws. in the garden, they pleased me by beginning immediately to express their anxiety that something shd. be done. There seems to have been some outward pressure fr. one or more parishioners. After some talk it was decided that I shd. draw up a letter to Ld. Lonsdale as a preliminary move.

   Mr W's cart going to Penrith I rode thus to Yanwath, & fr. thence walked to Newton in 65 mins. Found all well. The Bride & her sister called. A Sunday Sch. has begun at Newton!!

8. With 'the boy' 'up the fields', chopping pea sticks for Aunt J. etc. [Miss Jane Monkhouse].

9. Returned via Penrith. Had tea at the Vicarage.

10. **Sunday.** In the even. commenced a series of sermons on the 'Doctrines & Means of Grace'. Gave notice of coll[ection] for Nat. Soc. next week.

11. After writing a draft of a letter for Ld L. took it down to the Vic. & afterwards commenced to read the deeds in the Iron chest. Found that there is already abt. £40 in the hands of the Minister and churchwardens that may be applied to rebuilding the school, and that there is already a committee or body of Trustees for the School consisting of the Earl of Lonsdale, The Archdeacon, The Vicar ex. off. & 2 or 3 lay parishioners.

     In the afternoon returned the call of the Archdeacon, who rec'd me kindly. Having taken my papers with me we discussed the subject of the School. He approved of a Meeting after I shd. have ventilated the matter with the Trustees. Among School papers until late at night.

12. At Helton. Ventilated the school matter with Mr Branthwaite the only survivor of the original body of elected Trustees. Found him very willing to cooperate.

13. At the Castle Mr Benn [Lord Lonsdale's Agent] out. Heard the cuckoo & swallows. In the even. to tea at Askham Hall. A long talk with the A(rchdeacon). Pleasant.

14. Drove Mr & Mrs W. to Hackthorpe.

15. A preliminary School Meeting. Proposed to pension the Master who has held his appointment since 1804. The amt. offered £10. The endowment being only £12.10.0. Appointed by the Meeting its Secretary to conduct negotiations.

16. Drove the Ws. into Penrith where I had 3 or 4 hours for shopping. A talk with Mr Atkinson respecting establishing some kind of a Clerical Club in one of his rooms.

17. **Sunday.** Fair congregations. My sister Isa. to dinner etc. Aunt B. & J. to tea. After Evensong all walked round the most delightfully green Park.

27. Called at the Vicarage & Castle respecting School matters. Learned fr. Mr Benn that Lord Lonsdale was willing to grant us additional ground fr. the vil[lage] green. As yet he offered nothing more. Went on to Hackthorpe to attend Mr Robson's sale.

28. The Visitation at Penrith. A fine day. Sermon 'bosh'. Charge good.

29. Do. at Appleby; but unable to go.

31. **Whitsunday.** In even. preached on purity.

June

2. Being Mrs W's birthday, a small family gathering at the Vicarage. At length saw Mr Mawson, but beyond professions of being ready to assist in raising a school, he seemed disinclined to proceed. Talked of being busy etc. Carried him the papers he had offered to look over. In the afternoon walked to Newton. Very tired morning; but better even.

5. Rose early. Still warm & delightful weather. After tiring myself with 'work' had a long talk with Dr Jackson on 'Parochial Work'. In afternoon drove by Clifton, where I picked up 'the boy', to Askham. Found a letter from Mr Mawson declining to help with estimates. Another from Mr Barwise refusing L[ocum] T[enens] for Nt. Soc. in the Holme. Thence by Hackthorpe to Newton.

6. To Carlisle. Meeting of School Assoc. etc.

7. **Trinity Sunday.** Holy Com. 20. The 2 Ch'wardens carried off the alms between them! Quite positive [insistent] abt. using 'Holy Table' in preference to the Vestry. Branthwaite seemed too like his disagreeable brother in law Brown fr. whose presumptuous domineering we thought to have escaped on his ceasing to be Warden. Hope to begin with

monthly Com[munion] when the Wardens will have more practice. Learned fr. Arch. that Christie was *not* Ord. to All Hallows.

9. At Hackthorpe, detained all night by rain.

10. 'New Fair' [Appleby]. Very wet. Hope it may deter R. fr. going again.

11. A good day's Paroch. Work. Spoke to the 2 lay trustees abt. my obtaining an estimate fr. Mr Abbott, Helton; called upon him & arranged for his calling here on Saturday.

12. This being Mr Ward's birthday, it had been arranged that we were to have a 'pic nic' up Ullswater. Notwithstanding some showers yesterday & even this morning started with great hopes for the day because the barometer had continued to rise. By the time we had arrived in view of the Lake the rain ceased & the day became warm and serenely bright, in fact perfect for our work. Saw Airy Force to unusual advantage. Drove on to Patterdale, and thence home very well pleased & tired.

13. Found several difficult letters & other work irksome fr. the exhaustion of yesterday.

15. Started for London to attend meetings of National Soc. etc. Pretty well. After a pleasant journey arrived well. Took a cab. fr. E[uston] Ry Sta. & drove to Golden Sqr. Hatchells Hotel etc. but unable to find a lodging; went to 127 New B[ond] St & there Mrs Byers wd. not hear of my going elsewhere, & for the next 4 days made me very comfortable.

16. Saw Geo. Moore who repaid me 26/- the amt. I was out of pocket for free scholars. After service at Lothbury where I heard Dan Moore, retd. to Luncheon at 5 B. C. Yd. Thence to Grant & Griffins, & so to St Pauls where at 3 pm. was the Annual Festival of the S.P.G. Bp of Salisbury preached. Came on to Simpsons where we Secretaries were to dine. Home with Mr Byers.

[Three pages later]

121

June 1858

7. To London. Stayed in Bond St.

13. Preached at St Lawrence's, City.

14. To Tiverton, Bath.

16. Oxford – London.

17. Willesden.

18. Safely back to Askham.

July

19. Wrote to W.

[next page]

September 1859

17. Walked to the steamboat at Ullswater thence to Patterdale, whence after waiting 5 hour I took coach over Kirkstone for the first time. Dusk when we arrived at Ambleside. Mr Park not having ans'd my letter took a gig to Hawkshead. He had sent an explanation by letter to Grasmere. Thus I lost 7/6. Stopped at the Salutation. A good Inn.

18. **Sunday.** Abt. 8.30 started to walk to Grasmere. Passed Rydal Mount etc. It looked deserted, being 'shut up'. Entered the Vestry of G[rasmere] Ch. at 10. Rain prob. but hitherto dry. A fair Cong; but less than 2 or 3 weeks ago.

    Preached & obt. £7.15.2. After some fuss asked to lunch by Mr Jeffery. Thence he lent me an Umbrella to go a mile thro. the pouring rain to an *Inn*, where I had to spend my Sunday even.

19. After Breakfast I judged it prudent fr. the unexpected pace at wh. the money had gone to make for home. So I started to walk over Grisdale. Pleasant, hard & exciting journey. Home by steamer for 2/- by 3 pm.

20. At School morn. Mr Ainsworth after having to 'begin at the bottom' last Xmas has now got abt. 30 pupils into a more efficient state than I have seen here. Called at the Vic. where asked to come to Tea etc.

23. Went by Clifton to Newton, having been informed that my offer of security for H.B. as Station Mast. at [? Langham, ? Langholme, nr. Canonbie] was not deemed sufficient.

24. In the morn. with Aunt M. [Miss Jane Monkhouse of Newton d.1862] talked over her affairs. Astonished to learn her good intentions towards myself. At 1 pm on by Carlisle to Rockcliff.

25. A wet morn. so that my sermon for the Nat. Soc. only prod. £1.2.0.

26. Left Mr Toppin's hospitable roof & returned by Clifton.

27. At Helton etc.

29. 11.30. Started to go by Clifton to Newton for the Birthday at Wm Thompson's. A wet journey but pleasant even.

October 1859

3. Took drag back fr. Clifton. Tea with Aunt. Arranged further abt. her Will.

4. Tuesday. By Penrith. Attended Lecture at Farmers Club. Thence on to dinner at Askham Hall. Walked from P. to Low Close in 1 hour.

5. After 7 hours Parochial Work at School & just feeling very tired when the Mess's Sherwen drove up. Returned with them to Patterdale.

6. At 9 am. a very fine morn. We started to 'do' Helvellyn for the *first time*. We were 3 hours ascending, had a pleasant rest in the hot sun on the top, fr. whence we returned by the mines [Glenridding]. 6 hours altogether. Although less tired than I expected it was very agreeable to find Mr Rook's snug rooms the end of our journey.

7. Mr S. drove me back to L.C. [Low Close] fr. whence we went to Haweswater & thence back to dinner. After they left to Clifton.

8. After a day at C. [Clifton] putting up frame, gardening etc. to Arthur Haygarth's to tea.

9. **Sunday.** Fair congregations. A good week at school wh. is thriving well.

12. Had A. Haygarth, Mr Ainsworth & Brown to tea.

13. Tom Lane called. First time I had seen him since in Holy Orders. Much disappointed.

14. Drove Isa. for a pleasant even. at Strickland.

15. The Queen paper thro. [? bl]. Thence to tea at A[skham] Hall.

16. **Sunday.** Very wet.

17. Started for an Educat. meeting at Carlisle. Weather close & warm. Lord Brougham being expected the meeting was larger than formerly. The Bishop, possibly, because of the numerous clergy present, more tolerant & friendly towards the Nat. Society. Went on to Kirkandrews. Mr Pattinson also to tea. Much profess[ional] talk.

18. With Mr Brown on to Silloth. Unwell. Met at the Station by Hon. Mrs & Miss Morley.

20. Had a *cold* bath in the sea before 7 am., not having felt strong enough before. Much colder today. Visited the school alone.

21. Hard frost with a piercing N. Wind. Yet went out to find Mr Carrick. He engaged over the accident. For the third time he came to dinner. At 4 pm after some pleasant time left for Plumbland.

22. While at breakfast at Plumbland, there was a *snow* & hail shower. In the bright frost walked to Aspatria. At 4 pm Mr Watson drove me back to Torpenhow, where I received much show of hospitality; but rather sick, and unequal to enjoying it.

23. **Sunday.** So cold as likely to mar my collection. Peculiarly dull all the morning & obliged soon to come out of

Church, when I was sick & faint, but recovered sufficiently to preach. The Congregation & collection very poor. No
notice seemed to have been given of any sermon. Because
of my illness excused myself to the Misses Railton fr. my
visit to Smittlegarth, & sent a messenger to tell Mr
Sherwen that I cd. not Preach at Bolton Low Houses in the
afternoon. Before night much restored by warmth & quiet.
Some useful conversation with the New School Master.

24. In Mr Thexton's gig to Wigton, & so home, feeling pretty
well. Found 'charity' wanting.

26. The second day of the Brougham Coursing, & a rough
change in the weather. The frost displaced by wild sleet &
snow. [The day of the storm & 600 wrecks.]

November

4. At length another letter!

5. Wrote again, but storm hindered posting.

6. **Sunday.** Very high wind with rain. After morn. service rode
to Langwathby & preached for Nat. Soc. coll. £3.14.0.
Enjoyed the ride! Return for even. Serv. After some little
talk with Mr Townson abt. his proposal to exchange.

9. L's Birthday as I learnt on the ...

10.

13. **Sunday.** Congs. rather thin partly owing to the hay fire at
Lowther. In the even. preached on Schism with reference to
the intrusion of a 'Preacher'.

16. Had 'ownfolk' with Isa. & Pershaw [his brother and sister]
to dinner.

17. Sale at Park House; bought 13 lots.

18. Concluded a good week's paroch. work. The School has
now an attendance of more than 40. A better appearance
of feeling among people. Having found a greater ignorance
among *our members* here of their privileges than elsewhere,

& an unusual disposition to despise the Ministry, my efforts have been towards counteracting this.

19. Some letters, one official. The old dread of finding in each of these last an intimation that the [Nat.] Soc. cd. not afford my stipend had at length disappeared under the improving prospects of work. Yet I left it unopened for an hour or more, & it was well, for my old fears are now a fact. My distress wd. have been greater once than now although the evil is great enough. As another effort wrote to the S.P.G.

20. **Sunday.** Weather fine. Congs. fair.

22. A letter from S.P.G. informing me that I am just too late, the appointment of Mr Troutbeck at Dacre being nearly complete. So I must try again to exist on my £70.0.0.

23. A long round after school, by Helton Dale etc. Asked the Pearsons, who are abt. to emigrate to Australia, to tea. Notwithstanding that I had long ago volunteered to the Mother any help in my power towards getting them passage money fr. the Colonial Fund the poor fellows have ex[h]austed their own money in ignorance. I have never seen the place where the people looked as little to the Parson for advice etc.

24. In the afternoon walked over to Clifton to help in the removal of some planks; but came almost direct back.

27. **Sunday.** Began with Dr Goodwin's Advent sermons.

28. Understanding that it was Father's birthday, afternoon started to walk over. Before reaching Penrith I learnt he had sent for the Dr who overtook me at the last mile, & I was there in time to hold for a painful cutting operation at a dangerously inflamed hand.

December

1. After driving to my qrs & back by Clifton yesterday I left Newton again this morn. & the Patient much improved.

Agreeably surprised by the expressions of gratitude at my success in nursing.

2. A letter fr. Grace P. in Canada. While nursing I had managed to write a short letter to Peter.

4. **Sunday.** Very stormy weather. Congs. *very* small.

8. After 3 days of snow, wind & rain, clear frost this morn. Went to Kendal.

11. Congs. good.

12. At Askham morn. saw Archd. on Ch. rates etc. p.m. to Widewath etc. Returned in time for the first 'exhibition' of our progress at School. The audience much pleased so I learned afterwards. Mr Ainsworth walked with me at night & expressed as at length resolved on resigning unless something be done speedily to raise his stipend. Although it was late I was too tired & anxious to go early to bed.

13. At Clifton to meet Cleasby. [Note: Prob. Thomas Cleasby, Ing Hill, Mallerstang].

14. The cold intense. Walked to Penrith, returning for dinner at Miss Low's. There learned fr. Mr Ward that the Trustees were stirring ab. a collection. Returned in the even. Snowing.

15. Diocesan Inspection of Schools having come at last, we had arranged with Mr Simpson to visit our schools today. A greyhound coursing was the excuse for some of our best boys being absent; but nevertheless the Examination passed off better even than I had expected. Helton School was *worse*. A good supply of maps etc. wh. I had procured seem to have been neglected. The only boy in the first class did not know E. fr. W. on a map, and he poor fellow was kept there notwithstanding our offer to take him free at Askham.

   After dinner at Mr W's. called upon the Archd. with a message abt. a meeting of our Trustees tomorrow. Had much confidential talk abt. my taking the Mastership of Lowther School. I concluded that something was being done.

16. A meeting of the School Trustees. Only the 3 fr. Helton present, and they full of talk agt. a new building; however they had collected £4.0.0 & voted that the Master's stipend be increased to £25.0.0. per an. Afterwards drove the Ws. to Park View.

17. Back to Low Close were I fd. that Mr Townson had called.

18. **Sunday.** Very cold with some snow on the ground. S[unday] School & Church thin. Mr Townson came into the Vestry & said that he had proposed the exchange to Lord Lonsdale who made no objection! Afterwards Mr W. accepted Mr T. as my substitute. Since we had all experienced the disagreeable harshness of the Bishop decided if possible to avoid any communication. Another talk with the Archd. They meet on Friday.

19. Wrote to Govt. for papers towards obtaining a grant of books etc & a third time respecting Mr Ainsworth's payment as a Probationer. A long walk thro. the Parish. In even. enjoyed a little more of Dynevor Terrace [by Charlotte M. Yonge] & then had a spell at rubbing up my school work in anticipation.

20. More snow. Waded thr. the drifts to Askham.

23. Met Mr Simpson who had been examining the Lowther schools. Spoke of my appointment.

24. After being 2 or 3 days at Clifton aiding in the dispersion for the holidays, – home.

25. **Christmas Day.** Sunday. – Considering Weather congs. fair. The Ch. carefully dressed. In even. called on Archd. Learned that the Trustees had recom. me to Lord Lonsdale, also dismissed Atkinson [John Atkinson, the under master] & recom. a trained Master as second.

26. To Newton – very cold & wet.

27. Drove Isa. to Askham – so home.

28. Not feeling my cold etc – to the wet weather & icy roads

remained indoors. Finished after much enjoyment the reading of Dynevor Terrace.

31. Missed my sister at Askham. Returned tired & dull.

January 1860

1. **Sunday.** Very wet & windy. Well pleased with my sermons. At Lowther *no* congren's in aftern'n. We had 60 in even. The Archd. having expressed a wish to see me, as I had twice heard, called & learned that all was right fr. Lord Lonsdale. Only I was only allowed to hear part of his letter in wh. he expressed satisfaction with me & the prospect of a trained Master as second. I believe His Ldsp. left this appointment with me; but the Archd. seemed to conceal something & desire to have it appear that the appointment was with him.

2. Called upon the Archd. with Mr Ainsworth's testimonials. Altho. the Archd. professed that he wd. again write to Mr Rigg, he is I think only wasting time. Mr A. is *the* man. When speaking yesterday abt. my writing to Lord L. the A. said I must not say 'the suggestion of the Trustees', thus exposing the hollowness of all his trouble in making it appear my appointment was in any way with them. So I wrote as follows:

> My Lord.   Askham, Penrith. 2.1.60.
>
> Having learned that your Lordship approves of the suggestion of Mr Townson that I should take his place as first Master of the Lowther School, I beg to return my most grateful thanks for the appointment. Their sincerity I hope to prove by an efficient discharge of my duty. When desired by yr. Ldshp. I shall be happy to send the form of nomination.
> I am, etc. Jos. Brunskill

Too wet & stormy for Helton, so remained visiting in Askham. Gave J. Mounsey the letters etc. fr. 'My Lord' requiring a promise to alter or build before paying the stipend of £25. earned by Mr Ainsworth last year.

A long talk with Mr Townson partly relieved the discomfort caused by the now evident purpose of the Archd.

to continue his old plan of exalting himself at the cost of Master & School. He for the first time mentioned the supplemental bond wh. he said that *Lord Lonsdale* would require me to sign.

I mentioned the consequence to my poor friend Paget Wilkinson [Francis Paget Wilkinson, librarian of St Bees 1851, rector of Great Orton, 1857–59] (& might have added Livingston) [Thomas Gott Livingston, BA Oxon, Minor Canon of Carlisle 1855] of such an act. The A., said there was no analogy in this case but rather with that of a curate, seemed nervous & spoke of my accepting this paper being essential to my appointment. I answered that I wd. sign anything that they professed to be legal; but that as I imagined the Patron, Trustees, Master etc. were only such by virtue of authority from the Statutes, by these we must abide without adding or diminishing. If the Statutes were defective the Charity Commissioners were the power to grant a new scheme etc. Talking abt. Mr Ainsworth he said he would not only have to discharge his duties so as to satisfy the people, but please the Trustees. I answered that if he did his duty well that was surely enough for the Trustees. No, he replied; the Trustees claim the choosing of the books used in the school! And all this grasping for power for himself (for 'Trustees' is only a blind) in a conversation during wh. he had told me that the Statutes gave the entire superintendence of the school to the Head Master! Well, by God's blessing upon a prudent use of my varied experience I must try to secure my own position, so that I may be able to 'bear my own burden'.

17. Sent the Archd. a copy of Mr Ainsworth's testimonials & one for myself, also a letter on the delay. I mentioned that Mr A. was much harrassed by the suspense, and that I must have skilled help at starting. In even. walked to Penrith. At Threlkeld.

18. Called on Mr Barrett. Dr Monks Concert.

19. Disappointed abt. lodgings, went to the Castle to enquire after the empty house at [Lowther] Newtown. Heard the

Statutes of the School read. My position much weaker than I expected. After consulting with Mr Ward & Archd. wrote to Lord Lonsdale direct abt. the house. Heard that Mr A. was to be my second.

20. Again to the Archd. when I gave the desired memorandum. In even at Whale.

21. A wild stormy morn. with sleet etc. In even. to Clifton for Brougham Church.

22. **Sunday.** Started in a strong gale of wind & rain to walk to St. Ninians. Warwick accompanied me. Congr. 8!

23. To the Station for the M.L. & Penrith for H. & A.S. Snow & Darkness hindered my going to Newton. [These references obscure.]

24. Rode to Hackthorpe, got the school key & arranged for fires to [be] kept on. Called at Mrs Mawson's to say I wd. enter upon my new lodgings on Sunday even. On to the Archd's who said I might get the school limewashed & repaired. At the School found a letter fr. Lord Lonsdale returning my formal appointment complete. So I have at *length a freehold*! Hurried on through the dangerous snow by Low Close to Clifton thence to Penrith & so to Newton for a rest.

25. Wrote some 8 letters & began a Sermon.

26. Afternoon rode to Greystoke & had a pleasant talk with Lees. Returned thro. a fierce blinding snow storm.

27. Drove to Penrith thence with Isa. etc. to Clifton.

28. **Sunday.** Thick snow & very cold. Rode to St Ninians. Congrega. 7. In even. to my new lodgings at Lowther Village, ready for tomorrow's work.

29. Rose early & at nine to School. Found abt. 55 scholars in attendance. The poor boys generally dull & backward. The schoolroom ill arranged, & much noise. At noon Mr Ainsworth having as yet his old lodgings at Askham, came

with me to dinner. Back at 1 pm. Left abt. 3.30 pm. Through soft deep snow & high wind, walked to Low Close, & remained 'packing' till 9 pm.

31. At 3.15 pm. hastened to Low Close where the carts fr. Newton were waiting for me. Sent one load to Clifton & brought the other safely with me.

February 1860

3. Up to this Friday aft. all had gone pleasantly, & my health was rather improved than injured as I had written home to say, when the Archdeacon called & did me more harm than all the weeks work.

As he came in I noticed the chief old Agitator pass the windows (Miller) & so I believe fr. him & others the Archd. had been gathering gossip, wh. he expressed to the effect that the Parish was in greater ferment agt. me than my predecessor. Told me that I had been breaking a rule wh. the Trustees had made for my observance as to the hours of work & play, that I was quite at their mercy as to dismissal. As I knew my formal appointment gave the lie to this last I did not notice the insult. The grumbling I was prepared for; but that he should come, as of old to my sister, annoyed me *very* much. That a rule as to the management of the Scholars was to be made by the Trustees I protested agt. as a usurpation of my rights. The Statutes make me solely responsible as Superintendant of the School. I enquired particularly if there really was such a rule, wh. he assured me there was. Therefore denying its obligation I will give it some attention, lest the enemy who watches & writes down our time takes occasion to talk. 'The Trustees' have succeeded in bringing the position of all the officials connected with the Charity into *singular* contempt. Thus Messers Miller & Co. never imagine; but that I am bound to carry out any rule they can procure to be made. The Archd. professed to have come as my friend etc. for wh. I thanked him; but fervently hope to be saved fr. such friends in future. The mischief to my health was considerable. In the even. called on Mr Plumer.

4. Having some workmen at the school did not go to Clifton till afternoon.

5. **Sunday.** Again very windy & wet with hail etc. Walked to St Ninians. Cong. 12.

6. At noon, saw Archd. a few minutes. He acknowledged that they had neglected all examination in Latin etc! I had expressed a regret at not having had an ex. by Threlkeld.

11. From Clifton to Newton. Aunt M. poorly.

12. **Sunday.** Over snow white roads, & through bitterly cold frosts rode to Brougham [St. Ninian's]. Cong. 23. Dined at Whinfel.

18. At Clifton, Mr Wood called & offered Brougham. [Revd. J. Wood, rector of Clifton 1847.]

19. **Sunday.** Thankful to have only to go to Clifton Church, for the weather has again changed fr. yesterday. Wind & hurricane – snow etc. To Askham in even. Scolded by Mrs W. for not approving of their new scheme for school building. Took it patiently as being prob. my last!

22. My 34th Birthday. A letter from L. Just as I had concluded that as of old it wd. pass unnoticed 'Park View' at 3 pm. walked into the School, bringing a crowd of kind wishes, a nice present, & invitation to return with them. Roads nice and a pleasant walk. In the morn. I recd my reappointment as Organising Secty at £20.0.0 per an.

23. Walked fr. Clifton – morn. Even. at Coy Pond.

24. In even. after Preaching at Penrith on to Newton where I fd. Hannah very poorly. [? his half-sister Hannah b.1837].

26. **Sunday.** Drove fr. Clifton with co. to Brougham. In even Isa. returned to Newton.

27. More hurricane with snow. The snow wh. fell mainly on Tuesday remained till end of week. Hannah – Bronchitis!

March

[n.d.] **Sunday.** Drove fr. Newton; but disappointed in getting Co. to church. Cong. abt. 24.

8. Poor Ainsworth revealed his miserable position. Its effects on his appearance has been noticeable. He seemed most wretched.

11. **Sunday.** At Clifton. Isa. at Newton to see Hannah who is recovering. Mr Wood at Brougham.

12. **Weather** still wintry. Snow & frosty nights. The Archd. called & remarked as agreeably as he cd. abt. half holiday on Friday. He is pursuing his old plan of listening to accusations agt. the Masters till I much dislike his visits. Mr Mawson I now find has been slandering me busily fr. the first. Last Wednesday in school I protested agt. a story of Tom Mounsey's that I had never given a Latin lesson, & mentioned that I had been told of one boy boasting that he was a better scholar than his Master. From Mr Bland [J. Bland curate 1860] I learn that Mawson early applied to him to be private tutor, & that M. has since said that B. was the applicant!

    It seems therefore that I must face my persecutors or succumb. As I do not mean to do this latter, I shall (D.V.) to-morrow give the boy Mawson my opinion of his conduct, before his Peers.

13. After 'Roll Call', I began by telling the boys that I had to tell them of their disagreeables. It had come to be a case of kill or be killed, & I did not mean to yield. Naming Mr Mawson & addressing the boy I related what I believed to have been his unfair & persecuting system towards my predessors & self. Warned him of the consequences, & appealed to the boys on the ground that his slanderous system had injured the school in making the appointment undesirable, & must continue to mar its efficiency.

14. Having learned that Mr Mawson had used his opportunity when Mr Ainsworth was there at tea on the 24 ult. to talk

134

agt. me, naming as his authority Mr Whitwick, I feel more confirmed in my policy to take the Bull by the horns! At abt. 9 pm. Mr Mawson came to my rooms for an interview; but Mrs Scott very considerately gave me an opportunity to 'refuse to see him'. I had previously resolved to 'cut' him. Much talk afterwards with my kind Hostesses. As Mother & Sister they condemn M's conduct. I learn that Mr Whitwick [curate of Newton Reigny] has been busily defaming me in Penrith. Some reason to conclude that Mr Bland is dangerous.

15. The Archdeacon called at the school in the afternoon, & heard Scott & Mawson read a short chap. in Caesar. He was apparently well pleased; but I avoided showing any concern in the matter. Some talk afterwards abt. Mr A's threat of further proceedings for his pay at Askham.

16. In even. to Penrith. After Church with Tim Leech to Newton. Troutbeck preached & is improving. [Revd J. Troutbeck, vicar of Dacre 1858].

April

5. After some bother fr. Archd. gave Holiday for the Easter Week.

6. **Good Friday.** Began my duties as temp. curate of Penrith at Ch. Ch. Cong. good.

8. **Easter Day.** At Ch[rist] Ch[urch]. Services very grand. Com[munican]ts 64. Preached again in afternoon.

9. Monday. Snow storms etc! After a quiet week of needed rest at Newton, for I might not go E. went to Pen[rith] again on ...

15. Preached morn. at St Andrew's aftn at Ch. Ch. then after rest etc. at P. Vicarage on to Clifton.

16. Thence to reopen school.

22. **Sunday.** The past week very cold, with snow. This morn bright; but colder to & fr. Penrith than expected. Pr. morn at Ch. Church, even. at Old C. [? St Andrew's].

23. Penrith Sheep Fair. The snow wh. fell last even. still covering the costly grass fr. the sheep, wh. as we passed Penrith had generally moved to the hill. The best fields hardly green. From some cause cold & rain in face etc.

24. The Cattle Fair. A considerable covering of fresh snow last night; but no frost as yesterday. Our first field day at Cricket. The snow having melted, ground pretty well; but the wind dangerously cold.

28. By Kendal to Hawkshead.

29. **Sunday.** Preached for Nat. Soc. £2.12.0. No collectors in afternoon! Fine old church. In even. the cold wind gave place to rain.

30. Started to return at 7 am being driven to [Windermere] Ferry. Got safely back to School by 1.40. In even. to Clifton with Father – Mortgage.

May
– All this time fine sun & rain.

28. **Whitsun Monday.** Awoke at Newton to find the ground covered thick with snow! There being no frost however to mar the wonderful show of blossom. During this month all vegetation had made wonderful progress.

30. Mr Ainsworth stopped by Mr Mawson and again well scolded.

June 1860
11. At 8.16 pm left Penrith for London.

12. Arrived safely in Bond St early. Saw 'Xst. in the Temple', 'Denizens of ye Highlands' & ye Kensington Museum so as to get to the Meeting of Secretaries at the Sanctuary by 12 am. In the evening dined with Geo. Moore.

13. Saw 'Royal Academy' before Meeting. Afterwards to 'Lords'. At 9.15 started to return.

14. By abt. 7 am. got safely back to my lodgings. Much less tired than I expected.

16. To Greystoke abt. our examination.

17. At Penrith. Still some snow drifts on the Western Fells.

18. Hannah much better accompanied me towards Hack-thorpe.

20. Diocesan Inspector.

21. Fine evening. Good cricket. Law Harrison Esqr. called at noon fr. the Bank.

30. The half yearly ex. & distribution of Prizes. Quite as satisfactory as I expected. The Archd. – 5 weeks holiday. To Newton afterwards.

July
Penrith Sunday as usual.

1. After a quiet holiday spent mainly at Newton, interrupted mainly by the Bank.

August
6. Returned & reopened the School. There being less than 20 scholars I conclude the people wish a longer holiday!

October
7. **My last Sunday at Penrith.**

8. Returning by 'Mile Lane' this morn. noticed fresh snow on Helvellen. While leading hay during (I think) the first week in July the old drifts were still visible on the Western fells.

10. Much more snow on the Fells.

11. Wind a hurricane. Much corn yet to cut & more to carry.

12. Friday. Up to this time the late harvest or something has kept the average attendance below 30. All else very pleasant.

December

16. Received a second cheque fr. Mr Butler making £32.12.0 for six months I had taken Sundays at Penrith, almost always 'double duty'.

22. Ended my first year of School Work with more praise fr. the Trustees than I expected.

9

Hackthorpe
1860–1870

BRUNSKILL'S TENACITY, indeed pugnacity, in church matters is best seen against the poverty and humiliation of the curates' world. A typical example comes from the parish of Kirk-andrews on Esk near Longtown. As one enters the Georgian church there is a gravestone on the left, by the wall. It is to the Revd Henry Hodgson. He completed his studies at St Bees Clerical College in 1821, and was ordained by the bishop of Chester. He held four curacies in the next ten years; he was then appointed to that of Kirkandrews in 1832, and he remained in that lowly post for the next thirty years, doing duty for the rector, who lived at and held the rectory of Arthuret. When his pluralist master died in 1862 his kind patron Sir Frederick U. Graham of Netherby appointed him to Kirkandrews, for which there was no parsonage, with the handsome stipend of £911.2.4 a year of which £854.12.6. came from tithes.[1] Not many curates were so fortunate. He lived to enjoy this affluence for four years, and died in 1866. Many curates never obtained promotion and died in poverty.

Some time after his marriage Brunskill managed to rent a house from Lord Lonsdale in Hackthorpe, and from this base served his school on weekdays, and at weekends was available for occasional duty for the local clergy, doing weddings, funerals and Sunday services. This became the pattern of his life from 1860 to 1882. As far as school work is concerned there is little to record, except that the Trustees insisted on the right to choose the school books, long after the Education Act of 1870. Dr Jackson the rector and a trustee maintained that point until his death in 1877. It is arguable that he was right to do so in view of Brunskill's pronounced high-church views often trumpeted in the press, and especially when from 1867 he was the secretary of the newly formed branch of the English Church Union in the Penrith area. Not only were the lectures of the E.C.U. describing medieval ceremonies printed in the local press, but at times they featured as a counterblast to the doings of the Church Missionary Society printed in the same issue.

In those early years Brunskill was well dressed, good looking with a trim short beard, well cut frock coat, and every inch the parson determined to stand his ground. In later years when he added small parishes to his school work, he rode from Hackthorpe to his vicarage on Fridays, and back to school on Sunday evenings, these long journeys in all weathers took their toll. There is a photograph of him on horseback at Threlkeld rectory probably in the 1800s; his coat is of a more homely cut, his beard more ragged, his hat rather battered, all bearing the marks of a hard life struggling to keep a family, and holding a parish and school in double harness.

Lydia and Joseph Brunskill had the following children:

John Ritson, born 11 May 1865
Alice Mary, born 6 October 1866
Cyril Wane, born 12 August 1869
All these at Hackthorpe.

In 1872 he was made perpetual curate of Plumpton Wall near Penrith, when two more were born:

Isabelle Maud, born 10 November 1872
Lydia Violette, born 13 February 1876.

It is Alan Webster's tradition that his mother Lydia was born at Clifton; this is quite possible, as Brunskill seems to have had an aunt there whom he visited when he was curate at Askham. Indeed it is quite possible that more children were born at Clifton, especially if Brunskill was occupied with school during the week.[3] Some time after the birth of the last child, Lydia travelled home to Plumpton with the baby, caught a cold and died in the following June.[4] Brunskill was left with five children under the age of ten, with a school and parish to care for. His position must have been very difficult. We will return to this later. But it seems that Brunskill's sister Isabella became 'mother' to the children for a time.

Brunskill left behind dozens and dozens of press cuttings, a few from the national papers, but most from the local papers at

Kendal, Penrith and Carlisle. There were also the church papers, and to all he sent a regular stream of letters on all manner of subjects relating to schools, bishops and their unfair doings, horse-shoeing, the poor law, curates, church music, church patronage, architecture, and rabbits. The maddening thing is that more than half are not dated. As they cover a period of forty years, many are under a variety of pseudonyms, some of which he has initialled in pencil, so that is is only possible to select themes appropriate to each parish he served. His public letters developed from the time he went to Lowther School, and were at full flood when he was at Threlkeld.

He was fearless in attack, and in defence of the church, a radical Tory in politics, and determined in lecturing farmers at the Penrith Farmers' Club on the treatment of horses.

There is an interesting report in the *Penrith Observer* of the 8 May 1866. He appears to have affronted his Hackthorpe neighbours by fencing in some of the verge of the highway in front of his cottage. He was summoned by Joseph Powley of Rosgill to appear before the Hackthorpe Police Court 'for unlawfully erecting, or causing to be erected, certain posts in the parish of Lowther at the side of Heron Syke and the Eamont Bridge Turnpike Road, in such a manner as to reduce the breadth and confine the limits of the road.' He admitted that he had erected the posts, and that he had received notice to remove them. He was fined one shilling with costs. These squalls are the stuff of village life!

A year later in 1867 he raised another storm, this time in Penrith Parish Church. The Vicar, the Revd S. J. Butler took a holiday in May, and asked Brunskill to take his duty. Brunskill had never taken any notice of the Puritan survival of preaching in the Black Gown after the offices of Morning and Evening Prayer. He usually went from his pew to the pulpit without donning the gown. This custom survived in a few places from the days when Puritan preachers were intruded into parish churches, especially in the market towns such as Penrith, Kendal and Barnard Castle. I remember talking in the 1940s to a very old retired school teacher at Kendal, who remembered the days of Archdeacon Cooper in the last century. The Archdeacon decided to abandon the Black Gown in the pulpit, and these were her words: 'I remember the first Sunday he went up into the pulpit wearing his surplice, and HE LOOKED THOROUGHLY ASHAMED OF HIMSELF!'

Well, on his first Sunday Brunskill took Morning Service at St Andrews and went, as was his custom, into the pulpit in his surplice. The next weekend saw a furious crop of letters in the local papers, protesting at this innovation by the secretary of the local English Church Union, namely Brunskill. Clearly the Pope was stalking in the shadows; letters appeared from parishioners (1), (2), and (3); the bishop of Carlisle was written to by the churchwardens, and all was in an uproar. Brunskill wrote a lofty riposte to the *Penrith Observer*, saying that he did not take any notice of anonymous letters, but that he was always willing to given an explanation of his faith to any earnest enquirer. The storm soon subsided when next Sunday Brunskill brought his own gown and used it, while the more nervous parishioners prayed for the early return of the vicar from holiday.

Brunskill seems to have revelled in stirring up the church. In July of the following year 1868 a meeting of the E.C.U. was held in Penrith at the house of a Mr Metcalfe. The clergy present were an odd bunch. The Revds S. J. Butler, vicar of St Andrews; Thomas Lees, vicar of Wreay, Carlisle; Beilby Porteus, vicar of Edenhall; John Scott Mulcaster, rector of Gt. Salkeld; C. M. Preston, vicar of Warcop; Brunskill of Hackthorpe; C. J. Plumer of Elstree rectory, Edgeware, Herts; C. H. U. Pixell, BA, perpetual curate of Skirwith, then a high church parish; and H. Pixell, MA of Southbank, Leamington. There were also six laymen present. A paper was delivered on the subject of 'Burial of the Faithful Departed' from R. Brett Esq of Stoke Newington. The *Penrith Observer* carried two columns of the lecture describing the Catholic rites of long ago, with lights, incense, vestments, chanted psalms and so forth.[5] Heaven knows what the fellside farmers made of it in their weekend reading. But the humour of the situation was that on the reverse of the same page there was a long account of the meeting that same week at Christ Church Penrith on behalf of the Church Missionary Society. But, lo and behold, one of the clergy present was Mr

Mulcaster the rector of Gt Salkeld. He clearly was hedging his bets!

To return to 1867; on Saturday 6 July Brunskill went to Clifton to celebrate two marriages. When he arrived at the Clifton tollgate the keeper Sarah Watson demanded 2d. toll. Brunskill protested vigorously, claiming exemption as acting curate of Clifton. But he paid and went on his way; but he summoned her before the September Hackthorpe Police Court for demanding a toll from a clergyman exempted by statute. In cross-examination by Mr Shepherd a solicitor of Penrith, Brunskill admitted that he was not licenced curate of Clifton, but claimed to be curate of Askham, though his vicar, Mr Ward had died in 1863. Mr Shepherd claimed that a stranger going to take a service was not exempt, but only a vicar or curate going to take a service in his own parish. The Bench deferred judgement until the next Sessions. The outcome is not known.[6]

In the same week Brunskill was saddened by the death of his father John Brunskill at Newton on the 5 September aged 76 years. In his Will he left to his daughter Isabella all the furniture and other articles he received either on the death of his grandfather the Revd John Pearson or on that of his daughter Mary Ann, John's wife. The rest of his household goods he left to his second wife Hannah. Subject to the life interest of Hannah, John's estate (principally Bankfoot) was left to be sold, and the proceeds to be divided equally between his son Joseph, and daughters Isabella and Hannah, subject to the direction that 'any advances made to my said son Joseph in my lifetime for his preferment or advancement in the world shall be deducted from his third share'. He also provided that should his daughter Hannah be still a minor at his death, her mother shall use the income of her third share for her benefit during her minority.[7]

To return to the early years at Lowther, it is probable that about the time of Brunskill's marriage in 1861 he acquired his own horse, or more accurately a fell pony for his weekend transport to nearby churches. His attachment to horses was an old one, and, after the church, was a predominant part of his life. In a lecture before the Penrith Farmers' Club in July/August

1873 Brunskill paid tribute to the lessons he learned in boyhood at Newton from a farmer's son. This farmer's son in boyhood had been so attached to the horses, that when there was a forced sale, the boy had barred the stable door, and laid on the ground between the door and his pets. His tears were unavailing, and the horses were sold. But when in turn Brunskill was a boy at Newton this man, now head husbandman, taught Joseph all he knew about horses. 'For in the whole animal creation there is no creature like the horse in the interest he gives to mankind in any sphere of life and civilisation. In every age the horse has associated with man in everything great and beautiful ... The generous beast is eminently sociable, delighting to serve us, and there seems a fine sympathy attracting the more tender and manly parts of our nature'. The lecture filling two columns of the Cumberland Advertiser was devoted to kindness to horses, their eyes and feet.[8]

Brunskill became (rightly) a fanatic on the correct shoeing of horses. Alan Webster has the family story, that once when Brunskill was in London for a meeting of the National Society he went to Whitehall to see the horses of the Lifeguards. He went up to a mounted guardsman and asked permission to look at his horse's foot. Apparently permission was given, and Brunskill raised the horse's foot and examined the method of shoeing, to see how the army farriers did their work. Having satisfied himself, he lowered the foot, thanked the guardsman, and went on his way. Brunskill's lecture is extremely good, and still worth reading. He protested against the unnecessary use of blinkers, as depriving the horse of the full use of his eyes on all sides so that the animal is not startled. He also attacked the artificial methods of riding introduced by George IV, saying that cavalrymen should go to look at the Elgin Marbles in the British Museum to see how horses were ridden, and how not to rein them. While Brunskill was concerned with the whole horse, and its humane treatment, he reserved his main thrust in the appreciation and treatment of the foot. That smiths should know its structures, bones, hoofs, frog, cartilages, lamina, veins, arteries, and the nerves of which the foot is composed. He attacked the efforts of many crude and untrained blacksmiths who made their own shoes, drove nails too deep into the quick, and pared and rasped too much of the hoof for fancy effect, thus removing nature's protection of the more sensitive part of the foot. Brunskill's lecture of 1873 is perhaps the best thing he ever wrote. In 1869 he wrote an anonymous article in the *Cumberland & Westmorland Advertiser* praising the work of John Winskill farrier of Melkinthorpe and Penrith, who had abandoned making his own shoes, and was now using machine made shoes on the pattern of Mr. R. A. Goodenough, where the nail holes were smaller, and not likely to admit nails which would injure the quick. Winskill was a pioneer in the Penrith area, and no doubt Brunskill had his horse shod by him.[9]

In March 1894 Mr H. Pears, veterinary surgeon of Longtown delivered a lecture to the Penrith Farmers' Club on the structure of the foot of the horse and shoeing. Mr W. Graham of Eden Grove was president, and the MP Mr J. W. Lowther was also there with a number of leading farmers. It is interesting that there were also three horse-riding parsons there; J. Brunskill of Ormside; W. Lovejoy of Edenhall; and H. M. Kennedy of Plumpton. The lecture was a complete exemplification of all that Brunskill had been campaigning for for over twenty years. In explaining the structure of the foot he went into details which even Brunskill could not give. Mr Lowther added an informed comment from his examination, in the Natural History Museum at South Kensington, of the skeletons of horses and humans as to their bone structure. Mr Kennedy from Plumpton urged the new County Councils to institute examinations of blacksmiths undertaking shoeing. Brunskill pleaded for the adoption of shoes rolled by machinery, with countersunk nail holes. Mr J. M. Richardson of Carlisle mentioned that the Worshipful Company of Farriers had been formed in 1890, and two examiners had recently held examinations in Carlisle.[10] There is no doubt that Brunskill did much good in this field, and encouraged demonstrations at the agricultural shows at Shap and Keswick.

There is a pleasant little footnote to this. On the 22 October 1875 he wrote a letter from Plumpton to a local paper:

Domestic Service

Sir, Your correspondent, 'An Old Maid', makes a good suggestion that the girls of a family 'take a place' at home. I am a country clergyman cheered with daughters and sons. The girls are not being taught that one kind of work is menial and another genteel, and will, I believe, help us to live by lessening our subjection to the 'greatest plague of life'; and then, if ever needful, gaily and skilfully earn their own living. The boys are my regular helps in stable and garden, and with a horse at full work we have no other hired groom.

All stable work I find to be interesting, and, aided by little early advantage, I have, by practice since ordination, acquired what is considered to be a creditable skill in the craft, grooming being, in my experience, with fairly convenient arrangements, a pleasant and healthful recreation. Should some neighbours regard my work as infra dig, the more outspoken express envy at my independance; for unlike the tent making of a greater missionary, I have not only a resource against 'stamping out', but my occupation is a constant present gain in economy, safety, and many comforts.

B.R.[11]

Looking at these early years at Hackthorpe one cannot avoid the impression that Brunskill whether as the son of a small farmer, a junior clergyman, or the head of a country boys grammar school was like a chirpy cock-sparrow, who would not be put down by anybody. He made mistakes, but he worked hard to improve himself. He gave his whole heart and mind to his school, his church and family. His proving-ground was the school at Hackthorpe.

NOTES TO CHAPTER NINE

1. *Crockford* 1860 & 1866.
2. L.M. Press cutting September 1867.
3. Letter of Alan Webster 4 June 1989.
4. L.M. Letter of Richard Atkinson Brunskill 24 June 1876 to his niece Isabella Brunskill (Joseph's sister) on hearing of Lydia's death.
5. The clergy are placed from the Clergy List 1867.
   The press cuttings from L.M. & W.M.
6. L.M. Press cutting September 1867.

Brunskill's illustration of Wordsworth's poem 'Michael'

From Brunskill's illustrated 'Wordsworth'
His 7 year old daughter Lydia at the porch of Threlkeld Church,
in the part of 'We are Seven'.

7. L.M. Will dated 1 November 1849. C.R.O. Kendal.

8. W.M. *Cumberland Advertiser* 5 August 1873.

9. W.M. Two adverts of John Wilkinson, farrier of Melkinthorpe and Penrith, with communications, probably by Brunskill, on the new method of shoeing.

10. W.M. Cutting. *Penrith Observer* 13 March 1894.

11. W.M. Cutting 22/11/75. Presumably written from Plumpton.

NB
Since typing these pages I have come across a booklet entitled *Old Horseshoes* by Ivan G. Sparkes, Shire Album no. 19. pub. 1976, and on p. 24 a mention of the Goodenough shoe, which 'received a mixed reception in England'. It is a good introduction to the history of shoeing.

10

Hackthorpe & Swindale
1870–1872

THE FRACAS at St Andrew's Church, Penrith in 1867 over the black gown, and Brunskill's membership of the English Church Union, had a more serious side than an interest in old ritual; it was the deplorable condition of many country churches, and the slovenly way in which the sacraments were administered. In the Penrith district the parishioners still mention a fishing rector of the latter part of the last, and the first part of this century who kept his minnows in the font. I remember one clergyman who, after the administration of the Holy Communion with household bread, used to take a duster from a nail at the back of the vestry door, and dust the crumbs from the large paten on to the vestry floor. I am sure our Lord did not mind; but it was a very casual way of treating so sacred a reminder of One whom one was suppose to love. To Brunskill the E.C.U. seemed to be one way of exposing a scandal which brought the church into such contempt.

His first intervention on this point was also in 1867. The gist of the letter was to attack the bishops' condemnation of 'Romish practices' while worse scandals remained unchecked.

> Sir, During a ministry of over twenty years, spent chiefly in the diocese of Carlisle, I have seen something of the 'usual and sanctioned ritual'. I have frequently gone to Church at the appointed hour for service and found that the Pastor had been earlier, and had either 'got through the duty', or had disappeared without doing any.
>
> (In one or two churches the ante-Communion was read from the reading desk, while in another a Rural Dean said the Prayer of Consecration without touching the Bread or the Cup.)
>
> Various hymns and prayers are usually interpolated after the Nicene Creed, as also the ceremonies which accompany the change to the black vestment. In one parish where I was curate in charge there was no font, and the covering of the 'holy table' was so filthy and rotten that it dropped to pieces on removal. In another parish of which I was also in charge, I discovered the fine old font desecrated under the Vicar's pump etc. The prominent 'black

bottle' and large coarse pieces of bread at the Holy Communion were scandalous, and the consecrated wine which remained, I have seen drunk from tumbler glasses by men standing and talking in the chancel.

[Brunskill then asked, which course he should follow, these 'uses' or a more reverent use of the Prayer Book.]

February 25 1867   J.B. [1]

His most astonishing attack on slovenliness was in an (undated) article in a local paper on the state of affairs at Threlkeld, a church which he was later to serve as rector.

The parishioners and others who worship in the parish church of Threlkeld cannot be congratulated on the appearance presented by the interior of that sacred edifice. The window at the east end is in a deplorable condition. The panes are simply pasted over with a paper covering which was supposed at one time to produce the effect of stained glass but which now has become so torn and faded that it serves no better purpose than that of collecting dust and obscuring the light. All the windows on the north side have large cobwebs suspended from them, or at least they had last Sunday morning. How these aid divine worship we are unable to say. On the sill of the window over the communion table were two vases, empty, and innocent even of a single flower, symbolical it may be of the church which was almost empty, though sufficient of the natives might be seen loitering outside to fill it to overflowing. On the woodwork and panelling near the lectern, on the faded paint, the only marks visible were those made by the hair of the jaded reader. It would seem to be ages since a house-painter visited the place. Cushions, carpets, and footstools are in the same dilapidated condition. The choir now breaking down when it ought not, and anon breaking in when it should be silent, performed its part in a most melancholy way.

The clergyman who supplied the vicar's place on Sunday was obliged to come in himself and spread the 'fair' [?] white cloth preparatory to the administration of the sacrament, and, from a mean little half-pint bottle standing on the floor, to decant the wine which was to become the sacred symbol and element. We don't think that if the inspired Psalmist were to visit Threlkeld he would say of the parish church 'A day in thy courts is better than a thousand.' One felt inclined to doubt the practical nature of the religion professed by the worshippers there. After all a little attention to the house of prayer is desirable on the part of Christian churchmen.

> If funds are not forthcoming to fee some Keswick painter to
> clean up and renovate the building, at least some of the parish-
> ioners might spend an occasional hour scrubbing out the place
> themselves ...
>
> [It was signed] LEBAZI.[2]

One suspects that it was Brunskill himself who was the visiting
clergyman, sore at seeing so goodly an heritage being ruined.
But that it was his writing is proved by the initials J.B. he has
pencilled at the foot.

In about 1869 Revd C. H. B. Pixell perpetual curate of Skirwith (a member of the E.C.U.) whose Anglo-Catholic parish
was warmly supported by Christopher Parker Esqre, of Skirwith
Abbey announced in his Christmas letter to his parishioners
that he had arranged for a mission to be held in the parish
shortly after the next Easter. The gist of a long and intense
article was to encourage the use of sacramental confession. The
editor of the local paper, perhaps suspecting that the clergyman
was a crank, added this caption to the reprinted article:

'The Revd C. H. V. Pixell and his parishioners.'[3]

The missioner was none other than a well known and much
respected Revd George Body, later a canon. His visit stirred up
another wasps' nest. A furious protestant wrote to the *Penrith
Observer* that the Revd Mr Body was promoting 'gross super-
stition and debasing idolatry'. This was too much for Brunskill
who in a long letter pointed out that the bishop of Carlisle had
recently taken his family to hear the famous preacher at none
other place than Westminster Abbey. Mr Body also spoke at
Penrith and said 'that the work which we have to do is to rear
again our Father's church – worship as they worshipped our
Father's God – and so manifest the love wherewith we love our
Jesus'. Brunskill welcomed anyone who worked to improve the
standard of public worship, and of church music. Thirty five
years ago I was a regular visitor to Skirwith church and vicarage, in the days of Fr Wilson. The daily round of Matins and
Evensong (the latter often sung to plainsong) and daily Mass
and the Reserved Sacrament were a cordial to the soul. When
other churches were only used on Sundays, Skirwith church,

though a bit florid, reminded us of higher standards than the customary. That this was so was due to priests like Pixell and Body, and to some extent Brunskill, whose grandfather came from the mother parish of Kirkland. But Brunskill was a Prayer Book man rather than an Anglo-Catholic, though he did support those priests such as Machonochie, Tooth and Green who were persecuted by the Church Association and imprisoned under the Public Worship Regulation Act 1874, which aimed to suppress the growth of ritualism in the Established Church.[4]

There is a pleasant undated press cutting describing a festival of church music at St Andrew's, Penrith which epitomises Brunskill's persistent work for better and more cheerful services. Up to the time of rehearsal at 1.30 pm trains and vehicles of all sorts, carriages, chaises, gigs, and farmers' carts brought the choristers from the following parishes: St Andrew's, Skirwith, Addingham, Askham, Dacre, Great Strickland, Lazonby, Langwathby, Lowther, Melmerby, Skelton, Temple Sowerby, and Wreay. When the service began at 3 pm the whole body of the church was filled with congregation and unsurpliced choirs, while the surpliced occupied the choir stalls. The service was conducted by Canon Butler the vicar, and his curate Revd C. H. Gem, with the Revd G. F. Weston giving the sermon. The opening Procession rang to Baring-Gould's hymn, 'Daily, daily sing the praises, of the City God hath made'. The press reporter said that the 'outburst of song was most jubilant'. There is no doubt that Brunskill's hand was behind much of this.[5]

In the field of education the clouds began to gather. In 1869 the Endowed Schools Act, and the Education Act of 1870 showed that at last Parliament was about to reform education. Lowther school, and the three dame schools were soon to come under its provisions. Soon Brunskill was writing to the press protesting against the threat against ancient endowments, and more particularly the exclusion of denominational teaching from state schools. 'School-boardism' was his spectre, and the first step towards socialism.

In the middle of his school work and fears for the future there came a small change in his fortunes. On 20 February 1870 the Revd Thomas Sewell perpetual curate of Swindale died aged 73 years. He was a native of Swindale, one of several brothers who had taken orders. His brother had been vicar of Troutbeck. In the twenties Thomas was curate of Newton Reigny, but the call of his native dale was stronger. On 15 June 1850 the vicar of Shap appointed him to Swindale where he remained till he died. He was single, and lodged for many years with Jossie Green at Naddle. His stipend was £56 a year, at a time when the statutory wage for a curate was supposed to be not less than £80 a year. He was a 'tall, good-looking, square-shouldered, lang legged, girt striding man', equally at home on a fellside farm, or following a fox in the crags, or taking the plain Prayer Book services in the simple chapel. At the time of his coming there were eight houses in the dale, with a breadmaker, schoolmaster, and parson. The schoolroom and the chapel stood end to end. The average attendance of children was two or three. The little chapel was poor and damp, with ten pews. There was no font, and the communion table was plain and simple. There was one little bell rung by a chain from the schoolroom, which was not tolled until the parson approached, and then the few dales folk entered, some with a sheep dog. The surplice was donned from the desk, where it was left from the previous week. Often babies were baptised at home, occasionally from a basin in the chapel. All baptisms had to be registered at Shap church. Services were not always punctual; sometimes on hot days the parson would have a swim in the dub below the stepping stones, and as time was of little consequence in those parts, no-one troubled if the service was half an hour late. Once when Sewell took one or two children to Lowther to be confirmed by Montague-Villiers (bishop of Carlisle 1856–60, the bishop who had plagued Brunskill at All Hallows), the bishop rebuked him in the vestry for not answering a letter sent three weeks earlier. Sewell calmly replied that he would answer when he received it. These humble priests of these remote chapelries were sometimes men of great physical and spiritual stature; Thomas Sewell was one of these, a good man.[6]

On his death the Revd Stephen Whiteside vicar of Shap since 1863 offered the charge to his old friend Brunskill. He served the place from Hackthorpe on horseback, while continuing his work at Lowther school. He seems to have undertaken some repairs, for in the same year (1870) the roof was reslated, and a wooden ceiling added. There were further improvements under Whiteside in 1874. Brunskill's chief claim to our gratitude is due to his observation of some rubbish lying in a barn at the sale of the effects of Mr Hogarth, solicitor of Clifton in 1870. In a corner he noticed a panel of medieval glass, which had been removed from the east windows of Clifton church at the 'restorations' of William second lord Brougham. The east window had formerly contained a Calvary of 14th C. glass, with Our Lady with the arms of Engaine on the left, a crucifix in the centre and St John with the arms of Fallowfield of Gt Strickland on the right. The Engaine window was placed in the west window of the side chapel, the crucifix was destroyed, and the Fallowfield window was bought by Brunskill for 20s. The churchwardens were not interested, and Brunskill had the window repaired and placed in Swindale chapel.

In about 1944 when I was curate of Lowther I heard one Monday morning that there had been an explosion of gas at Clifton Church the previous Saturday. The rector's daughter Mrs Norma Gilbanks had gone into church to light the gas stoves on Saturday evening, and on her lighting one stove there had been an immense explosion which blew out all the windows. She was badly shaken, and lost the sight of an eye. I spent a whole morning picking up the bits of the Engaine window from the churchyard. The old rector the Revd W. M. Keys-Wells died the same year, and in his study there was found the Fallowfield window which had been returned to Clifton when Swindale chapel was demolished in 1933. When the east windows were reglazed the Engaine and Fallowfield windows were returned to their ancient places and look glorious against a quarry of clear glass.[7]

Though Brunskill's interests were mainly church and school, there was one side of his care which dated back to his experience in Sunderland, the lot of the poor and sick. In a letter to the *Penrith Observer* of 15 June 1872 he pointed to the overcrowded condition of the workhouses. Many years earlier he had pleaded for the erection of cottage hospitals, which would

take cases of serious infection out of the overcrowded workhouse wards, and keep them in separate cottage hospitals. He
pointed out that even a new workhouse would not remove
workhouse children from the corruption of their fellow
inmates. Readers of the life of the explorer Sir H. M. Stanley
will remember his experience at the hands of an usher in the St
Asaph workhouse. Brunskill wrote that for many years he had
waited for some sign from the Board of Guardians at Penrith
workhouse that they would consider boarding out pauper children. 'I would save money to the state and ratepayers by going
back to the only healthy and natural system, home life and
family ... These unloved girls or boys know of no fond heart
that will grieve if they do badly, nor a kindly welcome home
again when they return hearty and prosperous. Their very name
is forgotten for the number they hear in the 'Ward' they become
dull and wooden as the surrounding monotony. Their restoration to happy English life cannot be done by the rich so
naturally as by a kind cottager. Such a benevolent householder
is more powerful in this work of mercy than any Board or
Parliament.'[8]

When he became rector of Threlkeld Brunskill became a
member of the Penrith Board of Guardians and of the old
Sanitary Authority. He also took great interest in the Penrith
Farmers Club, and delivered a number of papers to the members, and took part in many of their discussions.[9]

Injustice to the poor made Brunskill very angry. On the 27
September 1881 he wrote to a Kendal paper protesting that two
Kendal justices had condemned to hard labour a man named
Thomas Johnson 'for the crime of poverty'. 'Early on that same
Sunday when this "criminal" was taking shelter in some shed or
hoghouse, I also met a shivering and coughing family. They
were not "run in", but while having some breakfast by a fire, I
had time to notice their very wet condition. The distance from
Keswick (to Threlkeld) is only four miles, and it was then fair
weather, so I enquired the reason, and believe that they had
spent the whole previous night on the road exposed to a
terrible storm of wind and rain. Why had they not sought
shelter in some cattle-shed? Because when the police denied

them a lodging and drove them out of Keswick it was too dark
for them to see any such shelter. A third bad case happened on
that same good day in London. What is described as "a poorly
clad and dejected looking man with a starving wife and
family", is denied justice by Mr Barstow, a London Police magistrate, because he had no money. The hapless casual had been
savagely kicked by two hirelings whose duty it was to provide
lodgings at a casual ward ... In England all power remains in
the hands of the richer class of people; but some think that they
hear the surging tide of "democracy", etc, the mastery by the
"common people".' J. Brunskill.[10]

Even in his last parish of Ormside Brunskill kept his eye on
the work of the Poor Law Guardians, and the food dished out
to the inmates of the Workhouses. A correspondent in the *Penrith Observer* complained of the waste of food in workhouses.
Brunskill replied that when he visited Kirkby Stephen workhouse he carried a motion that the paupers should be allowed
butter or jam rather than too much bread. In those days the
Local Government Board allowed a change from three gruels on
Saturdays for the boys and girls to suet pudding with syrup for
dinner. 'That plan worked very well for a time, but is not now
needed, as all the children who were formerly in the workhouse
are at present boarded out'. In general Brunskill felt that more
attention to variety in diet was being observed, with the result
that there was less waste.[11] It is interesting that boarding out
workhouse children did not get under way till the last part of
the nineteenth century.

In essence, because of his own experience, Brunskill was a
very just man, and was fearless in exposing the system of patronage in the church. On the 20 January 1872 he wrote to the
Penrith Observer about church patronage, that so much rested
with the Crown, bishops and cathedral canons, as well as the
vicar of Kendal in the Carlisle diocese. So many hard working
clergy were ignored by their superiors who promoted their
friends. Brunskill praised the then earl of Lonsdale, pointing out
that the two clergymen he had in his life appointed to the vicarage of Askham had each been curates in the diocese for over
25 years without any promotion from the bishops etc. It was

left to a lay patron to do what the church had failed to do. 'However there is evidence all around of young and stranger clergymen having been presented to livings. I once heard an old soldier apologise for his baldness by saying that it was caused by younger men walking over his head'. He must have sent a similar letter to the *Westmorland Gazette*, for on the 5 February 1872 he received this reply:

Ings Vicarage, Kendal.

To the writer of the letter signed 'Fairplay' in the Westmorland Gazette,

Sir, Allow me to thank you for your letter on Church Patronage. It is high time the matter was looked at properly. It may appear egotistic in me to say what I am about to say but "ex uno disce omnes" must be my excuse for doing so. On account of the delicate state of my dear wife's health as well that I thought a change would be beneficial both to me and the people, I have twice sought for preferment once from Lord Lonsdale and since from the Vicar of Kendal. In the former case I was told I had no chance because the majority of the Preston Patrick people had decided upon another candidate altho' he had but just attained the Priesthood. In the latter I could not be appointed to Natland altho' all the parishioners, with the exception of one great man, who never attends Natland Church, and who used his influence against me, *memorialised* the patron in my behalf.

I am a Westmorland man who from the love of his native County gave up £100 a year to get back into it & have twice refused preferment out of it.

Since I came here now nearly 18 years ago a new organ, a New School, & a new Vicarage have been built. While on the other hand I have seen what Sallust would call 'Non Homines', men who fraternised with Dissent & gave Christian burial to the unbaptised patted on the back & receive preferment after serving one or two years.

I write with no motive but that of love for our spiritual Mother the Church of England & to thank you very cordially for your letter & beg to subscribe myself,

Yr obliged faithful servant,

Thos. Fenton, vicar of Hugil and Ings, Kendal.[12]

Well, not many clergy could quote Sallust today! After serving Swindale for just under two years, Brunskill was appointed in 1872 to the perpetual curacy of Plumpton Wall near Penrith.

NOTES TO CHAPTER TEN

1. W.M. Folder of press cuttings.

2. W.M. Folder of press cuttings.

3. W.M. Folder of press cuttings.

4. W.M. Press cuttings. (1) Revd S.F. Green. (2) Revd A. Tooth. And a prayer slip for the Revd S.F. Green who had been in prison one year at mid-Lent 1882.

5. W.M. undated press cutting.

6. *Shappe in Bygone Days*. Revd Joseph Whiteside. Kendal 1904, pp. 59–87.

7. I recorded these details in a MS book which was later used by the Revd C.M. Lowther Bouch, rector of Clifton in a history of the church. The glazing was done by Abbott & Co. of Lancaster.

8. W.M. Brunskill to the *Penrith Observer* 30 January 1872.

9. L.M. From the Obituary to Brunskill in the *Penrith Observer*. He d. 10 March 1903.

10. W.M. Brunskill to *Penrith Observer* 15 June 1872.
    Brunskill to (?) *Westmorland Gazette* 27 September 1881.

11. Undated article to ? *Penrith Observer*.

12. L.M. Brunskill to *Penrith Observer* 30 January 1872.
    L.M. MS Letter 5 February 1872 Revd Thomas Fenton of Ings to Brunskill.

11

Hackthorpe & Plumpton
1872–1879

IT WAS perhaps unfortunate that the first twenty years of Brunskill's ministry coincided with the reign of two bishops, Villiers (1856–1860) and Waldegrave (1860–1869) both narrow evangelicals who would not countenance nor promote men of high-church leanings. In 1862 Waldegrave founded the 'Church Building and Benefice Association' through which 9 new churches, and 16 new parsonages were built, and 13 livings augmented. As Canon Bouch has recorded there were still 47 villages without a church, 51 livings with no parsonage, and 96 benefices of under £100 a year.[1] From the arrival of bishop Harvey Goodwin, former dean of Ely, in December 1869 the modern diocese may be dated. He introduced many consultative reforms, a diocesan conference in 1870, ruri-decanal meetings for clergy in 1872, and conferences in many centres in the diocese at which the laity and clergy met to consider questions put by the bishop. The first one held in the Penrith district met at the grammar school in 1872. In 1873 the bishop announced a Mountain Chapel Competition inviting designs. Brunskill at once dipped his pen, and on the 6 February 1873 wrote thus:

> A suggestion from the Bishop of this Diocese for an improvement upon the modern 'dandified' chapels which in too many places have superseded the venerable dale churches, brought from two gentlemen of Windermere liberal offers of money for a prize plan. Competition is restricted to architects dwelling in the diocese or Lancashire, and their drawings are now before the judges. I venture some remarks.

He then pointed out that the new buildings were for church rather than chapel people. That the description 'Mountain Chapel' is not appropriate to a dale church. He pointed out the need for plaster ceilings to keep out excessive heat, and drifting snow. That the windows should be glazed in thick glass to withstand gales; that the bell or bells should be in a tower which would form a porch, rather than hang open, with the ropes coming through the roof letting in cold air and rain. He very sensibly protested against the unnecessary heating systems under the floor when a plain stove would do, with a bright fire in the vestry.

His strongest complaint was against repeating the medieval plan of a large chancel cutting off the congregation from the clergy, when a simple apse could take the communion table. He also pleaded for attention to the acoustics of a building.

> And so I conclude with a hope that while a church provides for the people a comfortable shelter as a primary requisite and enables them to see and hear, it may be none the less characteristically beautiful.
>
> I am yours truly, Dalesman.[2]

In 1872 Brunskill was appointed to the perpetual curacy of the district chapel of Plumpton Wall near Penrith. The patron was G. Dixon Esq. and the stipend £62 a year. The mother parish was that of Lazonby where the rector Revd J. Heysham (1846–1877) received £551 a year.[3] Brunskill's predecessor's later stipend was £49. But as it was the rule of Queen Anne's Bounty that perpetual curacies in private patronage could not be augmented by capital grants, they remained at the bottom of the ladder until transferred to the bishop. Thus when Miss Dixon transferred Plumpton to the bishop in 1879 after Brunskill's appointment to Threlkeld, Plumpton was raised to £300 a year; while Brunskill at Threlkeld received £138 net. There is no wonder that he expressed himself forcibly against the system. A year after his arrival at Plumpton his chapelry was declared a separate parish.

The chapel of Plumpton Wall dedicated to St John was built in 1767 by subscription at a cost of £200, and erected at Salkeld Gate. The parson lived at Plumpton Foot, and in 1847 received £44 a year. In a New Year's letter to his flock in January 1876 Brunskill scornfully described it as a 'Club Chapel', where a few people, 'having joined in the expense, shared the area, and divided what they took to be their property by pens or "omnibus pews". But this "Chapel of Ease" has been since March 1873 the parish church of the district extending about two miles around; and I believe that the so-called seats are free to all the parishioners of Plumpton.'[4]

One of the clergy whom Brunskill got to know was the Revd C. H. Gem, curate of Penrith 1868–1874. He was a graduate of New Inn Hall, Oxford, and took his BA in 1862. He was curate of Thatcham, Berks 1862; Chaplain of Queens Hospital, and Professor of Classics at Queens College, Birmingham 1862–64; curate of Dudley 1864–65; of Tatchbrook 1865–68; and of Penrith 1868–74. He was appointed vicar of Torpenhow in 1874 on a net stipend of £312. The famous dean of Carlisle Francis Close at once opposed the nomination. Close was a powerful evangelical preacher, who did much work for the Cumberland Infirmary, foreign missions, church expansion, and temperance. He was much admired, but strongly opposed to the slightest whiff of high-churchery. On the 30 March 1874 Brunskill wrote to the *Cumberland and Westmorland Advertiser*:

> THE OPPOSITION TO THE APPOINTMENT OF THE REVD. C.H. GEM
> Sir, The opposition in Carlisle to the well-earned preferment of Mr Gem is led by Dean Close. Now, during many years he went about the country persecuting Churchmen who had choral worship, and surpliced choirs etc. such lawful usages in the Church of England were railed at as popery by Mr Close, of Cheltenham, till he was converted by getting a living of £800 a year, where, in a highly ritualistic church, his main business was to keep up a good surpliced choir. This well-placed ritualism, however much it may be now to his taste, has not brought him to see the inconsistency of his old persecuting spirit. He and his followers still seem to believe in their own infallible opinions as strongly as the Pope himself.

Pointing to the amount of work Mr Gem had done in Penrith in taking daily services, the number of communicants he had prepared in Confirmation, his raising money, and his work in the parish schools, Brunskill remarked that

> ... the number of poor in the church galleries will bear comparison with anything that can be shown by the boasting 'Evangelicals' from the empty pews of the Parish Church, Carlisle.
> Yours very truly, FAIRPLAY.[5]

Close had been perpetual-curate of St Mary's Carlisle 1858–68, while at the same time drawing his dean's stipend of £1,400 a year. Brunskill's pen was improving his style. There was an element of humbug in a rich dean opposing the preferment of a poor curate.

In 1874 Brunskill was himself in trouble. In the previous year he made some alterations to the seating arrangements in the church. It is difficult to recover from the veritable fusillade of letters he wrote in 1874 to the *Carlisle Patriot*, the *Penrith Observer*, and the *Cumberland & Westmorland Advertiser* what were the facts which led to his being delated by churchwardens Mr Kirkbride and Mr Monkhouse before the Consistory Court. He appears to have altered some seats to provide for a small choir, and his family. This was resented by the proprietory pew owners, and hence the uproar. There were several hearings almost verging on farce, when the churchwarden Monkhouse retired, and his place was taken by Thomas Sewell, a relation of Brunskill, who refused to support the action. The upshot was that Brunskill was ordered to restore the pews to their former state, and was fined £25, almost half a year's stipend. He is not always exact in his public letters. In a letter to the church *Guardian* of 25 June 1879 Brunskill complained of the cost of faculties: 'Here at Plumpton, having, as I believed the approval of the Bishop, Chancellor, and everybody else concerned, when in the exercise of my discretion as being officially responsible for the conduct of divine worship, I helped slightly to alter half-a-dozen unlawful seats in order that some of the congregation, and my own children, might kneel, I was worried by a long and disgracing suit in the diocesan court, and, with repeated fines, had to pay costs equal to one year's income from this "living".' Brunskill had for some time conducted a campaign against faculty fees, and after his conviction he asked publicly in a letter to the *Penrith Observer* of 9 July 1875 why the Earl of Lonsdale, who had prepared a grave for his family without faculty, but with the consent of the rector and churchwardens of Lowther had not also been summoned for Chancellor's fees.[6] He reserved his last shaft for Chancellor Burton who had tried him. C. J. Burton had been rector of Lydd in Kent from 1821 at a stipend of £1,247 a year. When in 1855 he was made chancellor he came to live permanently in Carlisle, leaving two curates to do his work. 'However I presume to ask what is this Chancellor who has done so much towards the ruin of me and mine? Is he not a clergyman who, leaving in notorious neglect his parish in Kent, obtains from some friend this place at Carlisle? ... This judge rules that parishioners have personal rights in the church and churchyard, but that they must not exercise these lawful rights till they have paid his fees for a faculty.' He then expressed his regret at having the misfortune of coming to Plumpton. They were unhappy days.

Among Brunskill's press cuttings is one which illustrates the capacity of the Church of England in its petty medieval courts to incur the maximum of odium over trivia. There appeared this account dated by Brunskill on 8 August 1876:

A 'Faculty' farce played out

Some time ago Miss Moordaff, an old lady residing at Seaton, was dragged into the Augean stable, the Carlisle consistory Court, by the Revd A. Hodges, vicar of Camerton, for having been guilty of the monstrous crime of enclosing a grave in Camerton Churchyard without first obtaining a faculty for the purpose. There can be no doubt that Miss Moordaff thought that she was acting legally when she made the enclosure, and that she had been misled in the matter. The case was heard by Chancellor Burton, who decided against Miss Moordaff, and even went so far as to threaten her with imprisonment if the enclosure was not removed. It was removed; a faculty was obtained for making another, which is now being done; and on Tuesday last there was a public demonstration of sympathy with Miss Moordaff, who has undoubtedly been the victim of as gross an act of clerical tyranny as the history of the nineteenth century supplies. Last week the courts decided in favour of the lady, and on Tuesday such a scene was enacted at Seaton as will serve to talk of for a generation. There was tea for all comers free – a bountiful spread. The forms from the neighbourhood were too few to seat the hundreds who gathered from all the district. After tea came the climax – the conveying of the railings from Seaton to Camerton churchyard. The procession was headed by the Flimby band; then came the ladies in carriages, the principal lady concerned having, as a tribute of sympathy and congratulation, the pony taken out of her carriage, which was drawn by six men. Next came, mounted and cloaked, with something like a sword which he brandished at the lady in front, an individual who was understood to represent the offending vicar. Then came one hundred men, each bearing a piece of the expelled railing, some mounting the pieces on their hats like cockades. Then followed four hundred people bringing up the rear, and so they came to Camerton Church, and each man laid his piece of iron within the gate, where the masons were already at work rebuilding the wall preparatory to the erection of the palisades which the lady had been obliged to remove – and had taken to her barn for safety – and now restored them in this fashion.[7]

Another running battle at Plumpton was over the development of the church school. In 1874 it had sixty children, and in 1874 the diocesan inspector of schools reported: 'In the higher division of Plumpton school the religious knowledge continues on the whole to be very fair. The children are generally below the average age, but their examination, both in Holy Scripture and in the Prayer Book, showed careful teaching. Great care will be required with the lower division, in which I would strongly recommend the use of pictures. The singing needs great improvement'.[8] Whether here or at Lowther Brunskill regularly sent to the papers any favourable reports of church schools. But dissent was in the air, and following the Education Act of 1870, several malcontents led by Mr Thomas Lowthian, and a Mr Sisson of the Pack Horse Inn in 1874 demanded a meeting of the ratepayers for the purpose of applying to the Education Department for the formation of a School Board, and to change the school from a church to a state school. One of the provisions of the Education Act was what was called the 'Cowper-Temple' clause which while permitting Bible instruction specifically excluded all denominational teaching, which in this case meant the Prayer Book catechism. The meeting was chaired by Mr Heskett of Plumpton Hall. This was a battle after Brunskill's heart. The recent report of H.M. Inspector of Schools was read, in which he stated that the school was conducted according to the standards of the recent Education Act. The report of the diocesan Inspector was also read, and the school accounts of recent years were pinned to the notice-board. That of 1873/4 read thus:

School endowment income £4.12.8.	Expenses: By managers for coals. £1.10
Botton's charity	£10.	Books	£1.
School pence	£30.16.4	Schoolmaster	£52.2.
		Making a total of £54.12.

Nearly all the books and school materials, as slates, maps etc. were provided free, and the charge was only at the rate of 3s., 4s., and 5s. a quarter. Moves were in hand to extend the school, and many gave donations on the condition that it remained a voluntary religious school. When a vote was taken there were nine votes in favour of a school board, and twenty-one against. Though the religious vote was strong it is probable that the fear of greater expense to the ratepayers was stronger. The school question was raised again in 1882, and this time Brunskill's successor H.M. Kennedy had a vigorous duel in the papers with Mr John Heskett over the same question. Kennedy proposed to raise £240 to enlarge the church school, and employ a second teacher; Mr Heskett of Plumpton Hall spoke out against the extravagance. The principal landowners seem to have been reluctant in their support.[9]

We have already seen that Brunskill's wife Lydia died on 23 June 1876. (A stained glass window was put up in her memory at Plumpton, but she was buried at Newton. When the new church was erected at Plumpton a brass memorial was erected in the chancel in its place.) John Langhorne has this letter, written the next day by Richard Atkinson Brunskill to Isabella:

> My dear Isabella,
> Please to present our united deep sympathy to your poor brother and those little children for the inexpressible loss which they have sustained. You must all have had a most distressing and trying time of it. But God's will be done.
> Poor fellow, will you please say all that is kind to him on our joint account. And, sad as it appears, yet how providential for your sorrow-stricken brother to have had your comforting help all through this severe trial, and which he will still greatly need, and none other can do as you can. May you be preserved and helped in your good office by giving comfort to the bereaved is the earnest prayer of us all and with our united love to you all.
> I am, My Dear Isabella
> Your affectionate Uncle,
> R. A. Brunskill.
> We thank you very much for the post cards. Your Aunt could not sleep on Thursday night until early morning, for thinking of poor Lydia.[10]

The year following Lydia's death a letter appeared in the

Carlisle Journal from a layman signing himself VOREDA (the name of the Roman camp in the parish) complaining of the injustice of the perpetual-curate of Plumpton receiving £60 a year, while the rector of the mother parish of Lazonby received '£700' a year. The figures given in Mannix & Whellan's Directory of 1847 are thus:

Lazonby parish	Rectorial tithe	£208
	Vicarial tithe	£247
Plumpton Wall	Rectorial tithe	£120
	Vicarial tithe	£207
Lazonby glebe		£80

The letter writer said that from Plumpton over £200 a year went to the rector of Lazonby, while over £300 a year went from Plumpton Street to Ecclesiastical Commissioners. 'In consequence of such an inadequate stipend (£60) at Plumpton we are practically left without a clergyman. We have him two days a week to be sure, Saturday and Sunday, but on the other five he is generally absent at Hackthorpe Grammar School, where he does get something for his services.' [11]

The tithe question continued to rumble on. On 23 November 1880 W. A. Hunter of Plumpton raised again the injustice of Plumpton tithes not benefitting their parson. 'I am almost glad that Plumpton is treated so shamefully. [Revd H. M. Kennedy] can hit and hit hard when he sets about it, and plainly he would not have hit at all if there had not been the local cause. ... I consider all tithes a nuisance and an injustice, [but] so long as I am compelled by law to pay them I would, of course, prefer to have them spent in the parish in which I live, and in which my property is ...' [12]

The rector of Lazonby followed the common practice of letting the collecting of tithes by auction, the lessee being given a percentage of the sum collected. The following notice appeared in a local paper in August 1881.

There will shortly be another tithe auction, this time at Plumpton in Cumberland. The churchwarden of this parish, being one of those who decline to pay any more tithes to the Rector of Lazonby till he proves his right to receive money for which he does nothing, has been threatened with legal proceedings. The usual ten days' notice having expired on the 9th, the churchwarden has set aside a pig and a cow to await the arrival of law officers. The complaint is that £800 per annum is taken out of the parish as tithes by the Rector of Lazenby, who renders the parishioners of Plumpton no service in return.[13]

Present-day church people have not the faintest idea of the resentment caused by tithe, not only (as in this case) to churchpeople, but more especially to dissenters who worshipped apart from the Established Church. In Wales and the West-Country the opposition was bitter.

But the subject which gnawed at the thinking of the poorer clergy was how to get out of the poverty from which there was little hope of escape. So many livings were in private patronage, and many pitifully poor, that despite the fact that they did not attract capital grants from the Bounty, curates aimed for the security of a poor benefice as better than nothing. It was here that Brunskill was fearless, if imprudent if he hoped for preferment, in attack.

Writing in the *Church Times* of 16 November 1870 on the subject of 'Hedge Parsons' past and present, men who were professionally ignorant and slovenly in their ministrations, he referred to the choice 'by our two recent alien bishops (Villiers and Waldegrave) of Hedge Parsons for Rural Deans (that) alone would prove the charge that professional ignorance was deliberately preferred. ... Under good bishop Percy we had union and strength for hopeful progress, which has not been equalled by the aliens, and the hill clergy were gradually rising to the higher standard of the better times. However, a good time is come again. There will be toleration for all who honestly strive to do their duty, and the scoldings which were all reserved for the zealous may reach the scandalously idle. In the famous Bishop of Alet you quote a good example, and in Harvey Goodwin we have pre-eminently the man qualified and ready to repeat the success of Nicholas Pavilon [sic]. [Nicholas Pavillon 1597–1677, Jansenist, exemplary Bp. of Alet, France 1630–1677. French biog. trans. into English & pub. 1869 & 1883]. From our new Bishop we shall have a brotherly guidance that will soon roll from my mountain home the present reproach....

May [Harvey Goodwin] be spared as Bishop of Carlisle till another generation has testified that he has boldly done his duty.[14] Piers Plowman.'

There is no doubt that Harvey Goodwin did much to embrace the broad spectrum of the clergy in his diocese. But one act of patronage roused Brunskill's anger. In 1877 the Revd James Thwaytes who had been rector of Caldbeck 1855–1877 died. His stipend was £436 a year. Brunskill, and perhaps a few more, hoped that one lucky man would be raised from the mud of poverty. But the bishop appointed W. F. Simpson, a minor canon and sacrist of the Cathedral. He had been ordained at Manchester in 1871/2; had been curate successively at Withington, Lancs 1870–72; Scarborough 1872–74; St James' Carlisle, and cemetery chaplain 1874–75; minor canon and sacrist of the cathedral 1874–77; and from 1875–77 lecturer and curate of St Cuthbert's, Carlisle. Simpson appears to have had private means, for in 1879 he was able to employ W. B. Tremenheere as curate. In a letter of 21 September 1877 to the *Carlisle Journal*, Brunskill expressed himself forcibly. These extracts are from a long letter:

> In June last year you kindly inserted a complaint from me that it is usual in this diocese to supersede the senior clergy, especially those who were ministering in remote parishes, and that the chances of preferment were almost confined to the staff and other prominent places. The Bishop, in answer to 'a person calling himself a curate,' gave a list of names which, I think, established the injustice. Now, it seems that his Lordship had added to the grievance by preferring a junior and comparative stranger to the desirable living of Caldbeck. Moreover, the lucky individual during the two or three years of his service in this diocese, if he has not been exactly laid up in lavender, has resided within reach of good society and Rose Castle, and from the defence set up in his own letter and that from Mr Cooper, it is confessed or boasted that he has held several well paid offices. In our rural simplicity we believed that recent reform had given a full salary to the minor canons and had set apart several livings to which these 'regular' clergy regularly succeeded ...
>
> In 1855, when Caldbeck was last vacant, there was, I think, in a Carlisle newspaper, some protest which was believed to have spoiled some snug plan for continued nepotism there, and about twenty years ago I heard Mr Thwaytes, then rector, express a

desire that he might survive and hold the benefice till the bad times of partizanship and favouritism had passed and the rural clergy had their fair rights in succession ...

Not known to the stranger bishops, they feel that insult is added to injury when these officials boast about giving livings according to merit ...

The policy which makes the country clergy feel themselves to be 'cuffed and disrespected' does not result in the greatest good to the largest number. There are the people in the parishes where they have no change in a generation. Yours etc. A CURATE.

The letter was initialled J. B. in ink.[15] Brunskill had been in orders for twenty-six years, the new man at Caldbeck six! There was, however, a pleasant sequel to Simpson's appointment to Caldbeck. He was then a bachelor. In due time he married Frances Fidler the daughter of an eminent citizen of Wigton, and a JP. The second son of this marriage was Frederick Arthur Simpson who was born in 1883. For education he went to Rossall and The Queen's College, Oxford, where he took a first in Modern History. He was ordained by bishop Diggle of Carlisle in 1909 to the curacy of Ambleside. In the same year he published his first volume of *The Rise of Louis Napoleon* – the second volume came in 1923 – which raised him to the first rank of historical scholarship. By 1911 it was clear that either Oxford or Cambridge would claim him, and in that year he was elected to a fellowship of Trinity College, Cambridge. He became a university lecturer, and in turn senior dean, and then dean of chapel. He was an accomplished preacher and writer of a high order. As the years passed and he retired from teaching he became one of the sights and characters of Cambridge, an eccentric. He lived till 1974, still occupying his college rooms, an elder statesman in college life.

Brunskill had every right to protest against the lack of promotion for poor clergy, but in this case it is possible that bishop Harvey Goodwin saw potential in the new rector of Caldbeck which others had not seen.

Another question must now be addressed; how poor was Brunskill? Admittedly he had now two homes to maintain, at Hackthorpe and Plumpton, and a horse. He had someone, initially Isabella, to look after his five children, and he had to educate them. On the other hand he received £160 a year from Lowther school and £60 from Plumpton, a total of £220. Not bad for a 'Country Curate'. Many would have been content with less.

We can make two comparisons. J. G. Mallinson was appointed to the perpetual curacy of Martindale by Mrs Clarke in 1877, with a stipend of £114. He lived there until 1891 when he retired to Southport. On the other side of Ullswater is the perpetual curacy of Matterdale, in the patronage of the rector of Greystock. John Bell was appointed in 1851 on a stipend of £115 a year. He was an old St Bees student, and in 1879 he obtained the external degree of BA at University College, Durham. In his later years his stipend was £128. He retired to Penrith in 1894 after a tenure of 43 years.[16] Poverty does not seem to have broken him! One wonders why, on his school salary of £160, Brunskill was not content to stay solely at Hackthorpe, and concentrate more on school and family, avoiding the constant journeys in all weathers on horseback. Perhaps the Education Act of 1870 made his future at Hackthorpe uncertain.

NOTES TO CHAPTER ELEVEN

1. *Prelates & People of the Lake Counties.* C.M.L. Bouch. p. 423.
2. W.M. Folder of press cuttings.
   (a) Printed broadsheet n.d. Mountain Chapel Competition.
   (b) Letter to *Westmorland Gazette*, 6 Feb. 1873.
3. Clergy List 1872.
4. L.M. Printed New Year's Letter to the Parishioners of Plumpton, Jan. 1876.
   Brunskill describes himself as Vicar.
5. W.M. Folder of press cuttings. Letter by Brunskill 30 Mar. 1874.
6. W.M. Folder of press cuttings. Five press cuttings including that of the *Carlisle Patriot* 23 Oct. 1874 giving details of the Consistory Court.
7. W.M. Folder of Press cuttings.
8. W.M. Folder of Press cuttings.
9. W.M. Folder of Press cuttings.
10. L.M. MS letter of R.A. Brunskill 24 June 1874 to Isabella Brunskill at Plumpton Vicarage. Isabella Brunskill was then the widow of Joseph Brunskill, solicitor, who d. 9 Sept. 1872 at 13 Belsize Square, London, aged 34.

11. **W.M.** Folder of press cuttings. Letter to *Carlisle Journal* 1877 on the livings of Lazonby & Plumpton from Voreda.

12. **W.M.** Folder of press cuttings 23 Nov. 1880.

13. **W.M.** Folder of press cuttings 19.8.81. probably by Brunskill who has initialled the cutting 'B'.
    Hist. Gazetteer & Directory of Cumberland, Mannix & Whellan 1847, & repr. 1974. Lazonby & Plumpton Wall.

14. **W.M.** Folder of press cuttings. Letters to *Church Times* 16 Nov. 1870. For N. Pavillon see: *A New General Biographical Dictionary*, by Revd Hugh James Rose, vol. X. 1848.
    The Biography of N.Pavillon bp. of Alet was translated from the French into English by a Layman of the Church of England, and published in 1869 and 1883.

15. **W.M.** Folder of press cuttings. Brunskill to *Carlisle Journal* 21 Sept. 1877. Clergy Lists 1874 & 1879. Jas Thwaytes & W.F. Simpson. *Crockford* 1896 for W.F. Simpson, whose income for 1877 is given as £410 net and house.

16. **Martindale parish.** (J.G. Mallinson) Clergy Lists 1876–1887. *Crockford* 1892.
    Matterdale parish. (J. Bell) Clergy Lists 1876–1887. *Crockford* 1895.

NB:
In the matter of curates' wages, when I was curate of Askham & Lowther from 1942–44 my wage was £220 a year, and from 1944 at Kendal Parish Church £280.

For Canon F.A. Simpson see: *A Last Eccentric*, by Eric James, 1991.

12

Lowther School, Hackthorpe
1860–1882

SERIOUS THOUGH the disputes at Plumpton had been over tithes, church schools, and the arrangement of the church, they were secondary to the growing knowledge that sooner or later the Lowther schools would be faced with changes under the Endowed Schools Act 1869. For years Brunskill had conducted a vigorous press campaign to keep the issue of religious education in schools before the public. In January 1872 bishop Harvey Goodwin of Carlisle was invited to give a lecture at Penrith Grammar School on the subject of Education. The press reports stated that the leadership in educational reform in the district had been undertaken by Mr Gordon the headmaster, 'whose indefatigable exertions in the cause of education are worthy of public thanks'. There is no doubt that Mr Gordon's exertions reported in the press, and through the high standards of the school, had stirred the public mind to look at the condition of the village schools. The bishop in his lecture dwelt on the general development of education, and avoided the touchy subjects which he described as 'amounting to an educational storm'. Fierce controversy ranged around several points: 'There is the question of the payment of fees to poor children in Church schools, the religious difficulty as to the reading of the Holy Scriptures, with or without explanation, in Board schools, the doings, past, present, and future of the Endowed Schools Commissioners, and several others'.[1]

In the same issue there was a letter from 'The Master of a Country Grammar School' protesting at the remark of Mr Gordon that boys of thirteen or fourteen came from the country grammar schools to 'finish' their education at this school, and that such boys could neither read nor spell, and were equally ignorant of geography and Scripture history. It is possible that Brunskill was the writer. He asked Mr Gordon 'in common fairness to the said masters (of country grammar schools) (1) to name the schools whence he has received such boys, or, (2) withdraw his statement. It might be interesting to know what proportion of boys who have begun their studies under Mr Gordon stay with him to "finish" them. For the credit of schoolmasters I must ask the Revd S. J. Butler if he can name any "academies" in the neighbourhood which are "conducted by persons who have not succeeded in some other profession" '.[2]

By 1871 it had become apparent from the investigations of commissioners sent into the counties by Parliament that the old parish schools, some with good endowments as at Lowther, but the majority with few, that educational provisions were totally inadequate. As we have seen, there was the boys' Grammar School at Hackthorpe, a girls' school at Hackthorpe, and two dames' schools at Whale and Meltinthorpe. There was an inadequate school at Askham, and the small school at Helton. At the centre of this part of the Eden Valley was Penrith with its grammar school, together with six charity schools:

> Robinson's, 1661 for poor girls
> The School of Industry, at Netherend
> The National School
> The Wesleyan Day School
> The Infants' School 1828
> The Mechanics Institute.

In all there were about sixteen academies in the town.[3]

What were Brunskill's objections to the Education Acts of 1870, 1873 and 1876? Basically that under the charitable provisions of the old parish schools the Church of England was dominant, could teach Church of England doctrine, and could teach the three Rs. under the All Seeing EYE of God; and sent children into the world believing that their use of their talents was answerable to God. Experience of the needs of the population in Sunderland, not to mention the needs of the northern market towns which had increased by the coming of the railways, should have reminded Brunskill that the Church as well as the old endowed schools were incapable of meeting the needs of an expanded population. Basically he believed in a benevolent and radical Toryism, which at its best was an enlightened paternalism, doing much for the poor. On the other side of the debate were the dissenters, politically and socially disadvantaged, who were treated by the establishment as second-class, not only in their chapels but also in the nonconformist British Schools. When I was curate of Lowther (1942–44) I used to visit a Methodist family in Melkinthorpe. One day the married daughter of the house said to me: 'In the eyes of you church people we Methodists are regarded as second-class citizens'. Despite all the best, and it must be added the worst, efforts of the Established Church, the chapels had given a homely religion and political hope to the poor. The doctrinal and political arrogance of the clergy and gentry drove the poor into radicalism, and ultimately caused the secularisation of the schools. The Cowper-Temple clause of the 1870 Education Act was the first and logical step in that direction.

Brunskill's ideals were summed up in a sermon he preached at Threlkeld church on 14 November 1880 (later printed) entitled 'Educational Liberty'. In his opening words he mentioned 'the struggle to establish in this dear realm of England the revived Paganism coming in from France. With the crisis in the French Government of the last few days fresh before us, we are entitled to form some judgement according to fruits. The leaders topple from power, while boasting how they have employed it to close some four hundred voluntary schools, and drag thousands of Christian teachers from their homes, to starve in the streets. These oppressors of liberty, having tasted the sweets of revenge, may proceed further with other schools, or, having sown the wind, they may reap the whirlwind, as did the last Emperor Napoleon. More than thirty years ago, when speaking in Whitehaven, for some Ragged Schools there, I contrasted the priceless value of our English freedom in educational work, with the way in which that mighty ruler drilled all French children, and marched them like his soldiers to his secular schools. Well, I saw twenty years go by, and then those scholars rose against their instructor, and the broken Emperor fled for shelter to England.'

Brunskill objected to religion being taught as an educational extra, when it should be a thread running through life, the home, the school, conduct, and later life at work and in the home. 'Christian teaching is expressed in the hymn "Do not sinful action, speak no angry word, ye belong to Jesus, Children of the Lord".' 'You must strengthen the hands of the Christian teacher by showing that you *care* for religious education. You must not leave it to chance, and you must be doubly careful to carry on good school influence at home.' At the end of his sermon he said: 'We labour to make people Churchmen from their youth ... We mean that the child shall grow up with a feeling that he belongs to a great society, with a great history.'[4]

Thus to Brunskill School-Boardism which taught the Bible as though it were just another history book was depriving the child of the faith which gave meaning to life. Unfortunately the old schools were inadequate to new needs.

Brunskill's most intelligent and often entertaining opponent was the editor of the *Cumberland and Westmorland Advertiser*, to which paper Brunskill sent regular letters under a number of pseudonyms. His letters were often too long, nostalgic for the good old days, and lacked the brevity which would commend his subject to the reader. One letter to the Advertiser *was* short and to the point: he protested that in a previous issue the paper had appeared to jeer at religion:

> Sir, I venture to send a protest against some editorial remarks in last week's Advertiser, which are apparently a jeer at religion. You seem to say that Christianity is only a something to be taken into the labour market, and that there it has no value. We believe that the hope of a Christian is not only a personal comfort, but also that a genuine belief in there being a *duty to God* as well as a duty to self and neighbour is of marketable value, and that a school where the children are habitually treated as being under the all-seeing eye of a living God, is more likely to train useful members of the State than where the pupils are under secular influence only. This, our belief, we act up to by giving labour and money to education, and such a conscientious opinion having the largest amount of fruit to show in English Elementary Schools, is I think fairly entitled to toleration. With much regret that I should have to write to so old a friend as the Advertiser, I am, yours obediently,
>
> A Churchman

[The letter has been initialled in pencil: J.B.]

The Editor's reply occupied a long column. He accuses the Churchman of tilting at a windmill of his own creation. The editor ventured to 'differ with a remark of our Vicar [of Penrith] that the "religious teaching of the schools was the FIRST essential of education", and my remarks were intended to combat his opinion and express my own. In the first place there is as much difference between religion and the religious teaching of the schools, as there is between prime Cheddar and Willimoor; and it was the teaching, not the religion that I fell foul of. Don't for a moment think that I think that clergymen, or for the matter of that ministers of all denominations, are going to delegate their functions to the schoolmaster yet a bit. Here is "Churchman's" confusion. I spoke of things terrestrial, not celestial; material, not etherial, and made the broad statement that from a realistic point of view the youth whose only acquirement, attainment or accomplishment was his *religious knowledge*, would have a very poor chance of getting a living in these matter-of-fact-days. ... I don't think it can be gainsaid, that the youth who can only take the "religious knowledge" of the schools to market, may walk from John o' Groats to Lands End seeking employment and finding none. His wares are not marketable. When he applies to an employer will he be asked any of the following questions: How long is it since the creation, and was there more than one, or how long did it or they take: Who commanded the sun to stand still, and how long did it stand? How many wives and concubines had Solomon? How long was Jonah in the whale's belly? How many people did Samson slay with the jaw bone of an ass? Who cut off his locks when asleep? How many fox's tails did he tie together and set fire to? Who was the robber and murderer who accompanied Jesus Christ from the Cross to Paradise? (I only learnt this myself from the *Yorkshire Post* on Good Friday). How many epistles did St Paul (not the Swinton full-back, as was stated by a juvenile the other day in answer to an examiner's question) write to the Corinthians, and what were they about? Not one of them.

Again, traverse the columns of "wanteds" in a daily newspaper. See if it is required in any of them that the person applying for a situation as cook, slut, or housemaid be versed in religious knowledge. In my experience I only remember a case that would at all apply, and it is hardly to the point. It was that of a Rector of C _____, who wanted a housekeeper, and he tacked on to the advertisement, "No Wesleyan need apply". In these matters I hold that teetotalers are more consistent than Christians. To be an abstainer is to hold an extra qualification. Let me repeat that in this matter-of-fact, material age, the three r's must be there, and all there, and that the fourth r may be there, but that it must hold the fourth place. Do the good, rich people, and some of them are portly, ever think or know how much more difficult it is for poor people to be good than for themselves? Have I like "Churchman" been tilting at a windmill?

Now, Mr "Churchman" I have the advantage of you; I know you; I know you are a lover of animals, and that your best efforts have been used for many years on their behalf; and I put this to you – Would you engage a man to look after your horses simply because he could tell you the height of Balaam's Ass, and the length of its ears? I guess not. You would ask him what experience he had had; how long he was in his last place, if he was kind and gentle with the beasts in his charge, and took an intelligent interest in them. And if he could answer these questions satisfactorily, it would be no bar to his engagement if he was ignorant as to how many animals Noah took with him into the ark, and how he fed them!'[5]

Well, Brunskill continued to write on the subject of School Boardism for a number of years. But the fruit of the Education Acts, and the benefits received by the children of the poor of the expanded towns were referred to at the foot of a letter written at Penrith on 16 May 1891. A correspondent calling himself 'Cumbrian' had written to complain of the needs of children in the Castletown area of Penrith, and the proposal to expand the Brunswick Street school. A respondent calling himself 'Citizen' referred to the Statistics of the Education Department of 31 August 1890, proving the benefits of the new Board Schools.

SCHOOLS FOR OLDER SCHOLARS

	Church of England Schools	Board Schools
Number of children on the registers	1,464,314	1,200,452
Average number in attendance	1,202,731	990,732
Percentage of passes in reading, writing and arithmetic.	88	91

Specific subjects

	Church of England Schools	Board Schools
Number of girls for whom a grant of 4s. per head was paid for cookery.	9,699	52,491
Passes in algebra, stages i, ii, iii.	6,232	11,034
" " euclid and mensuration, stages i, ii, iii	113	352
" " mechanics, scheme A	345	7,553
" " mechanics, scheme B	12	94
" " principles of agriculture	481	244
" " chemistry	123	951
" " sound, light, and heat	97	470
" " magnetism and electricity	427	996
" " Latin	124	95
" " French	1,162	3,315
" " animal physiology	3,073	6,801
" " botany	484	735
" " domestic economy, stages i, ii, iii (girls)	3,939	10,724
" " other subjects	61	291

This was a remarkable record of schools many of which had not been going for fifteen years, let alone the twenty years since the passing of the Act. And it was against this rising scope of elementary and higher education that Brunskill struggled to maintain his position at Hackthorpe. Let there be no mistake; he was moved by the highest ideals as a churchman and a teacher to do the best for his boys at Hackthorpe. But the system was out of date. The boys were taught at the grammar school, the girls at the girls' school at Hackthorpe, and the infants at the dames' schools at Melkinthorpe and Whale. In addition he had to hold his own in his parish, first at Plumpton, and later at Threlkeld. In 1871 he inserted this notice in the Penrith papers:

Promotion. A correspondent sends the following:- We have just read in a Glasgow newspaper, among a list of appointments to places in Her Majesty's Civil Service, the name of Richard Parker from Melkinthorpe, Lowther, who, like his elder brother before him, has been preferred to the full privileges of a clerk in the Glasgow post-office, after having successfully passed through all the probationary duties and examinations. These two youths have not had to seek the favour of patronage, but as the sons of a frugal husbandman, have been brought up or educated according to the old fashion. For them there was no dread of the school board constable. To honour and succour father and mother is even yet a popular principle about Lowther. Accordingly, as the seasons for planting, barking, harvesting, &c. came round, they learned to labour in woodcraft and agriculture, and so helped to earn their own living. In the intervals they attended an efficient free school till of age to enter the Civil Service, and build on the self-education of after-life. And now that they are fairly launched on life's voyage to try the world in a great city, we would send 'just a kind memento' in the phrase of the Ayrshire Ploughman, who bids his dear young friend

> 'To catch dame Fortune's golden smile,
> Assiduous wait upon her;
> And gather gear by every wile
> That's justified by honour.
>
> Not for to hide it in a hedge,
> Nor for a train-attendant,
> But for the glorious privilege
> Of being independant.'[7]

That sums up Brunskill's philosophy splendidly. He and James Ainsworth continued in double harness at the school. Ainsworth married the mistress of the girls' school (the date has not been discovered) and after this the following notice appeared in a national newspaper:

LOWTHER GRAMMAR SCHOOL, Westmorland – One mile from Clifton Station, N. & N.W.R. and 3½ hours from Manchester, 'Founded in 1697 [sic] for the education of gentlemen's sons ... Here is clearly a nucleus for a middle-class boarding school.' – Recent Parliamentary Report. Headmaster, the Revd JOSEPH BRUNSKILL; second Master Mr JAMES AINSWORTH. The education is classical and commercial. The school is situated in one of the most healthy and beautiful localities in Westmorland. The second master receives a few boarders, the terms for which are:- Under ten years of age, 25 guineas; above ten, 28 guineas per annum. – The SCHOOL TERM BEGINS

January 15, and ends June 21. – Reference kindly permitted to the Venerable the Provost of Queens College, Oxford and others.[8]

How long this continued is not known. Whether it was this which sparked off local resentment, is not clear. The trustees received a number of letters of complaint, and as a result they engaged the services of the Revd C. H. Pares, one of H.M. Inspectors of Schools to conduct a formal inspection. He had formerly been a fellow of Pembroke College, Cambridge (1857), and had been ordained by the bishop of Ely in 1863/4. From 1857 to 1864 he was an assistant master at King's School, Sherborne; and from 1864 one of HM Inspectors of Schools, living at 2, St George's Crescent, Carlisle.[9] Dr Jackson, who had been one of the trustees when Brunskill and Ainsworth were appointed in 1860, was still rector of Lowther and now receiver and chairman of the trustees.

A full meeting of the trustees was held on the 29 August 1877. The trustees present were Sir R. C. Musgrave, Bart; the Ven. Dr Jackson; Richard Burn Esq, and The Hon. William Lowther MP. The three teachers were required to be present, and the letters of complaint were read in their presence. The report of the Revd C. H. Pares was also read, which contained the damning sentence 'that the Educational results do not correspond to the outlay'. The trustees decided that the augmentations to the teachers be discontinued, Brunskill's of £80, Ainsworth's of £35, and Mrs Ainsworth's of £30. The small salaries of Margaret Crowden and Sarah Bowness at the two dames' schools were increased by £6. Thus Brunskill was left with his basic salary of £80, Ainsworth £60, and Mrs Ainsworth £30. In addition Ainsworth was ordered not take any private pupils after 31 December next.[10] The trustees also required that all school books had to receive their approval, and that the timetables of school hours and classes be kept in a conspicuous place in the school, and that school holidays should not exceed eight weeks in the year, and that extra holidays could only be given by permission of one trustee.

When the trustees met on the 7 January 1879 Dr Jackson had died, and the chair was taken by Mr Burn, in the presence of Sir R. C. Musgrave, and the Revd T. B. Tylecote the new rector. It was reported that an action at law had been commenced by Mr & Mrs Ainsworth against The Hon. William Lowther MP, Richard Burn Esq. and Sir Richard Musgrave, Bart, in the Queens Bench Division of the High Court of Justice, claiming the discontinued augmentations of £35 and £30 respectively up to 24 June last. The trustees agreed to instruct Messers Little & Lamonby, solicitors to defend the action. They also agreed that as Ainsworth had continued to take in boarders against the instructions of the trustees, the opinion of Mr F. Vaughan Hawkins should be sought as to the power of the trustees to dismiss.[11]

It will be noted that Brunskill did not share in the action taken out against the trustees. In the same year 1879 he was appointed by Lord Lonsdale to the Lowther rectory of Threlkeld, four miles from Keswick. His position was still the same, teaching five days at Lowther, and doing parish work at weekends and in holidays. At a meeting of the trustees held 4 August 1880 notice was given to the teachers that 'an enquiry will be made respecting the observance of the orders made by the trustees at their Meeting of 9 August 1879.'[12]

An adjourned meeting of the trustees was held at the Girls' school at Hackthorpe on 25 September 1880, at which the four trustees were present. A copy of a Memorial was received, which had been addressed by the Inhabitants and Ratepayers of the parish of Lowther in vestry assembled to the Charity Commissioners, containing certain allegations of neglect of duty against the teachers of the Boys' and Girls' schools at Hackthorpe. A copy of these charges had been sent to each teacher calling their attention to them. Written replies were received and read from Brunskill and Mrs Ainsworth, while Ainsworth attended and made an oral statement. It was resolved that as Brunskill and Mrs Ainsworth had wilfully disobeyed the Rules and Regulations of the Trustees of 9 August 1879 they should be dismissed as heads of their respective schools at the end of the present term.[13]

It seems that both began an action against the trustees for wrongful dismissal. For, at a meeting of the trustees held 16 November 1880, they agreed to seek the advice of the Charity

Commissioners 'whether in view of the possible contingency of the present Head Master and Mistress successfully disputing the validity of their dismissal the Trustees would be justified in applying, and whether the Charity Commissioners would sanction their applying any portion of the funds of the Endowment in paying the salaries of the Master and Mistress now to be appointed, until the contingency be determined.'[14]

The position was distressing in the extreme with all the teachers remaining entrenched subsisting on their basic salaries. At the Meeting of the trustees on 9 September 1881 Ainsworth applied to have the augmentation to him and his wife restored. It was 'resolved that in view of the changes about to be made in the Government of the School the Trustees do not feel justified in granting it.'[15]

On 16 February 1882 a public notice appeared in the local papers from the Education Department under the Endowed Schools Act and amending acts concerning the schools in the parish of Lowther mentioned in a Scheme of the Court of Chancery, dated the 10 February 1831 and of the Endowments thereof. 'The Committee of Council on Education have approved a Scheme for the future management of the Foundation, and notice was given that unless within two months a Petition is presented to the Committee under section 13 of the Endowed Schools Act 1873, the Scheme will be approved without being laid before Parliament. Copies of the Scheme may be had from Hackthorpe Post Office, or the Charity Commission price 4d. each.'[16]

The Scheme was approved by Order in Council on the 3 May 1882. A new body of governors was appointed, and at the end of the current term (or a later one if approved by the Charity Commission) 'the old schools shall close, and the teachers shall cease to hold office'. They were given life pensions on the foundation: the Revd Joseph Brunskill £30; Mrs Charlotte Ainsworth £12.10d.; Mr James Ainsworth £40; and Sarah Bowness £10. The surviving school or schools were constituted elementary schools under the Education Act of 1870, and religious instruction was to be given in accordance with the principles of the Christian Faith, subject to the power of the governors to alter the regulations governing the school after proper notice. Eventually Hackthorpe school became the elementary school for the boys and girls of the whole parish. Two further Orders were made in 1887 and 1894 for the government of the schools and its assets. A final Order of 18 October 1909 transferred from the Lowther Foundation: £3,570 Consols to Appleby Grammar School, and £3,000 to Penrith Grammar School. By then Joseph Brunskill was dead, but the Order continued the annual pensions for life: The Revd James Ainsworth £40, Mrs Charlotte Ainsworth £12,10s., and Miss Sarah Bowness £10. [17]

The Ainsworths came off best. In about 1880 he started to study for the external degree of BA at Trinity College, Dublin, which he obtained in 1883. In the year of his dismissal he was ordained deacon by the bishop of Rochester, and priest in 1883. He was curate successively of St Augustine, Bermondsey 1882–1886, and St Matthew, Brixton 1886–7. He was vicar of St Luke's Bermondsey from 1888 to 1908.[18] He died in about 1914.

By the summer of 1882 Brunskill was permanently at Threlkeld, a poorer man. But his old boys did not forget him, and a small 'jellied' circular letter was sent by the Revd Jas. E. Potts, BA of Orsett, Essex to as many former pupils whose addresses they could recall, some as far away as W. Campbell, Adelaide, Australia; George Harrison, Tipperary; John Potts, South America; and many more in Britain, in Lowther and Askham parishes. Among his relatives were E. Ritson of Jarrow and J. Ritson of Sunderland. John Langhorne has the barometer which was presented to Brunskill.

> To the Revd J. Brunskill, Head Master of the Free Grammar School, Hackthorpe; and James Ainsworth, Esq., Second Master of the Free Grammar School, Hackthorpe.
>
> Dear Sirs, – We the undersigned, former pupils of Hackthorpe School, desire to express to you our regret at the painful circumstances under which, we hear, you are about to retire from what must appear to you – and to a great extent rightly – your thankless labours there during 22 years.
>
> We feel that we owe much of our subsequent success not only to the intelligent industry with which you grounded us in ordinary subjects of an elementary education, but also (in the case of some

of us) to your careful cultivation of classics, French, drawing, and mathematics, as extra subjects.

Nor do we remember with less pleasure or gratitude the particular attention given by both of you to the teaching of religious knowledge, or your kindly care for our comfort, or the refining discipline which has been materially helpful to us in the various states of life to which we have been called.

We sincerely hope that amongst your reminiscences of the old school, after your connection with it has ceased, you may derive some degree of pleasure from this expression of our hearty sympathy, esteem and gratitude.[19]

None of the trustees subscribed.

NOTES TO CHAPTER TWELVE

1. L.M. A/C in *Penrith Observer* 9 Jan. 1872.
   (a) The Grammar School lecture by the bishop of Carlisle.
   (b) Letter from 'The Master of a Country Grammar School.'
2. Ibid.
3. *History, Gazetteer & Directory of Cumberland*, Mannix & Whellan 1847. p. 293, Penrith Grammar School, p. 298 Academies in the town.
4. A Sermon on Educational Liberty, preached at St Mary's Church, Threlkeld 14 Nov. 1880 (by the Revd Joseph Brunskill). (L.M.)
5. L.M. *Cumberland & Westmorland Advertiser*, April 8. (Year not given).
6. W.M. Letter of 'Citizen' to a Penrith paper, 16 May 1891.
7. W.M. Folder of press cuttings, dated in ink 1871, and initialled J.B.
8. W.M. Folder of press cuttings, page 1.
9. *Crockford* 1882.
10. The minute-books of the Trustees of the Lowther Charity Schools are at the Lowther Estate Office, Penrith, and have been photocopied by courtesy of Mrs Anne G.S. Bennett the Clerk to the Trustees.
    Minutes of the Trustees 10 Nov. 1832.
    Minutes of the Trustees 29 Aug. 1877.
11. Ibid. Minutes of 7 Jan. 1879.
12. Ibid. Minutes of 4 Aug. 1880.
13. Ibid. Minutes of 25 Sept. 1880.
14. Ibid. Minutes of 16 Nov. 1880.
15. Ibid. Minutes of 9 Sept. 1881.
16. W.M. From folder of press cuttings.
17. From copies of the Orders supplied by the Charity Commission, Graeme House, Derby Square, Liverpool, L2 7SB.

Orders of: 3 May 1882.
13 Dec. 1887.
19 June 1894.
18 Oct. 1908.

18. *Crockford* 1914. Ainsworth probably died 1914, as his name does not appear in 1915.
    Crockford of 1880, Preface iv has a consideration of bogus degrees bought by clergymen. It added that the BA of T.C.D. did not require residence. It also added that the Divinity Testimonium at T.C.D. did require two years' residence.

19. L.M. Press cuttings n.d., but 1882: Lowther Grammar School.
    L.M. The 'jellied' letter is dated Nov. 1881, signed by James E. Potts, and posted from Orsett, Romford, Essex.

NB:
V.C.H. Cumberland II, 1968 ed. p. 113 contains a warm appreciation of the work of bishop Harvey Goodwin 1869–1891. A man of science and a mathematician, he put the diocese on its feet.

13

Parson of Threlkeld
1879–1893

BRUNSKILL'S TIME at Plumpton was not happy for domestic and public reasons. In addition, the gathering clouds at Hackthorpe from 1877 made his future uncertain. The removal of his augmentation of £80 in August that year reduced his income from all sources from £220 to £140. It is significant that when Mr & Mrs Ainsworth commenced an action in the High Court for the restoration of their augmentations in 1878, Brunskill did not join them. The rectory of Threlkeld in the gift of the earl of Lonsdale became vacant in 1879 and Brunskill was appointed. The Clergy List gives the stipend as £120 a year, while Crockford has £148 gross and £138 net, with a population of 381.[1] In short it matched his old reduced income, except that until 1882 he had the basic wage of £80 from school on top. I can detect no animus by Brunskill against the Lowther family in later years, as he supported the Lowther political interest in the county, and held Tory meetings at Threlkeld in their favour. It is clear that lord Lonsdale appointed him to Threlkeld to resolve a difficult situation at Hackthorpe. Brunskill's resistance to dismissal from August 1879 to the summer of 1882 I think was a plain attempt to get some sort of annuity out of what he considered to be a freehold. The £30 for life was the result. Threlkeld was four miles from Keswick, and 13½ from Penrith, and a much longer ride to Hackthorpe.

The second change in his life was his marriage on the 9 of January 1879 to Rebecca the fourth daughter of the late John Simmons of Bishopsgate and Dalston, London. The marriage took place at St Peter's Church, Belsize Park, Hampstead. It is a fair assumption that as Brunskill's widowed sister Isabella Brunskill lived at 13 Belsize Square, Hampstead, the introduction was through her.[2] Rebecca thus took over Joseph's rectory at Threlkeld to care for him and his children.

There is an extraordinary story attached to Threlkeld church told by William Hutchinson the Cumberland historian, who knew the man in question. In the second half of the seventeenth century one Alexander Naughley was an episcopal clergyman at Stow in Midlothian. He was a considerable scholar and a friend of Gilbert Burnet (1643–1715) when he was professor of Divinity at Glasgow University from 1669. In 1682 when a number of episcopal clergy were dispossessed for refusing the Covenant Burnet helped them to find places in the English church. It is said that Naughley was banished from Scotland, and, putting their two baby sons in panniers on either side of a little Scots Galloway pony, the parents walked into England and came to Threlkeld. The 'curacy' of Threlkeld was then pitifully small, being worth between £8 and £12 a year, and, as no-one else would take the place, Naughley was appointed. He was a learned and pious man, and, despite his poverty managed to send one son Alexander to Edinburgh University where he took his Master's degree. His father dying shortly afterwards, the son was appointed 'curate' of Threlkeld where he remained for 57 years. As the father had been a good man, the parishioners were happy to accept the son.

In order to augment his miserable stipend he taught astronomy, navigation, mensuration, and other branches of mathematics. He was also of great reputation as a classical scholar. 'He lived in the most homely and slovenly manner. His usual fare was a crust of sour brown bread, boiled in plain water, seasoned with a little salt, and boiled in his only pan, which he never washed. His only luxuries in diet, which he ate with superior enjoyment, were messes of oatmeal. His hearth was seldom cleared of embers, and his whole apartment was strewn over with books and papers, intermingled with his household implements. His dress was the meanest in the parish; he wore wooden clogs, and never indulged his neck with the luxury of a neckerchief, or any kind of covering.'[3] Towards the end of his life he became deranged, and cut himself intentionally with a knife. He survived, and when Hutchinson the historian reproached him he said: 'Well, at any rate, it is better to be so than to go mad.' After this he became sottish, grovelling and mean in the extreme. His voice was so piping that his congregation, even when they could hear him, no longer heard him with pleasure. He died in 1756 in his 70th year.[3] The church must be divine to survive such periods!

By the time Brunskill went to Threlkeld in 1879 his five children were aged as follows: John Ritson (1865) 14; Alice Mary (1866) 13; Cyril Wane (1869) 10; Isabelle Maud (1872) 7; and Lydia Violette (1876) 3. There is no information as to their early education. The assumption is that the boys went to Appleby Grammar School, and the girls to the Clergy Daughters' School at Casterton. As the early admissions registers of both schools are lost, the point cannot be proved for all. Much of their schooling would be met by charitable grants for the children of clergy.

In 1884 Brunskill applied to the Worshipful Company of Leathersellers for a grant for his son John Ritson then at Queen's College, Oxford. The application, which was printed, contained three testimonials.

(a) From C. Threlkeld Esq. MA Headmaster of Appleby Grammar School, saying that J. R. Brunskill had been at the school for five years from the age of 12 to 17; that he had won an Exhibition to Queen's College; that he was worthy of any assistance the Leathersellers Company can grant him.

(b) From Dr J. R. Magrath, Provost of Queen's College, saying that he has been in residence since Michaelmas last, and that his conduct and diligence have been excellent.

(c) From Revd Edward Melford Mee, Fellow & Tutor of Queen's saying that J. R. Brunskill had been in residence since October 1883, that he had been diligent in attendance at lectures and his studies. 'He will do credit both as a student and a gentleman to your Company's choice.' ... 'I know he is MUCH in need of pecuniary assistance'.

His father added a summary of the boy's school career; that when ten he had passed first class in religious knowledge in the examination of the Carlisle Diocesan Education Society; that in 1880 he passed the Cambridge Local Examination; that from 12 to 17 he had been at Appleby Grammar School; and as head boy had won a Hastings Exhibition to Oxford. He had won all the school prizes open to him. Finally 'that his father, now

Rector of Threlkeld, Keswick, has during a ministry extending over thirty three years, not enjoyed an Ecclesiastical income that would give, on average, £75 a year! (Threlkeld Rectory, 24 March, 1884.)'[4]

It is possible that until the age of 12 the children went to the local village church school, or perhaps into Keswick. John Langhorne states that when his mother Isabelle Maud was a child at Threlkeld the family was very short of money.

Apart from the fellside farms in the valley, there were a number of mines on the sides and at the base of Blencathra or Saddleback comprising Woodend, Gategill, Bleasgill, Glenderaterra, and Saddleback Old Mine. The ores they produced were copper pyrites, malachite, galena, cerussite, blende, iron pyrites, and sulphate barytes.

There was also the Threlkeld Granite Company producing granite-concrete flags, non-slippery paving setts, and granite macadam and tar macadam. Some of the mines failed and revived according to the fortunes of the local landowners. During the years 1881 to 1901 the Gategill Middle Level, and the Woodend Low Level gave employment to an average of 100 men and boys.[5] It is the family tradition that Brunskill was concerned for the welfare of the miners, and their families. Among them were a number of Welsh miners.

In 1883 there was a debate in church circles in London on the lack of provision for church services in Welsh to serve those who had left the Principality seeking work. The archbishop of Canterbury had voiced this criticism. Brunskill rose to the occasion in a letter of 21 July 1883.

> This [neglect] may not be so general as is supposed, and there is, probably, no necessity for 'the Welsh who migrate to England gliding to the Non-conformist Meeting House'. Before this happened here, among the workmen in a granite quarry, I found, by aid of letters commendatory, who among them was most able and willing to help his comrades, and we have well attended services in the church on Sunday afternoons and Thursday evenings especially for the strangers who only as yet understand their native Welsh.
>
> J. Brunskill[6]
>
> The Rectory, Threlkeld,
> Keswick, July 21, 1883.

In Alan Webster's folder of press cuttings there is a long article in Welsh giving an account of this hospitality mentioning Mr Brunskill, and the assistance of Robert Humphreys.

No account of Brunskill's life would be complete without a reference to his consistent advocacy of justice for the poor, going back to his early days at Sunderland, which was expressed in a radical Toryism. I have already referred[7] to the case of a poor man and his wife and family spending the night in the wind and rain between Keswick and Threlkeld which raised Brunskill's anger in 1881. He was fearless in exposing any injustice to the poor. In 1865, when still a young schoolmaster at Hackthorpe, he wrote to the *Penrith Observer* on the 30 September:

> Because there is much public indignation I beg to enquire publicly why the coroner appears to have been driven from his duties by the noise of false economies. On Tuesday, the 19th a woman was found dead out of doors at Newton, yet somehow the body was buried without the decent enquiry of an inquest. Again, on the following Monday, at Plumpton, a frightful death occurs at a saw mill; but there is no inquest respecting the condition of the machinery.
>
> ENGLISHMAN.[8]

On the 13 November 1872, when he was at Plumpton he wrote to the *Carlisle Patriot*:

> In a recent article you spoke of there being in Carlisle a growing feeling against police-made law. Some of my neighbours have suffered what they believe to be lawless wrong from the superintendent of police at Penrith. While employed in the praiseworthy industry of herding a cow upon the unenclosed land by the road side he procured their punishment by the magistrates. May I ask the chief constable or any other authority under what law of this realm of England the penalty was inflicted? Mr Fowler is still driving about threatening these honest workers with his further vengeance for what he presumes to call their wilful law-breaking.
>
> I am, yours truly, JOS. BRUNSKILL[9]

On the 27 November 1879 A NATIVE (presumably Brunskill) wrote to the *Penrith Herald*:

> Some ten days ago, I was grieved to see on the platform of the Penrith Railway Station two decent-looking men, who were tightly

chained together jauntily ordered by a policeman into a train for Carlisle. One of the men at least I had long known as a steady and obliging ostler at a Penrith inn. Since that time I have not been able to learn anything respecting these seeming criminals, unless it be that they were the two inhabitants of our town sent that day by Dr Wickham to Carlisle Gaol. Even by the police reports printed in the newspapers, there had been nothing laid against them beyond the fault of begging, yet they were disgraced and severely punished. I have read that Magistrates consider they can inflict nothing sharper than hard labour, upon bread and water diet; and while the poor men are at this moment probably in dark cells, I have the liberty to pity the mad transformation caused by turning a most kind and benevolent physician into an unfortunate Magistrate. Were these men given in charge by the neighbours to whom their begging was a nuisance? And by what law were they handcuffed? ...

Now, if Dr Wickham will allow his honest nature fair play, he will help these 'beggars' to get justice; and then having £20 apiece in their pockets, he will 'give his advice', as he has done to hundreds of distressed people in Penrith, and guide them to what Colony they may best emigrate and make a living for themselves. While life and hope remain men will do something against hunger. And a few months ago I travelled with a smart, well-mannered young man, who was being taken to gaol for begging, chained as if he had been a murderer, who said he would thankfully emigrate anywhere. And we reckoned that the money being wasted over his punishment in gaol, might have been used to a better end ...[10]

The same magistrate, Dr Wickham, and the Penrith Bench figured in the London *Echo* about the same time. A man had tramped from Burnley to Glasgow and back vainly seeking work. He got many a drenching, and spent many a shivering night under a hedge, or in the lee of the corn-rick. Having gone from factory to factory in Glasgow seeking work, and failing, he turned his weary feet homewards:

Yet a northern newspaper tells us that at Plumpton, on his way back to Burnley, this wayfarer was arrested by a detective on being seen coming from a house, and eating bread. Poor fellow, perhaps he was breaking a long fast; but his wan face, dusty clothes, broken shoes, and general appearance no doubt stamped him as a tramp, and, for the nonce as a beggar. 'What have you been doing?' 'Asking for bread; and if I had not stood very much in need of it I would not have begged.' A touching but fatal confession. He was taken before the magistrates, and informed by Dr Wickam that these guardians of public order had come to the decision to send every man found begging a month to gaol. As the prisoner, however, was probably not aware of this fact, Dr Wickham gave him only seven days. Seven days imprisonment to a man whose only crime was hunger, and who was convicted on no other evidence than his own statement to a constable? ...

As a rule, we may explain that the Penrith Bench of magistrates are in the habit of showing the greatest leniency to tramps. Many are brought before them who are simply cautioned and discharged; but it has come to the knowledge of the Bench that the begging system is becoming a positive nuisance. It would be well if such large towns as Glasgow and London were to look a little more carefully after their poor, instead of driving them into the country to beg, steal or starve.[11]

Religious controversy entered into a letter from Brunskill as late as 4 December 1893. It appeared in a Penrith paper:

Intolerance at Penrith Workhouse.

Allow me to ask how many of the farmers who acted as Poor Law Guardians to hinder the Church folk in our Workhouse from their lawful and usual rights to the ministry of a clergyman, are themselves dissenting ministers? When these farmers have disestablished the parson, will their own ministry seem to be on a higher level? Surely these country Guardians were elected to attend more than ONCE a year, and for some better work than, according to a Yankee proverb 'getting their own axe cheaply ground', and regardless of that public nuisance, Mr James Thom. I dare sign myself,

A CHURCHMAN.[12]

The Mr Thom here lambasted was a member of the Penrith Board of Guardians who had incurred the anger of A POOR MAN in a letter to a Penrith paper on the 20 August 1882, for insisting on questioning applicants for Poor Relief in public to their great distress. The usual practice was for a few experienced men to know from previous experience how to sift evidence of character and thrift without publishing all remarks made on these delicate subjects.[13] It is greatly to Brunskill's honour that the severity of the Vagrancy Laws, and the Poor Laws were exposed.

The reader will recall that when Brunskill was curate of Mallerstang, the early pages of the diary were full of news of the battles in the Crimea. There was a very strong patriotic streak in him, and one of his great heroes was Colonel H. C. Lowther MP who had served at Corunna and Waterloo. As a young man he had ridden at Corunna for sixteen days with little rest; at Waterloo he had ridden the eighteen miles from Quatre Bras to Brussels without change or rest. It was as a horseman that Brunskill admired him most, not only in war but on the hunting field, and on the occasion when he drove his carriage and pair from Lowther to Carlisle for a cricket match. He sat for 55 years in the House of Commons. 'He was no mere talker about Reform; but in his own house, and upon his own estate might be seen the two cardinal points of an English gentleman, love of God and love to our neighbour. ... Once on telling him about some wholesome improvement upon a property in Westmorland in which he was interested as a trustee, he remarked to us almost by way of apology for giving an opinion on a question of pure air in rooms, that upon his own property in Rutlandshire he had transformed all the old cottages into houses with five rooms each, every house (about 40) having a separate yard and pump, and all the rooms being laid with warm wood floors etc. This is the reform which Mr Disraeli lately summarised under the three heads of A Porch, and Oven, and a Tank, and must cure the real canker of our social system, by effectually enabling our rural poor to help themselves. So will the cottager close his ear against radical balderdash when he knows he has a true and able neighbour under the roof-tree of the hall and castle. Such men as the late Colonel Lowther are the real patriots when they prove to the poor man that his daily comfort and happiness are the chief aims of statesmen.' So highly did Brunskill revere his memory that he kept a photograph of him in uniform, wearing his Corunna medal.[14]

When in about 1888 Brunskill convened a Conservative meeting in Threlkeld Church of England School, to support the candidacy of Mr James W. Lowther, 'He [Brunskill] said he used to attend the great dinner which was given at Penrith every year on the birthday of [Mr Lowther's] grandfather, who had done more for the working people of this country than anybody else. (Hear, hear). He served working men by causing the

London and North-Western Railway to be made in that part of the country. He had more to do with bringing that railway over Shap Fell than any other man, and if it had not been for him probably there would have been no railway over there now.'[15]

These extracts bring out Brunskill's political beliefs; but he was not above a little political venom. In 1889 the Liberal interest held a political meeting at Threlkeld in favour of Mr Wilfrid Lawson. Brunskill wrote this report:

> A meeting of Radicals was held here last night. Mr Anderson, Keswick, was chairman, and was very abusive of Tories and Primrose Leaguers when introducing Mr Lawson. This gentleman was considerably below his dull level, except in his misrepresentation of those who differed from him. His speech fell very flat, and for his resolution only four hands were held up. A Mr Carrick fiercely attacked taverns, and the members of the Royal Family because they did not visit Ireland; and Mr Arlosh delivered such a tirade of abuse against England that Mr Lawson promptly repudiated his strong language. When Mr Arlosh had worked up his denunciation of tyranical government, the climax was carefully put on the long-drawn-out word BALFOUR. But the speaker was chilled. The flattered 'democracy' before him made no response. [16]

This link between the church and politics is somewhat frowned on today. I remember about thirty years ago, a Westmorland vicar telling me that when he was appointed by Hugh Cecil earl of Lonsdale to a market-town vicarage, he was advised by his lordship's agent at Lowther: 'His Lordship hopes that if he appoints you to the Vicarage, you will bear the Conservative interest in mind'. 'Certainly', said the vicar, and promptly voted Labour. Well, so the wind blows!

At the apex of Brunskill's political creed was loyalty to the Queen. In May 1867 when he was at Hackthorpe he was invited to preach the sermon at St Andrew's Church, Penrith, before the Cumberland & Westmorland Yeomanry. It was a 'loyalty' sermon, and occupies 1½ columns of the *Penrith Observer*. His text was 'Honour the King' (Romans XII, 1.) He said that 'the feeling of personal love towards the Queen, which we call loyalty, was fostered by every service in the worship of the Church of England. There was something like the tie of children to a parent existing between a Christian Queen and a Christian people ... And now is not loyal obedience to the Queen as the fountain of law and order, especially a duty for Englishmen? ... If we find it hard to keep the law; if we are tempted to forget our loyalty to the Queen, our merciful Lord has promised to give all who seek Him the grace and help of his Holy Spirit.'[17]

NOTES TO CHAPTER THIRTEEN

1. Clergy List 1880; *Crockford* 1880.

2. L.M. The marriage is in a press cutting of London weddings 9 Jan. 1879. That Isabella lived at 13 Belsize Square, Hampstead comes from the funeral notice (L.M.) of her husband Joseph Brunskill, (a solicitor) who died there 9 Sept. 1872; there is also a letter (L.M.) from Lydia, Joseph's wife at Plumpton vicarage of 10 Sept. 1872 addressed to Isabella B. at 13 Belsize Square, Hampstead sending condolences to Isabella on her husband's death, aged 34. He was buried at Hampstead Church 13 Sept. 1872. This Joseph Brunskill was the son of Richard Atkinson Brunskill who was born at Sandford, and bapt. at Warcop in 1801. See chapt. 1. R.A.B. died at Earlsdon, Coventry 7 April 1877 aged 76, and was buried at Coventry Cemetery 10 April 1877. (L.M. Funeral notice). John Langhorne says he was a solicitor. Revd Joseph's son John Ritson B. (who died at Dormans) was buried in the adjacent grave (intended for Isabella but not used) at Hampstead in 1946.

3. *Hist. Directory & Gazetteer of Cumberland*, Mannix & Whellan 1847 p. 266.
   Hist. of Cumberland, W. Hutchinson 1794, p. 422.
   D.N.B. Gilbert Burnet 1643–1715.
   Hist. of Cumberland & Westmorland, J. Nicolson, & R. Burn 1777, II, p. 374. The account of the Revds Alexander Naughley, father & son, have been conflated from several sources, and one of Hutchinson's observations has been softened.

4. W.M. printed testimonials in favour of John Ritson Brunskill 24 Mar. 1884.

5. *Mines & Mining in the Lake District* 3rd ed. John Postlethwaite, 1913, pp. 96–105; p. 101 for the output of the mines 1881–1901 & labour force. The Threlkeld Granite Company is advertised at the end of the book.

6. W.M. Folder of press cuttings. 3 cuttings of 1883 probably from the church *Guardian*. The Welsh article is dated 3 Sept. 1883.

7. Chapt. 10. ref. [10]

8. W.M. Folder of press cuttings: Englishman to *Penrith Observer*, 30 Sept. 1865.

9. Ibid. Jos. Brunskill to *Carlisle Patriot*, 13 Nov. 1872.

10. Ibid. A Native, to *Penrith Herald* 27 Nov. 1879.

11. Ibid. Extract from London *Echo* printed in a Penrith paper n.d., but c.1880.

12. Ibid. A Churchman to ? *Cumberland Herald*, 4. Dec. 1893.

13. Ibid. A Poor Man, to a Penrith paper, 20 Aug. 1882.

14. Ibid. Press cutting initialled J.B. in ink, n.d. but probably after the death of Colonel Lowther in 1875.

15. W.M. Folder of press cuttings: Report of Conservative meeting at Threlkeld c.1888.

16. Ibid. Mr Wilfred Lawson at Threlkeld dated by J.B.? 12.89.

17. Ibid. *Penrith Observer*, 28 May. 1867.

14

Threlkeld
1879–1893

THE FINAL break with Hackthorpe School in the summer of
1882 left Brunskill free to develop his interests. In 1882 he and
Dr A. W. Stirling of Westfield House, Stapleton were elected fellows of the Royal Meteorological Society, 30 Great George
Street, Westminster. (He does not appear to have continued his
membership of the Pharmaceutical Society.) There were a number of experimental weather stations in Cumberland and Westmorland, and Brunskill started one at Threlkeld, which he continued during his time there. Some of the major reports were
published, his were not. Brunskill had been raised in the Eden
Valley, every spring under the shadow of the 'Helm Wind'. This
is a strong east wind, which forms a great bar of rolling cloud
in the lee of the western edge of the Pennines, while the cold
wind rushes down the lower slopes. At a meeting of the
Meteorological Society held in London in June 1884 Brunskill
contributed a paper, which was read for him, on the subject of
the Helm Wind, and the thanks of the Society were conveyed to
him.[1] For a number of years he sent regular weather reports to
the local press. In one year he stated that 'during the latter half
of this June, from the 17th to the 28th two and a half inches of
rain were registered as having fallen at Threlkeld experimental
station in nine days. Yet, notwithstanding this so-called wet
period, fine hay was dried and carried without the aid of any
more costly machinery than rake and fork.'[2]

In the same year, 1884, John Ruskin of Brantwood, Coniston,
published his book *The Storm Cloud of the Nineteenth
Century*, and this was read by Brunskill. This was an old theme
of Ruskin's, going back to the visit which he paid as a young
man with his parents in 1842 to France and Switzerland, which
led him to study the true form of rocks and clouds; 'not as a
scientist, to class and analyse them; but to learn their aspects
and enter into the spirit of their growth and structure'.[3] This
was the theme expressed by Ruskin in the first volume of

Modern Painters published in 1843, the fruit of his strict evangelical upbringing: that the broad landscape, the lofty mountains, and swirling cloud formations reminded man of the
divine Creator.[4] In the *Storm Cloud* book he dipped into the
works of Homer and the Greek classics to describe the cloud
formations around mountains, plague clouds, typhoons, the
high clouds of summer, and the west wind at Coniston which
'comes down on the lake in swirls which spurn the spray under
them as a fiery horse does the dust'. 'I shall not forget having
had the good fortune to meet a vigorous one on an April morning, between Hawes and Settle, just on the flat under Whern-
side, – the vague sense of wonder with which I watched Ingle-
borough stand without rocking.'[5] Eminent painters, and poets
such as Wordsworth, were quoted in their description of sky
and cloud formations, some as portents of disease. After its
appearance Brunskill wrote to Ruskin, perhaps with the Helm
wind in mind, and received this brisk reply:

> Brantwood,
> Coniston, Lancashire.
>
> Mr dear Sir,
> I am extremely obliged by your letter, though you have read
> with little attention, or never at all – what I wrote of the plague
> wind. It has nothing to do with mountains or plains or places –
> but is an European change of atmosphere.
> – But please send me all you can get of the late debates of
> Met(eorological) Society.
> Most truly yours,
> J. Ruskin.   (Rec'd. 17.12.85.) [6]

(Ruskin had contributed an article to the first volume of the
Meteorological Society in 1839.) Brunskill sent him a copy of
his lecture on the Helm Wind to the Society in 1884, and on the
5th February 1886 Ruskin replied as follows:

> Brantwood,
> Coniston, Lancashire.
>
> My Dear Sir,
> Your papers are deeply interesting to me – and I will order my
> publisher at once to send you the papers of mine referred to – and
> any others likely to be of service in contributing facts for your
> consideration – and trust that I may yet be spared a few years to

enjoy looking at the underside of the sky with you. Whether I shall ever see it from the other, Heaven knows – I will write again when I have carefully read the notes on the Helm. I do not myself know it, though I have been in rough Yorkshire winds. Our Coniston Helm bursting down on the lake is bad enough!

Yes, I wish I could have seen Blenkathra with you. The straight way up him, from your church – is to my mind the finest walk in the district.

Ever faithfully & respectfully Yrs.

J. Ruskin.[7]

The publisher sent a copy of the *Storm Cloud* book, which had been inscribed previously: 'The Revd Joseph Brunskill, With the Author's true regards, 22 December 85.'[8] The correspondence developed rapidly, for Brunskill's next approach was to send several offprints from the Cumberland & Westmorland Antiquarian Society transactions of articles by the Revd W. S. Calverly, vicar of Aspatria, on early sculptured crosses in Cumberland. Calverly was a considerable authority on the subject, which after Calverly's death was taken up by the Prof. W. G. Collingwood. Up till then Calverly had written about the crosses at Dearham (1880), Gosforth (1882), and Isell (1885). He was to add more, St Michael, Workington, Aspatria, Lowther, Cross Canonby and Plumbland in 1887; Bewcastle, the tympanum at Bridekirk in 1892, and the coped tombstones at Gosforth in 1897.[9] The three early pamphlets elicited the following acknowledgement, which was copied by one of Brunskill's children, possibly Lydia:

Brantwood,
Coniston, Lancashire.
19th Feb. 1886.

Mr Dear Sir,

Your delightful letter and papers & Mr Calverley's [sic] admirable pamphlet have been in, & on, my mind – not to say also heart – ever since they came. They gave me much to think of, & to hope from your happily observant & earnest tempers– and I wanted to write at more length than I am able. I must delay at least my thanks no longer.

I hope if I continue to recover strength – (the long cold and darkness have thrown me back) – to give you at least pleasure by my sympathy – and to your friends – that of teaching me what I have need especially of learning, if I am ever to complete my own bits of eccles. history; for I have never yet been able to decipher the meanings of those northern sculptures.

I am more happy than you will believe, by this late & brief acknowlegement, in being made acquainted with your work and yourselves.

I am, Yours affectionately,
J. Ruskin.[10]

It is possible that Brunskill's interest in Ruskin dates from the lecture given by Canon H. D. Rawnsley before the Keswick Literary and Scientific Society at the Keswick Library in November 1883, of which he kept the press report. One passage from Ruskin was much to Brunskill's liking; he had been speaking of the medieval sculptor who carved the stern statues on the European gothic cathedrals:

> Do not mock at them, for they are the signs of the life and liberty of every workman who struck the stone; a freedom of thought and rank in scale of being, such as no laws, no charters, no charities can secure; but which it must be the first aim of all Europe at this day to regain for her children.
>
> Let me not be thought to speak wildly or extravagantly. It is verily the degradation of the operative into a machine, which more than any other evil of the times, is leading the mass of the nations everywhere into vain, incoherent, destructive struggling for a freedom of which they cannot explain the nature to themselves. Their universal outcry against wealth, and against nobility, is not forced from them either by the pressure of famine, or the sting of mortified pride. These do much, and have done much in all ages; but the foundations of society were never yet shaken as they are this day. It is not that men are ill fed, but that they have no pleasure in the work by which they make their bread, and therefore look to wealth as the only means of pleasure. It is not that men are pained by the scorn of the upper classes, but they cannot endure their own; for they feel that the kind of labour to which they are condemned is verily a degrading one, and makes them less than men ...[11]

It is necessary to be clear what was Ruskin's philosophy at this date. In childhood he had been reared in the strictest Puritan tradition of his mother. Volume I. of *Modern Painters* reflected that faith. The second volume of 1846 expressed the view that the painting and sculpture of the Middle Ages reflected the Christianity of the times, when there was no distinction between

Protestant and Roman Catholic. At a later period he was discouraged by the failure of Protestantism in its dealings with social problems, and he seems to have lapsed from any definite creed, and to have taken refuge in a generous morality. From his examination of Greek art and sculpture he seems to have been led back to a belief in spiritual power; that there is nothing more contagious than Faith, and ultimately that Faith which inspired so much European art and sculpture. By the time that he came to live at Brantwood in 1871 his faith in Christianity was restored, not to the dry and insular dogmas of his childhood, but to a catholic religion, neither Romanist nor Protestant, but truly Christian and well founded in Faith.[12]

From 1871 he issued from Brantwood a monthly letter to the workmen and labourers of England called *Fors Clavigera* in an attempt to form an Utopia in England – to make a 'merrie England' enrolled under the banner of St George. He attempted to found model farms and industries none of which succeeded. These experiments included the revival of the hand-made linen industry in Langdale, and the establishment of a cloth industry at Laxey, Isle of Man. From his time as Slade Professor of Art at Oxford (1870–79; & 1883–4) he also established several schools for Art. This introduces the second of Ruskin's writings to have a strong influence on Brunskill. He obtained a copy of Ruskin's advice to children from *Fors Clavigera*. It is an interesting example of that direct evangelical religion of the heart, which has for long been a strong ingredient in English and Welsh nonconformity, going back to John Wesley and Benjamin Ingham both of whom were strongly influenced by the Moravians. Perhaps Brunskill, whose religion was very churchy, might have found a certain appeal in the directness of Ruskin's approach. His first advice to children was 'You should always, in whatever you do, endeavour to please Christ (and He is quite easily pleased if you try); but in attempting this, you will instantly find yourself likely to displease many of your friends or relations; and St George's second order to you is that in whatever you do, you consider that no manner of disobedience to your parents, or of disrespect and presumption towards your friends, can be pleasing to God. You must therefore be doubly submissive; first in your own will and purpose to the law of Christ; then in the carrying out of your purpose, to the pleasure and orders of the persons whom He has given you for superiors …'.

His second 'advice' was 'say to yourself, every morning, just after your prayers, 'Whoso forsaketh not all that he hath, cannot be my disciple' – meaning that you are to give all you have to Christ to take care of for you. Then if He doesn't take care of it, of course you know it wasn't worth anything'. After this surrender, whatever is entrusted to you, look 'on yourself as a little housemaid set to keep Christ's books and room in order, not as yourself as the mistress of anything'.

Though his remarks were addressed to girls, his advice on dresses combined his artistic eye and interest in rural industries. 'Dress as plainly as your parents will allow you; but in bright colours (if they become you) and in the best materials – that is to say, in those which will wear longest. When you are really in want of a new dress, buy it (or make it) in the fashion; but never quit an old one merely because it has become unfashionable. And if the fashion be costly, you must not follow it … Your walking dress must never touch the ground at all. I have lost much of the faith I once had in the common sense … of average English women, by seeing how they will allow their dresses to sweep the streets, as if it is the fashion to be scavengers.

'If you can afford it, get your dresses made by a good dressmaker, with utmost precision and perfection; but let this good dressmaker be a poor person, living in the country; not a rich person living in a large house in London. "There are no good dressmakers in the country." No, but there soon will be if you obey St George's orders, which are very strict, indeed, about never buying dresses in London.

'Learn dressmaking yourself, with pains and time, and use part of every day in needlework, making as pretty dresses as you can for poor people who have not time nor taste to make them nicely for themselves. You are to shew them in your own wearing what is most right and graceful, and to help them to choose what will be the prettiest and most becoming in their own station. If they see that you never try to dress above your's, they will not try to dress above their's.'[13]

Though Brunskill was to differ with Ruskin over the extension of the railway from Windermere to Ambleside, he remained a fervent admirer of his teaching on the stature of the craftsman and his work, and of course of the old dalesmen. Till Ruskin's death in 1900 he collected many cuttings of his letters, slipping them into the *Storm Cloud* book. The proposal to extend the railway to Ambleside had roused the wrath of William Wordsworth in 1844.[14] In 1866/7 a Parliamentary Bill was proposed for the same purpose. A Lakes Defence Society was formed, money rolled in, and furious letters appeared in the London *Standard*, the *Manchester Courier*, and the *Birmingham Gazette*. Many of them were from comfortable middle-class people writing on behalf of the working classes.

On the 7 February 1877 Albert Nicholson and Wm. Bell, hon. secretaries of the Manchester committee of the Lakes Defence Society, wrote to the press thus:

> There are thousands of clerks, warehousemen, &c., and a growing number of the operative class who are in the habit of repairing to the Lake District for rest and recreation, and the peculiar charm of the district for them is that its central part is free from those railways and smoky chimneys of which they have too much in everyday life. On their behalf we make this appeal, in the hope that a sufficient number of members of Parliament may be induced to vote against the Bill to secure its rejection on Second Reading ... If made, the Railway will benefit a contractor, an engineer, and (possibly) a few tradesmen, and would inflict injury upon every English lover of Nature for all time.[15]

Ruskin the artist and Christian was concerned with the beauty and nobility of the Lake District, as well the skills of its ancient dales' people. Wordsworth in an earlier generation had dreaded the invasion of the new rich from the industrial towns, buying up the smaller farms and turning them into 'gentlemen's residences'. This was praiseworthy; but the economic forces from the new industries were against the old-time dale farmers. In 1895 the Royal Commission on Agriculture reported to Parliament on the condition of agriculture in the counties. The Cumberland report was written by Mr Fox Wilson, and took into account the agricultural depressions in the 1820s and the 1840s. He recorded that the old customary estatesmen were more heavily laden with family charges which their ancestors had put on their ancient farms, and were paying more in interest charges, than ordinary tenants paying rack rents to a landlord. The most telling evidence came from Mr F. Grainger who owned 168 acres at Holme Abbey, which had been held by his family since 1605. His table shows the gradual extinction of the estatesmen in the parish of Abbey Quarter in the Wigton Union, Cumberland:

Year	Number of statesmen	Number of leaseholders	Average size of holdings
1604	83	none	42 acres
1648	81	6	54
1780	51	9	58
1812	38	18	58
1837	30	20	100
1864	21	29	100
1894	9	41	100

It is fair to suggest that neither Ruskin nor Wordsworth, nor the Manchester Lake District preservationists, fully understood the financial plight of the customary estatesmen farmers. Of course Wordsworth in his poem 'Michael' had romanticised the cost of ancient family loyalties. There were however those who did understand the economic forces against the dalesmen. J. Overend of Hawkshead, writing in the *Manchester Courier* of 1 March 1887, assailed the opponents of the Bill from the Lakes Defence Society, that they 'are chiefly composed of gentlemen who favour the district with their presence during the height of the season, and are not poor in the sense the appeal (to prevent the extension of the railway) would have the public believe.

But those who support are residents all the year round – namely tradesmen, farmers, landowners, and others who feel the difficulty they labour under in competing with the outer world. They know that this line does not affect the beauties of the lakeland, and I feel sure, Sir, that public opinion will shortly listen to the cry against this cruel opposition, emanating from wealthy bodies, and wealthy men, made by promoters and supporters (of the Railway Bill) who depend for their livelihood on competing in the public markets.[17]

It is John Langhorne's tradition that Canon Rawnsley and Brunskill clashed publicly over the Railway Bill. Brunskill's letter to the *Manchester Courier* of 26 February 1887 put his view clearly:

Sir,
    The fate of the railway extension from the present terminus at Birthwaite (Windermere) to Ambleside now depends on evidence being found that the line will injure the Lake District scenery and the enjoyment of the public.

    Some quarter of a century ago, there was stern witness borne by 'sentimentalists' against the railway from Penrith by Keswick to Cockermouth, because the route, after a view of Helvellyn, goes almost round Blenkathra and Skiddaw, crosses at the foot of Derwentwater, and runs along the western shore of Bassenthwaite Lake; intruding, by many bridges, upon singularly fine scenery. And by this easy conveyance multitudes of the public have enjoyed in 'Moorish Skiddaw and far-reaching Saddleback, the proper types of majestic form'. Yet, residing in the centre of the district, and searching during several years, I have failed to find any person who will now bear witness against the railway. I have had cruel experience of the toil or cost between Birthwaite and Ambleside or Rydal, and I believe that there is increasing danger from such coach travelling, while the excessive vehicular traffic on the soft road injuries by mud and dust, those tourists who can walk.

    On behalf of the horses, which are commonly driven to Keswick and back (46 miles), I would plead that their journey be shortened by this almost hidden railway. In my opinion the 'tripper' may be decoyed to Stockghyl once; but the farce will not be repeated, and the famous letters written to the Morning Post 40 years ago, by the greatest lake poet, show that he would not now have hindered this cheap, safe, and clean mode of travelling, but would have extended his cordial welcome to the large numbers whom his writings have educated to relish the picturesque natural scenery of 'Wordsworthshire'.

    Yours etc. J. Brunskill Threlkeld Rectory.[18]

Brunskill and Wm. C. Ainsley Esq. MP were attacked in the *Manchester Courier* of March 1887 by a Mr John Walker of Bury. Ainsley was accused of wanting the value of his land to increase by the coming of the railway; and Brunskill was told:

To hear a country parson growling about 'the cruel experience of the toil and cost between Windermere and Ambleside' is most amusing. He not only has the coach at his disposal but the cheap and regular steamer and then again the distance could be done comfortably afoot in an hour and a quarter.

The writer made a fair point that the coming of the northern railway had not improved the economic condition of the customary 'estatesmen' farmers, who were declining in number year by year. He quoted an article in the *Ambleside Herald*:

The promoters (of the Bill) hope that the wants and interests of the 8,000 resident proprietors will not be easily set aside at the howling cry of united fillibusters (sic) who, if left uncontrolled, would cause our lovely Lake District to become the retreat of the grizzly bear, the grazing ground of the wolf, the region of brigands, and the land of ferns, thistles and underwood; 'blackmail' would be levelled on all intruders, then our lovely Lake District would become a 'heaven on earth', tryanny and oppression would reign supreme.
                    Yours &c. John Walker[19]

We do not know whether Brunskill approached Ruskin on the subject of the railway extension; it is possible that he did; for the following letter appeared in the *Birmingham Gazette* after 'a Cumberland gentleman' had approached him on the subject:

Brantwood, Coniston, Lancashire.
March 1, 1887.

My Dear Sir,
   I do not write now further concerning railroads here or elsewhere because they are to me the loathsomenest form of devilry now extant, animated and deliberate earthquakers, destructive of all wise, social habit, or possible natural beauty; carriages of damned souls on the ridges of their own graves.
                    Ever faithfully yours,
                    John Ruskin[20]

Others less heavenly-minded wrote to ask whether Ruskin had never travelled by rail between Coniston and London, or Oxford. For months the Lake residents were in high fever until the Bill was abandoned. Though Brunskill's contact with Ruskin did not survive this final exchange, Brunskill remained a fervent admirer, collecting and savouring his writings.

No less important to Brunskill was the philosophy of Wordsworth, who did so much to immortalise the qualities of the ancient dalesmen from whom Brunskill himself had sprung. On the 14 January 1801, Wordsworth had written to Charles James Fox from Grasmere:

> In the two poems, The Brothers, and Michael, I have attempted to draw a picture of domestic affections, as I know they exist among a class of men who are now almost confined to the north of England. They are small independant proprietors of land, here called statesmen, men of respectable education, who daily labour on their own little properties. The domestic affections will always be strong amongst men who live in a country not crowded with population, if these men are placed above poverty. But if they are proprietors of small estates, which have descended to them from their ancestors, the power, which these affections will acquire amongst such men is inconceivable by those who have only had an opportunity of observing hired labourers, farmers and the manufacturing poor. Their little tract of land serves as a kind of permanent rallying point for their domestic feelings, as a tablet upon which they are written, which makes them object of memory in a thousand instances, when they would otherwise be forgotten.[21]

Wordsworth's appreciation of the circumstances and character of the old northern estatesmen was soundly based from native experience, and sound reading. A number of local histories had appeared before and after the foundation of the Board of Agriculture in 1790, and the County Reports which it commissioned. He had seen the changes which had overtaken these people from 1770 to 1810.[22] His *Guide to the Lakes*, 1810, has a more accurate understanding of the half feudal and half proprietary origin of the northern customary farms than a number of modern economic historians have appreciated. The dales' communities were a close-knit society, where each family spun from its own flock the wool with which it was clothed; it was that homely serge which Richard Watson wore when he left Heversham to enter Trinity College, Cambridge in 1757. The rest of the farm wants was supplied by the produce of the yarn carded and spun in their own homes, and carried to market, either under their arms, or more frequently by pack-horses which went in trains to the nearest markets. When Brunskill went to Mallerstang in 1853 he saw the end of that old world which Wordsworth, Ruskin and Rawnsley worked so hard to defend.

Even 'Poet' John Close (1816–1891) of Kirkby Stephen, the composer of much poetic balderdash, wrote accurately of the frugality of that world up to the first half of the nineteenth century in Mallerstang:

> The people usually wore homespun cloth, and even yarn-knitten hose; the women, linsey-woolsey skirts and bedgowns (prints and cottons were then unknown); buckles in their shoes on sundays; on weekdays clogs and pattens. Diet – porridge and milk for breakfast; and those who could rear a pig, had bacon and potatoes for dinner, or oatcake, and rye bread and milk. One hundred years ago [i.e. about 1760], only two pigs were fed in the dale; now about forty each year.

Wordsworth was not alone in appreciating the quality of old-time people in the north at the beginning of the nineteenth century. Thomas Carlyle so described the people who lived around Ecclefechan with their heavy-laden, patient, ever-attentive faces at the Meeting House; also the thrifty, cleanly poverty of those good people.[23]

As early as 1882 Brunskill conceived the idea of assembling an album of photographs illustrating many of Wordsworth's themes: Gratitude, Courage, Poverty, Compassion, Resolution and Independence, Home, Faith and Duty, Frailty, Foresight, Gladness, Affection, Sport and Content. Brunskill who had sprung from these ancient peoples, enlisted the services of G. P. Abraham, photographer of Keswick, and assembled a collection of about thirty photographs of people and places. Many of them have his own children illustrating Wordsworth's themes. One has a view of his old father at Bankfoot holding cards for carding, while his half-sister Hannah stands beside the family spinning-wheel. He sent a few of these photos to the Wordsworth scholar, Professor Wm. Knight of St Andrews for his opinion, and received this reply:

Nov. 9, 1882   University,
                                      St Andrews, N.B.

Mr Dear Sir,
    Many thanks for your note of the 4th inst. & the accompany-
ing photos, illustrative of Wordsworth. If you carry out the idea
to *any extent* with success, I think a little volume in album form
of illustrations of Wordsworth in this way wd. be excellent.
    I have been urging Greens at Grasmere to (?raise) a vol. of
photographs of *Localities* associated with the Poet, especially at
Grasmere. If you could bring out a volume of photographic
illustrations of the Poems, like those you have sent me, they
would be even more valuable. Have you tried the *Waggoner*, or
the *Brothers*?
    I shall be much interested in your experiments.
    Yours very truly,
    William Knight
P.S. I return the photos with many thanks. W.K.[24]

Thus encouraged, Brunskill assembled his album, and printed
this prospectus:

Wordsworthshire

I have always loved to wander over the physical scenes inhabited
by men whom I have known, admired, loved, or revered, as well
among the living as the dead.
    Professor Knight, Secretary of the Wordsworth Society, in his
delightful book 'The English Lake District as interpreted in the
Poems of Wordsworth', writes, 'Not only was the "mind of man"
(as he says) "the haunt and the main region of my song", but
nature was nothing to him apart from man. Still further, it was
man as social man in relation to his fellows, man organised in
society, that chiefly interested him.

The Right Honourable Lord Coleridge, writing to Brunskill
(21.11.82) said:
'The photographs are very successful pictures. The idea of
illustrating Wordsworth by the living men and women of the
present day is new to me. Through Wordsworth's works the
scenes are seldom long absent from my mind.' [25]
    Unfortunately the album was never published, but it remains
a valuable record of the loyalty, character, and independence of
the northern estatesmen.
    There was one photograph of Brunskill's daughter Lydia

before the porch of Threlkeld church sitting in the grass by a grave. Under it he has these lines from Wordsworth:

> *We are Seven.*
> A simple child
> That lightly draws its breath,
> And feels its life in every limb,
> What should it know of death?

Lydia inherited the album, and in after years was disgusted at being called a simple child.

Apart from these literary interests, Brunskill's main thrust was agricultural. In 1887 the Royal Agricultural Society held its third annual show at Newcastle, and one of the stands contained a collection of hides taken that week in Newcastle market. They were punctured with hundreds of small holes inflicted by warble fly, rendering the hides useless, not to mention the suffering to the oxen. A lady entomologist from the Royal Agricultural Society sent leaflets which described the damage to hides, and the easy remedies which could be applied. The report added this: 'The secretary to any of our local agricultural societies may apply to the Rector of Threlkeld, who has been entrusted by the Newcastle Hide Inspection Society with some of their specimens for further exhibition, and who is also co-operating with Miss Ormerod [the entomologist] towards 'warble suppression'.' [26]

In January 1891 Brunskill reported to a local paper the advantage of Agricultural Colleges in teaching better methods of farming and dairy work. As some of the agricultural farms had incurred losses, the chairman of the Aspatria Agricultural College expressed his gratitude that they had not tried to carry on a farm. Brunskill added: 'Assistance upon the old line of scholarships may be more safely adventured by a public body such as a County Council, than by setting up some costly new experiment which might compete unfairly with good private work.' [27]

In June 1892 the British Dairy Farmers' Association came to Penrith, and Brunskill sent a long article to a Penrith paper giving a list of the most interesting places the delegates could visit. On the following day he attended, as was his custom, the annual dinner of the Penrith Farmers' Club. During the toasts the chairman paid tribute to the clergy of the Church of England and the other denominations; he mentioned especially the affection they had for good bishop Harvey Goodwin who had just died. The reply was given by Brunskill who was pleased to be reminded of the kindly feeling which had always existed between the clergy and their parishioners in that district. After mentioning the late bishop, he said that their new bishop Bardsley had studied agriculture in Sweden where the people often made their own farm tools. He added that 'it had been a hobby with him to impress upon young agriculturalists with who he came in contact that they possessed great skill in that direction. He had tried to collect hand-made flails, and wooden cowbands; that he was quite certain that they possessed the skill if only they would make use of it.'[28]

Apart from farming, Brunskill was not afraid to remind magistrates in public of their duty. 'Threlkeld, – A correspondent reports that a disgraceful affray occurred recently, in which two miners, father and son, and their dogs inflicted such severe injuries on a young man named Holiday, that he had to be removed to Carlisle Infirmary, where he still lies in a very precarious condition. The facts will doubtless be elicited by an enquiry in a court of justice.'[29]

There are several reports of childrens' treats being given at the rectory. One from 1889 has this: 'Among the games of cricket, tennis, and football, which helped to make a bright afternoon, was the old English game of goff. Some of the bats played with, had been imported by Mr Brunskill from Montreal twenty-six years ago [probably for Lowther School], before the game was known to this generation at home as 'lacrosse'. In the evening, after tea in the schoolroom, handsome parting memorials were given to Miss Brunskill by the children, and also by members of the parish choir.'[30]

The last cutting concerned an old schoolmaster friend from Brunskill's Leeds days, a Mr Preston. He was born in Westmorland; his first school was at Kings Meaburn, and he then moved to Ireby. As he held a first class teachers certificate from his Leeds days he joined the staff of the Durham Training College.

For some years he was head of an eminent school at Stockton, where he became ill. Brunskill persuaded him to take over the church school at Threlkeld for his health's sake. He was a keen musician, and led the village Glee Club and the church choir, and gave great pleasure. After only a year at Threlkeld he died suddenly in May 1890, aged 54. After a church service the members of the Glee Club and the Choir bore his coffin to the station for burial at Stockton.[31]

NOTES TO CHAPTER FOURTEEN

1. W.M. Press cuttings: *Penrith Advertiser*, 24 June 1884; 'Local & District'. W.M. *Carlisle Patriot*, 13 Nov. 1883. Letter of Wm. Marriott, Asst. Sec. of Royal Meteorological Society.

2. W.M. Press Cutting. n.d. note by Brunskill.

3. *Life & Works of John Ruskin*, W.G. Collingwood 1893, Vol. I. p. 102.

4. *The Art Teaching of John Ruskin*, W.G. Collingwood 1891, p. 154.

5. W.M. *The Storm Cloud of the Nineteenth Century*, two lectures, John Ruskin, 1884, p. 120.

6. L.M. J. Ruskin to J. Brunskill, rec'd 17.12.85.

7. L.M. J. Ruskin to J. Brunskill, Ambleside postmark 19 Feb. 1886.

8. W.M.

9. *A Bibliography of Cumberland & Westmorland*, Henry W. Hodgson 1968, p. 44.

10. W.M. Letter of Ruskin to Brunskill 19 Feb. 1886, copied by one of his children.

11. W.M. Press cutting of Rawnsley's lecture; in *The English Lakes* (a newspaper) 17 Nov. 1883.

12. D.N.B. John Ruskin (1819–1900)
    The Art Teaching of John Ruskin, W.G. Collingwood 1891, p. 154 et seq.
    The Life & Works of John Ruskin, W.G. Collingwood 1893, I. p. 102 for earlier period.

13. W.M. Press cutting extract from *Fors Clavigera*, in Ruskin Book, n.d. see ref. (5) above.

14. *Guide to the Lakes*, Wm. Wordsworth 1835 ed. repr. 1977, pp. 147 et seq.
    With Wordsworth's letters to the *Morning Post* on the Kendal to Windermere railway 1844.

15. W.M. Press cutting: Albert Nicholson & Wm. Bell to the London *Standard* 7 Feb. 1877.

16. The Royal Commission on Agriculture, England Report. Mr Fox Wilson (Assistant Commissioner) on the County of Cumberland 1895, pp. 32-33. (Sect. 51). P.34 refers to Bailey & Culley's report of 1797.

17. W.M. Press cutting, J. Overend to the *Manchester Courier*, 1 Mar. 1887.

18. W.M. J. Brunskill to the *Manchester Courier* 26 Feb. 1887.

19. W.M. John Walker to the *Manchester Courier* 8 Mar. 1887.

20. W.M. Press cutting, J. Ruskin to the *Birmingham Gazette*, 1 Mar. 1887.

21. Letters of the Wordsworth Family 1787–1855. Collected by William Knight, 3 vols. 1907. p. 138. Letter of Wordsworth to Charles James Fox 14 Jan. 1801.

22. *Guide to the Lakes*. W. Wordsworth op. cit. pp. 60–66.

23. D.N.B. 'Poet' John Close (1816–1891).
    Once a Year; Tales & Legends of Westmorland. J. Close 1860, p. 75. Old Times in Mallerstang.
    Carlyle's Reminiscences, Everyman edn. 1932. Tribute to Edward Irving.

24. W.M. Letter in Wordsworthshire, photo album. Wm. Knight to Brunskill 9 Nov. 1882.

25. W.M. Printed prospectus in photo album above.
    Prof. Knight took up the idea of an illustrated Wordsworthshire in:
    Through the Wordsworth Country, by H. Goodwin & Prof. Knight 1887.
    The English Lakes, painted by Mr Heaton Cooper, described by Wm. T. Palmer 1908.
    Wordsworthshire. An Introduction to a Poet's Country, Eric Robertson & illustrated by Arthur Tucker of Ashleigh, Windermere 1911.

26. W.M. Press cutting 30.8.87.

27. W.M. Press cutting, 'Model Farms', a letter of Brunskill 27.1.91.

28. W.M. Press cutting. Article in a Penrith paper; British Dairy Farmers' Association. 6.6.92.
    Ibid. Account of Penrith Farmers' Club dinner 7.6.92.

29. W.M. Press cutting. (? Penrith) *Herald* 27 Jan. year omitted.

30. W.M. Ibid. 24.9.89. Childrens' treat at Threlkeld.

31. Ibid. *Penrith Observer* 27.5.90.

15

People & Papers (1)

AS BRUNSKILL's father had eight brothers and sisters, it is possible that by now the family is related to about half the farming families of north Westmorland! But there are scant references to relatives in the surviving papers. In his early days he had an aunt at Clifton, and other relatives at Askham, and Hackthorpe. There was his father John, a yeoman farmer at Bankfoot, and his uncle Joseph a tenant farmer at Sewborwens, both at Newton. In 1867 at the time of the Clifton toll-gate case, there is a reference on the back of the press cutting to a Penrith solicitor Mr Brunskill appearing in a magistrates' court. This may have been Richard Atkinson Brunskill, an uncle whose son Joseph married parson Brunskill's sister Isabella. In the late 1890s, there is one reference to a George Brunskill, perhaps an uncle visiting Brunskill at Ormside rectory. Thus the references are few, and the dispersal of the family requiring more study.

As a clergyman he was a 'convinced churchman', strong minded, well informed on church history, the Prayer book, and local history. As a member of the Wordsworth Society, the Royal Meteorological Society, and the Cumberland and Westmorland Antiquarian Society his interests were wide. He never failed to attend diocesan conferences, and spoke regularly; he attended at least one Church Congress at York; and of course his membership of the Penrith Farmers' Club, and his long interest in horses, and farming methods, and the growth of Agricultural Colleges were central to his life as a country parson. In church matters he was an old fashioned high churchman; his churches were well repaired and maintained. But the adornments of his churches were simple, far from the inferior ornaments into which Anglo-Catholicism has descended in our day. A cross and two vases of flowers were the total extras on the Holy Table at Ormside. The country people would not tolerate more. His churches were clean and bright.

In early years Brunskill preached from a full written text, latterly from notes, but from a well-constructed theme. Three of these summaries survive on St Stephen, St John and the Epiphany. Here are his Epiphany notes:

> 'Epiphany – gospel –
> Meaning of Epip.
> To what Gentiles manifested.
> Hour – Birth of Xst. m(essage) to Magi.
> How star = to Magi's guess.
> At Jerusalem – Bethlehem.
> Gifts &c. of Magi.
> Xst. mani. to Gentiles that God's Grace – to *all* men,
>   by Angels to Jews, & star g.
> Zeal and courage of Magi.
> Learn from Festival.
> True wisdom, not in possessing a great understanding, but *using*
> No man to (o) great for religion.
> Readily obey divine calls.
> Courageously – duty.
> Outwardly express – mind.
> Gifts of Magi –
> (a) Charity. Riches to be used.
> (b) Prayer. Constancy & fervour.
>   Modesty, humility, faith.
> (c) Mortification. Not only avoid *sin*, but all occasions and liberties.
> Commemorate – Manifest: by great thankfulness, because *by enlarging Way* of *Salvation* we Xst. (Christians) Pity – Heathen.[1]

On the negative side his high churchmanship, and his radical Toryism would not countenance dissent or 'school-boardism', indeed any deviation from the Christian faith taught in the Prayer Book, which in his view led to Socialism; on the other side members of an established church, whether clergy or landowners are often blind to the faults of 'churchmen' which forced poor people into the chapels.

The religious divide between church and chapel, and in the old days between Liberal and Tory, in the dales is far deeper than most people realise. In my view it goes back to the agrarian grievances of the northern tenants which led to the Pilgrimage of Grace in 1536–7, and the subsequent hanging of the ringleaders. There was scarcely a northern manor where the tenants did not have a struggle with the lord over rents and manorial fines, often ending in Chancery. The acute poverty in the dales in the mid-eighteenth century drove many into the market towns seeking work and alienated many from the established church. In the alleys and yards of northern market towns such as Richmond, Barnard Castle, Kendal, Penrith and many more they found dissenting meetings of Calvinists, Quakers, Lady Huntingdon's Connexion, Benjamin Ingham, and later John Wesley worshipping in the Christian way, yet apart from the old order. The dale chapels preserved the Faith for an alienated people, conscious of past wrongs, yet still believing in the Gospel brought by unpaid local preachers.

In the upper Eden Valley with which I am best acquainted the theological roots of dissent are very deep. Among my heroes there are four who should never be forgotten:

John Boste (1543?–1594) of Well Inge, Dufton became a fellow of Queen's College, Oxford, became a Roman Catholic, was ordained priest at Rheims, returned as a mission priest, and for twelve years evaded arrest, and kept the Catholic Faith alive in the north, was captured and racked in the Tower, and finally brutally hanged, drawn and quartered at Durham in 1594.

Francis Howgill (1618–1669) of Todhorne, Grayrigg, was converted to Quakerism in 1652, and with James Naylor held the first Quaker Meeting in Mallerstang in that year, and in London in 1653. He was banished from Ireland by Henry Cromwell. He was arrested at Kendal in 1663, and tried at Appleby in 1664 and condemned to perpetual imprisonment in Appleby gaol for refusing to take the oath of allegiance. He died there in 1669, the saint of early Quakerism.

Benjamin Ingham (1712–1772) studied at Queen's College, Oxford, ordained and with John Wesley was much influenced by the Moravians. He built up a circuit of 80 chapels in the Midlands and the north, with a few in Westmorland based on Pear Tree Chapel, Kendal. He did much to give new life to old dissenting groups of Presbyterians, Independents, and Quakers in the mid-eighteenth century. His registers of Birks Chapel, Warcop reveal a diligent pastor of a wide scattered congregation. His movement collapsed on his accepting Calvinistic Sandemanianism in 1760.

Stephen Brunskill (1748–1836) of Orton was of Sandemanian parents, who after 1760 turned slowly to Wesley's preachers. Brunskill took over the chapel of Lady Huntingdon's Connexion in Kendal, and on his return to farm in Orton began his life's work in found-

ing Methodist chapels in the dales and villages. He was a pioneer
of Westmorland Methodism.

These men, so different in theological concept, were of heroic
faith, and gave their lives to serve people estranged from land-
lords and church. While it is easy to deride Joseph Brunskill's
dislike of 'dissenters', there is no doubt that he was the right
man to raise English country churches, from the squalor to
which the spent evangelical movement had reduced them, to
places of beauty and worship. In the Church of England he was
a man for his time.

One of the strong threads of Brunskill's life was his affection for
his sister Isabella. After leaving home she worked at Hackthorpe, and was two years younger than he. One of her ad-
mirers was Joseph Brunskill, the son of Richard Atkinson
Brunskill her uncle. There is this delightful letter from London:

Balsall Street, April 9th 1849.

My Dear Cousin Isabella,

I am sorry that you should compare my promises to pie crusts;
you being the elder I waited for you to write first, and was very
much pleased, and *always* shall be to receive a letter from you.

I am happy to hear you are enjoying yourself at the pretty village of Hackthorpe and should be greatly pleased were it in my
power to join you. I assure you I retain *too* lively a remembrance
of all my pleasures and kind Friends in Cumberland and Westmorland to forget you.

At this time I am enjoying my Easter holydays with my dear
parents, Grandpapa and Grandmama (who beg to be kindly remembered to you all) minus Eggs and Oranges, but in their place
a plentiful supply of excellent *Cheesecakes*.

Please to give my kind love to all my Aunts, Uncles, and Cou-
sins, not forgetting Emma Ward and yourself; in the meantime

Believe me to remain,

Your affect. Cousin,

J. Brunskill.[2]

The Emma Ward was of course the daughter of the Vicar of
Askham. I have not found the marriage of Isabella and this
Joseph. It is possible that he followed his father as a solicitor in
London. Isabella and Joseph went to live at 13 Belsize Square,
Hampstead. Joseph died there on 9th September 1872, aged 34,

and was buried in Hampstead churchyard.[3] Isabella continued to live there for some years. Parson Brunskill's wife Lydia wrote this comforting letter on receiving the news:

> Plumpton, 10 Sept. 1872.

My dear Isabella,

The sorrowful tidings of your sad bereavement has just reached me, and need I assure you of our deep sympathy under this very severe stroke. You who have borne life so bravely under all the painful self sacrifice which your dear invalid's long sufferings required of you, have I feel sure (?been) as a Christian with this dreadful trial. You have the comfort of knowing that you were able to soothe him and tend him to the last. I can assure you our thoughts have been constantly with you. We feel thankful that you could have the comfort of yr dear friend Miss Jackson's presence. She will I am sure be comforting to you in yr desolation.

Joseph had gone to Hackthorpe before Miss Jackson's letter came this morning. He was very anxious for news, but could not wait for the Post. I am sorry to say he is far from well – he is quite worn out when he comes home in the evenings. Although he makes no complaint. But I feel often very anxious about him, and wish it were possible to withdraw from the school – But I do hope it may be managed soon. We both felt very much grieved that he could not come last week, & yet I felt that it would be a risk for him as travelling and anxiety affect him seriously. He felt he would be of little service to you.

I have not been well for the last few days, or I should have written you on Saturday – I am obliged to rest frequently & take care. You must not think my silence arises from thoughtlessness, for indeed my dear Isabella we do grieve with and for you under such a heavy burthen.

May our Heavenly Father continue to support & strengthen you. With dearest love to you all.

Yours affect. sister Lydia.[4]

Some time after the funeral it seems that Isabella came north, for there is this undated letter from Lydia, still on black-edge paper:

> Plumpton Vicarage, Thursday.

My dear Isabella,

I felt sorry to know you were from home yesterday on one of my rare visits to Penrith. But I hope Johnnie's note reached you, and that you will all come to celebrate his birthday wch we purpose to keep on Saturday. Comrade will be at your service; only fix the place and time. We dine at one. I am writing Mrs Ward by this post, hoping she will come to tea – & don't be startled! I asked Mr &Mrs J. Simpson to come also in the afternoon – the lady seems to be socially disposed, and really I pity her, she is very unaffected and kind.

I expect my sister in law from Clifton, now, you must come, I hoped to have seen you yesterday & felt so grieved when Joseph said you were going from home.

I think I must have knocked myself up with horrid cleaning – wishing to make the most of my time whilst I had Aunt Mary. I have been so unsatisfactory lately. (? Isab) is growing so nice, so intelligent & right.

With warmest love

Yr. affecte sister Lydia Brunskill.[5]

During most of 1872 Lydia was expecting her fourth child Isabella Maud, who was born on the 10 Nov; she is John Langhorne's mother. The above letter is therefore from 1873. Lydia bore her fifth child, Lydia Violette (Alan Webster's mother), on 13 January 1876 and died on the 23 June 1876 and was buried at Newton. One of the first to help Joseph after her death was Isabella his sister.

As we have seen, Lydia and Joseph had five children, and we will deal with them in brief. **John Ritson Brunskill was born 11 May 1865.** His main schooling was at Appleby Grammar School. He obtained a Hastings exhibition to Queen's College, Oxford, and graduated BA in 1887, and MA in 1890. He was ordained deacon in 1888, and priest 1889 at Chester. He had two curacies, at Portwood from 1888, and at Bowdon 1893 to 1906. Bowdon is south-west of Altrincham. On the creation of the new parish of Hale, south of Altrincham he was made the first incumbent (1906–1924). He built a handsome church, St Peter's, Hale, and is commemorated in the chancel. His widowed aunt Isabella gave up her house at Hampstead and went to keep house for him for the rest of her life. She died on the 8 Sept. 1910 and was buried at Hale. She left her estate of £1,958.6.4. to John Ritson[6] In 1924 he became vicar of March Baldon with Toot Baldon in Oxfordshire where he remained till 1930. He returned to Cheshire and took temporary duty at

Stockport 1930, Alsager 1931, and Wilmslow from 1934. He ended his days at the Homes of St Barnabas, Dormans, Surrey; he died in 1946, and was buried in the spare grave intended for his aunt Isabella beside her husband Joseph in Hampstead Churchyard.[7] At some point he inherited Bankfoot in Newton, but sold it in about 1925.

Alice Mary was born 6 October 1866. On the 5 October 1889 she was married at St Mary's, Threlkeld to James Ritson from Sunderland and working for the Ritson Shipping Company. The service was taken by John Ritson Brunskill. James Ritson was born in Sunderland in 1862, and obtained his master's certificate in Sunderland in 1887. He served as a mate on the *Olive Branch* from 1887–9, and as master of the *Myrtle Branch* from 1889 to 1892. On the 31 January 1893 he succeeded Henry John Ritson as captain of the *Willow Branch*, which sailed for Singapore. His wife went with him. She died of fever on board ship on 24 May 1893 aged 26, and was buried in the Red Sea. Her husband died on board ship on the 28 August 1893 aged 32, and was also buried in the Red Sea. Lloyd's received the report of his death on the 7 Sept. at Calcutta.[8]

Cyril Wane was born 12 August 1869; he would thus be 21 in 1890 at Threlkeld. His early schooling is not known. According to John Langhorne he worked for some time at a 'milkhouse' (dairy) in Penrith. In 1899 Gen. Sir Redvers H. Buller was appointed to command the British forces against the Boers in S. Africa. Cyril had joined the reserves of the Royal Dragoons, and by 25 April 1899 was serving at Gen. Buller's Staff H.Q. at Ladysmith. From that date until January 1902 Cyril and his sister Lydia at Ormside rectory exchanged letters; Lydia wrote weekly, and Cyril replied as often as his duty allowed. There was a very warm bond between the two, and Cyril always addresses her as 'Dearest Lydia', and he concluded most of his letters: 'Believe me, your loving brer. Sybil', the childhood mispronunciation of Cyril. Alan Webster has a large packet of these letters covering Cyril's service in the Boer War 1899 to 1902. They are worth a separate study, giving an ordinary soldier's view of events. The following described the relief of Ladysmith:

C. Squadron,
Royal Dragoons,
Ladysmith.
March 10. 1900.

Dearest Lydia,

Thank you very much indeed for your long and welcome letter of Feb. 1st. recd. last Sat. (Mch. 3rd). You will have seen in paper how at last the Boers have been moved from here & that Ladysmith was relieved on Feb. 28th.

All the troops engaged in the relief made a sort of triumphal march in last Sat. (Mch. 3.) & then our Brigade went into the Tin Barracks about 2 miles above the town. It was terrible to see the troops who have been here all the time. Just like ghosts, & their eyes sunk in & looking fit to drop. They must have had terrible times & no sleep to speak of. There is a fever camp about 2 miles out where there are about 3,000 sick. There are very few horses left & those are all skin & bone. The town itself does not seem much worse for the bombardment; the Town Hall got a nasty knock, right in the Clock Tower. Of course all the shops were closed though they are opening now again, & as the railway is open thro' to Colenso today, soon all will be well.

It was the most impressive sight one could ever see. The gaunt & haggard troops trying to cheer, & could not; everywhere a look of desolation & decay, & most of the Civil population in mourning & trying to wave handkerchiefs, but could not control themselves sufficiently to cheer, being mostly in tears poor things. There was a makeshift band near the town hall, & they played for all they were worth. They say they could not have hung out much longer, so it is as well our Gen. was no longer in getting here. We hear Ld. Roberts keeps fighting with the Free Staters & beating them, but we hear nothing of what is going on North of here.

On Monday I was sent as Personal Orderly to Gen. Buller, so am at his head quarters at present, The Convent, which stands about 100 ft. right above the town. It seems an easy job enough, as there is a Corpl. of the Military Mounted Police here & we take it day about unless both are wanted at once. Of course it is much better here than being with the Regt. both for duty & accommodation & everything.

Lord Basing told me on Sunday that I was selected from the whole Brigade (!) & he was certain I wd. do my best etc. Our Col. (who is Brigadier you know) also said the same. Our duties are to follow the Gen. whenever he goes out & take dispatches etc.

I have had 2 or 3 good rides so far, twice nearly to Colenso (10 miles each way) & on Wed. the Governor of Natal visited the Town Hall & Hospitals etc. The Gen. and all his staff were there

& there was some speech-making & much cheering. The Naval Brigade have mostly gone back to their ships, they are going home I believe to be paid off. Poor things they all look very bad, & they have lost a great number thro' disease during the siege.

I was very glad to see Isabel had been able to be over home for a few days. It wd. be a nice change for her, as it must be frightfully lonely at Hutton at times, specially when it rains so, & days are short. Hope you have got a servant by this time, as it must be rather tying (& tiring) over so much running about.

It is really wonderful how everyone's spirits have gone up. Kimberley, & Ladysmith have been relieved, & old Cronje is safely at Cape Town. I wonder how much longer this wretched war will drag on now. As you say the lives *wasted* at Spion Kop, are really awful. There is no doubt though that our people are tremendously handicapped by the guns. At Spion Kop, you may have seen a mention, that 'had the Mountain Battery only been there in time' etc. This is a *wicked deception*, as our Mountain Batt. have 7 pounder *muzzle-loading* guns using powder which makes smoke like a house on fire, & very short range. The Boers' Pom-pom wld have *smashed* it in a twinkling, so perhaps it is as well for our poor Mountain Gunners they were not there in time.

Some seem to think this war is nearly over, at least as far as we are concerned in Natal. But now I am on 'Bullers Staff'! you may be sure I am as safe as at home, where I soon hope to be. The Regt. has gone back to Colenso, better water etc there, but here we have the best of everything including filtered water.

Did you get any acknowledgement of the socks yet? They are *very* useful & nice. Thank you ever so for them. I will put the proper address in my letter to Father as if you sent letters to the Regt. they will take longer.

This is my day 'on', but the Gen. is not going out till evening. It is always either 8 am or 5 pm – Please thank Isabel very much for her jolly letter in case I dont get one sent off to her. I am writing this in plenty of time for the Mail. It will be Easter before you get it – It has been very hot all this week, & this is an awful place for dust. Hope this will find you quite well as am glad to say I am.

With much love, Believe me Dearest Lydia, Your afft. brer. C.W. Brunskill.[9]

Cyril's affection for Lydia seems to have been as close as that of his Father for Isabella. It was fortunate that Brunskill had trained Cyril in horsemanship at Thelkeld rectory. General Buller had been defeated at Spion Kop in January 1900, and at Vaal Krantz. His leadership was severely criticised at home, and though he had relieved Ladysmith it was not till 27 August 1900 that he finally defeated the main Boer army at Bergendal. He reached Pretoria on the 10 October, and after being thanked by Lord Roberts he reached England on the 9 November. He resumed the command of the Aldershot division in January 1901, but was removed from command in October 1901. His statue at Exeter was inscribed 'He saved Natal'.[10]

Corporal Cyril Brunskill's return to Ormside in 1902 will be referred to later. In 1903 he emigrated to Canada, his father having died earlier that year. He announced his arrival on the 1 July. Cyril's first letter home as an immigrant is too good to omit:

> Winnipeg, Man.
> July 1st. 1903.

My dearest Lydia:
    Just a line to let Mother & you know that I arrived here safely this morn. about 4 am. (This time is 7 hours behind your time.) The journey by train was not so bad & we made fair time after Sunday. There were two special trains made up from Quebec; the first got in last night. The distance from Montreal to here is 1424 miles & farther from Quebec. There is plenty of demand for all kinds of labour here, both experienced & inexperienced & I will have no difficulty in getting something to start on.

    This is what is called Dominion Day & is a general holiday, so that there is not much business to be done now today. This morn. I went to the Immigration Office & entered my name for employment. The office is now closed but will be open all day tomorrow, & there are a lot of places on their register waiting for applicants, mostly farming. I was almost afraid of finding a scarcity of work here as one has heard so much of that lately; but there is plenty of work of all kinds here, & I daresay by this time tomorrow I will be in something. As far as I can see it will be best to go on a farm for a time and in that case I will secure myself over the winter.

    It seems rather queer to be here at last after being on the move so long. The sooner I can get into something the sooner I can send you an address. I need not say I am very anxious to hear how it goes with you all.

    The Post Office here was not open to-day for enquirers' letters, only those having private lock up boxes, but I will be there tomorrow morn. & get anything there may be.

    There are some Creameries near here I believe, but I have not been able to do anything yet about seeing anyone in them. I hope

Dear this will find you quite well. I have been thinking a lot of you lately & wondering if you are at Bowdon yet. It must seem a very dismal outlook for you just now.

These few hurried lines are only to reassure you as to my being able to get employment here, or hereabouts. It may not be much at first, but it will be a start. It is nice and fine here now, but there was a severe thunder storm last night.

With much love to you Dearest Lydia & hoping you are quite well.

Believe me, Yours ever.

C. W. Brunskill.

Cyril wrote again the following day:

> Winnipeg, Man.
> July 2.

My dearest Lydia,

Just a line of good news. I have got a start on a cattle ranch about 400 miles West from here. The address is Mr McGregor, Lake View Ranche, Moose Jaw, S.K.T. (note nr. Regina.)

The money is only about 10 dollars for the 1st. month but it is a grand country there & it is a start.

After 2 tries I found Mr Burrell in yesterday 7 pm. & stayed till 10 pm. He is very nice. All this morn. & till 2 pm. at the Immigration Office, then I called on Canon Coombes. He was out but I am to go back at 6 & after that must see Mr Burrell again. I leave here at 7.30 am. tomorrow. So you can guess I am in a tear. – I think the ranche will be all right. I am longing to hear from you again. The Post Office man said there was nothing for me there.

Well Dear you will I know excuse this scrawl. I will try & write from the train to-morrow.

Please tel Isa. I am in too much of a tear to write to her. I hope you are quite well Dearest.

Much love from, Yours as ever,

C. W. Brunskill.[11]

John Langhorne recalls that his uncle Cyril worked for some time on a ranch, and with his savings and a government grant acquired a quarter section of land in Alberta as part of a government land settlement scheme. A whole section was 640 acres. Then after some time he managed to build his own house, and on the 19 October 1910 he was married at Arthur Vale church, Alberta by the Revd A. D. Currie to Emily Whitaker. The farm was six miles from Huxley, and half way between

Calgary and Edmonton. In 1930, when John Langhorne's father retired from the farm at New Hutton the Dr advised him to take a long holiday, for his health. William and Isabelle Maud Langhorne accompanied by John went to Canada for seven months, and stayed with Cyril and his wife. The condition was that John had to get a job while he was there, and he went to work for a bachelor farmer; it was a very rough and ready life. His parents helped on Cyril's farm at the harvest. The farm was two thirds ploughing, with a few beef cattle, and one milk cow for the house. Before Cyril's wife died in 1952 he erected a wooden house near her brother's farm, and Cyril's farm was let. The rent in those days was based on the profit of the year's crop. After his wife died Cyril went blind and later went into hospital at Calgary. After a cataract operation he regained his sight, and resumed his letters to his sister at Hutton. John Langhorne has a collection of these. Cyril died on the 24 November 1955 aged 86, and was buried beside his wife. There were no children. John Langhorne was left the farm and was advised to sell it, which he did. During the Second World War John Langhorne served in the Eighth Army in North Africa, at El Alamein, and in Italy.

NOTES TO CHAPTER FIFTEEN

1. W.M. Three sermon notes, n.d. St Stephen, St John, & Epiphany.

2. L.M. Joseph Brunskill s.o. Richard Atkinson Brunskill to Isabella Brunskill 9 Ap. 1849.

3. L.M. Funeral Notice of Joseph Brunskill 9 Sept. 1872.

4. L.M. Lydia Brunskill at Plumpton to Isabella Brunskill in Hampstead, 10 Sept. 1872.

5. L.M. Lydia Brunskill (at Plumpton) to Isabella n.d. c.1873.

6. *Crockford* 1944 John Ritson Brunskill.
   L.M. Letter of John Langhorne 26.11.1989.
   L.M. Will of Isabella Brunskill widow, of 5 Christ Church Terrace, Iffley, Oxford 13 Oct. 1910.

7. Letter of John Langhorne 26.11.1989.

8. W.M. MS. Paper of John Ritson Brunskill n.d. giving marriages of:
   Alice Mary Brunskill to James Ritson, 5 Oct. 1889. Threlkeld.

Isabelle Maud Brunskill to William Langhorne June 17. 1908. Hutton.
Cyril Wane Brunskill to Emily Whitaker, 19 Oct. 1910. Alberta.
Lydia Violette Brunskill to John Webster, 6 Aug. 1913. Hale.
Lloyds Register of Shipping 7 Sept. 1893 at Guildhall Library, London,
by courtesy of Miss J.M. Wraight, Principal Reference Librarian.

9. W.M. A large packet of letters from Cyril Wane Brunskill to his sister
   Lydia at Ormside Rectory, during his service in the Boer War 25 April
   1899 to Jan. 1902.

10. D.N.B. Sir Redvers Henry Buller (1839–1908).

11. W.M. See note (9) above. Two letters of Cyril to his sister Lydia (after the
    death of Revd Joseph Brunskill) from Winnipeg 1 July and 2 July 1903.

16

People & Papers (2)

Isabelle Maud Brunskill was born 10 November 1872

ISABELLE WAS educated at Oxford High School, where in 1887 at the age of 14 she obtained an Education Certificate with honours in Division I.[1] In 1896 she was teaching at Kilburn, St Augustine's Girls' & Infants' School, London; on the 29 October 1898 the Education Department informed the headmistress Miss E. Ayckbowm that Miss Isabelle M. Brunskill had passed her examination in the subjects for a second year, obtaining a place in the third division of the Class List, and was thus recognised as a Certificated Teacher, and entitled to receive a certificate after probation.[2] She also held the Certificate of the 'Tonic Sol-Fa College' of May 1895.[3] After her London period she went for a short time to teach at Standish outside Wigan. In later years she recalled that she could easily tell the time in the morning, when the miners were going to work in their clogs. At 6 am the sound of the clogs along the street was fairly leisurely; by 6.30 am. the sound was fairly fast; by 7.45 am the men were running. In May 1899 she was appointed head of New Hutton School near Kendal, lodging the next nine years at the Vicarage with the Revd W. & Mrs Pearson. On the 17 June 1908 she was married at New Hutton to William Langhorne, a small farmer. The service was taken by the Revd W. Pearson. William Langhorne and his father had been shoemakers, and when his father took the farm (Raw Green) of 29 acres from the Underley estate, William had to learn farming. He gave up shoemaking on his marriage. John Cyril Langhorne was born 27 March 1909. Mrs Langhorne gave up teaching on her marriage. The small farm was never very lucrative and at times was a 'bit of a scrat'.

When I was curate of Kendal in 1944–48 I had the pleasure of meeting Mr & Mrs Langhorne, and she lent me the first part of her father's (now missing) diary to read. It covered some of his lecture notes at St Bees, some of the lectures of Dr Hook at

Leeds, his time at Mansergh, and the early days at Mallerstang. There was a quaint old-fashioned dignity and courtesy about Mr & Mrs Langhorne which I have never forgotten, a courtesy and dignity coming from a different age and way of life. I have already noted that when Mr Langhorne gave up farming on Dr's orders in 1930, he was advised to take a long holiday. In April Mr & Mrs Langhorne with John went to Canada and stayed for seven months with Cyril and his wife in Alberta. They returned to Hutton for Christmas. Mrs Langhorne died at New Hutton on the 12 November 1954 aged 82, and Mr Langhorne died on the 22 July 1958 aged 82. Both were buried at Hutton.[4]

Lydia Violette Brunskill was born 13 January 1876, according to Alan Webster's tradition at Clifton. Her mother died in the following June, and as her father did not marry Rebecca Simmons till 1879, there were three years when there was no 'mother' at Plumpton Vicarage. It is Alan Webster's tradition that at least the younger children did not take too easily to Rebecca. John Langhorne describes her in widowhood as 'a fierce old lady'. Lydia was only three when her father went to Threlkeld, and seventeen when he went to Ormside in 1893.

Alan has written this about his mother:

My mother was born at Clifton and her mother died through travelling by coach on a very cold day far too soon after her birth. She was baptised Lydia Violet, both of which names she greatly disliked. She had fair hair and was precocious and pretty. One of her first remarks was 'Carry I straight, don't bend I', when she was being moved around by elder brothers and sisters. At the age of 7 she illustrated the photographic Wordsworth by sitting, to her disgust, as 'a simple child' outside the porch at Threlkeld church. In her teens she was a keen tennis player and was incited by the Tractarian family to cycle through Keswick with tennis rackets under her arms on a Sunday in order to disgust the Keswick Convention.

On arrival at the Clergy Daughters' School at Casterton with another child, the entire school was warned against the two new arrivals on the ground that their fathers were Tractarians. She had no idea what the word meant, though it sounded like a dangerous infectious disease, and, not unreasonably burst into tears.

She believed herself to be less bright than her brother John who went to Oxford or her sister Maud who went for teacher's training. She remained at home helping her step-mother and her father with the house and parish, especially at Ormside. Afterwards she went as a church worker or assistant at the vicarage to A. J. Tuck, a cultured wealthy vicar at Ewhurst, close to Bodiam Castle in Sussex. It was there that she met my father who was working in the same parish. They naturally came together both with a north country background. My father came from St Bees and followed the northern tradition to Queen's College, Oxford. His father was a Whitehaven solicitor with a family of seven, connected with other Cumberland families – Alexanders, Fidlers and Parkers. Earlier generations were in shipping in Whitehaven; much the same background as the Ritsons in Sunderland.

John Webster and Lydia Violette Brunskill were married at St Peter's Church, Hale, by the Revd A. J. Tuck on the 6 August 1913. This was the church where her brother was vicar 1906 to 1924. John Webster had been ordained deacon by the bishop of Worcester in 1901, and priest in the chapel of Rose Castle, Carlisle in 1902. He was then appointed to the curacy of St Luke, Barrow in Furness, until 1905, where he remained two years. He was appointed to Wrenbury in 1915.

> They had a difficult beginning; the first baby was still-born, and John was given the living of Wrenbury in Cheshire by the rector of Acton, Canon Moore with whom my father was collaborating in the production of the Greek Patristic Lexicon published after World War II by Professor Lampe. Part of my mother's task during the engagement was to pack up the slips on which the lexicon was built and send them off to the basement of Pusey House.

Alan Brunskill Webster was born on the 1 July 1918. He has a wonderful story about his scholar father. There was a T.B. sanatorium at Wrenbury and at one point there was a Jewish patient there. As John Webster was also a Hebrew scholar he went and read the psalms to this patient in Hebrew – a gesture which was much appreciated. Alan also adds:

> My mother worked extremely hard from 1916 to 1935 at Wrenbury, especially founding the Guides, helping to build a new Sunday School Hall, introducing the choir to new music (she played the piano quite well, as did my father), and working very hard in the garden. She was a fluent and interesting letter-writer and many of her letters survive.

At her funeral at the end of the Second World War (she died 5th May 1945 aged 69) the village came together in a surprising way and a half-muffled peal of bells was rung. She was shy, fair-haired, intelligent and often very funny – obviously remembered by people in Wrenbury as more human and more approachable than my father. It was their custom to visit together on bicycles, sometimes joined by me: they could never afford a car.

John Webster died on the 4 September 1935, and was buried at Wrenbury.[5]

This concludes a short account of Joseph Brunskill's five children.

One of the changes introduced by Brunskill at Threlkeld was to hold an annual Harvest Festival. This pleasant custom had been initiated by the Revd R. S. Hawker, vicar of Morwenstow in north Cornwall on the first Sunday in October 1843. On the 14 October this account appeared in the *Penrith Observer*.

Harvest Thanksgiving
Threlkeld

The annual harvest thanksgiving services were held here on Sunday last, and the two collections at the church were given for the relief of brethren whose crops and homes have been wasted by the raiding Boers in South Africa.

On another occasion it was reported that the Anniversary of the Queen's Accession was observed in church:

The vicar, while explaining the blessings enjoyed in England from long settled peace, urged his hearers to maintain their loyalty and hereditary respect for law as a sacred thing, the ability to make and keep good laws coming from God's blessing, and he mentioned a curious historical fact, showing that the miseries following on a disputed right to the Throne were not so remote, even in this favoured country, but that he had heard a relative talk [probably Miss Jane Monkhouse of Newton] about them having taken place in her own experience. She would tell how some of her neighbours would flee into hiding as the troops of King George or King [Prince] Charles came near, in 'the rising of 1745', and how the unsuccessful were destroyed as rebels and had their property confiscated, she rode behind her father on a 'pillion' to Penrith in 1746, when six gallant men, after a long imprisonment in the

229

dungeons at Carlisle Castle, were barbarously put to death upon
the Fair Hill. One she saw pleaded hard to be let go back to his
wife and children. He was no 'rebel', and knew nothing of kingly
politics, having only, when ordered, saddled and followed his
master, yet his dripping head was held before the crowd of Cum-
brians as that of a 'traitor'.

This was strong stuff for a country congregation.[6]

One of the most delightful letters to survive was addressed to
Brunskill on the 16 November 1889 by Leonardo Cattermole,
of Norton Chambers, Gt Ormond St, W.C. He was the son of
George Cattermole (1800–1868) the famous artist. The son had
written something to the press about the treatment of horses,
and more particularly better methods of shoeing. His letter is a
reply to a response from Brunskill. The front of the envelope
has the drawing of a horse's foot, with the legend underneath
TUTUS ET FORTIS, and on the back is the sketch of a packhorse with the motto:

PACK'OS WOA – BISCUM.

Revd J. Brunskill, Threlkeld by Keswick.

Thanks to you, gentle Sir, for yr. letter. You will see, per enclosure, that I in 1886 wrote just as you do re 'frogs'. Thanks for
pamphlets. The carriage I told you of that I used to drive belonged
to my dear good friend Mrs Hugh Law Lushington (of
Rodmersham) who rented Patterdale Hall from the Marshalls.
The race with the Mail was from P. Hall to Penrith. Lor! what a
great deal I could tell you of sweet days spent there, and at
Debdale Hall; which the L. family rented from Col. Coke previously. Mrs Lushington was (R.I.P.) my sister Georgina's god-
mother. En passant Georgina is a devoted horsey one: she married
C. Sumner the Judge's son, and Winchester's grandson, and Can-
tuar's grand-nephew! She lives in California, at Los Angeles.

I am chatting away, because you imply that you like chat in yr.
'isolation'. You love Horses, that is our ground of 'Freemasonic'
acquaintance. When you are in London, let me know, and I will
show you some of my pictures of them. I paint figures as well, as
I suppose you know, and of course you know who my Dad was,
the George Cattermole of whom you may have read in the 'Dictionary of National Biography', Then of the Time, and all the Art
Dictionaries &c :- Roget is just writing a life of my father, noticing, as has been done before: his stage-coach driving. He was a
friend of Cotton, Sykes, d'Orsay &c. Read 'The Letters of Charles
Dickens' you will be interested. I supplied those to my father,

about his illustrations to 'Humphrey's Clock'. 'Dickens by Pen and Pencil' is just coming out. I have contributed 'A dinner at George Cattermole's, with a sketch of Dickens in a chair of Bryon's* (*Footnote: Lady Byron, at Lady Blessington's, gave my father the ring Byron had on when he swam the Hellespont). My father took Byron's rooms of Bulwer with all the furniture, in the Albany, when Bulwer left them. Bulwer had them direct from Byron. Bulwer was (Lord Lytton) one of our oldest and best friends.

I will look out for the 'Pall Mall' you mention. You shd. ask yr. bookseller to get you 'Odds and Ends, by Leonardo Cattermole', pubd. by Effingham Wilson, 11 Royal Exchange 1/-. It might do good in your parts. I am just doing some Coaching views in Watercolours, having just finished a life size picture of Saint Francis de Sales, which I have presented to the Temperance League of the Cross: I being a R.C. are you horror struck? My family are all Ps., but we had many friends R.Cs., some Jews and Greek Ch; and all pull together as jolly as sandboys. Perhaps you know the name of the Revd Richard Cattermole, B.D. who, with Stebbing, edited the 'Sacred Classics', and wrote various works on Ecclesiastical matters. He was my uncle.

A horse dealer informs me that there are more Horses used in England *now* than in the Posting days. We have many coaches in summer; and there is a London to Brighton four horse Royal Parcel Mail, which runs all the year and pays well. I always feel that a railway desecrates, hardens, pollutes a place, and that coaches are charming addenda to a secluded district. How charming it was to hear, at Patterdale, the coach horns. I used to ride one of Lushington's mares, 'Amazon' all about your country. I rode her one hot aftn. fr. Patterdale Hall into Penrith and back without dismounting. She was a large highbred ewe – necked one, safe to trot down *those hills* at 10 miles an hour! Strange that the Proprietor of the Ullswater Hotel was a Mr Bowness. I visited the Pritts and Coll. Salmon on the Lake.

In a coach builder's shop, here in London, is a man who used to drive the *three abreast* Pooley Bridge & Penrith Coach, by wh. I have travelled. I hope they are not cutting up your lovely Country with the abomination of railways desolation. I think I remember a Keswick and Patterdale Coach, with a rather tinpot horn, four stalwart 'slummockers' a fossil coachman and 'slow lemur' guard! Charming days, those at Patterdale. I have kept a diary, so can bring to memory such concentrated delights, 'visions of joy, passed long ago; moments of bliss', which death with *his* arrow and cupid with *his* have put a period to.

You write of 'isolation', I am prone to it. There is nothing better to bring one's mind into a condition of healthful harmony and peace, than *Isolation*; retreat it may be called, add to this, simply as a sanitary matter, (without the religious aspect at all) temporary abstinence from flesh meat and alcohol, and one *lives*: may be far more conscious of the pleasure of existence than in the feverish whirl of a debauched and noisy world, seeking rest and finding none in the hollowness of Society.

Here endeth &c!

Yours faithfully, Leonardo Cattermole.[7]

This was written on four sides of 4½ in. x 7 in. notepaper!

By 1890 Brunskill was 64, and it seems that he became increasingly anxious for the provision of his family. John Ritson was a curate of Bowden; Alice was married to James Ritson of Sunderland, a master mariner; Cyril was working in the Penrith area, before going into the army; Isabelle was aged 18, having finished her schooling, and not yet teaching; and Lydia was 14, and probably on the point of leaving school. If a clergyman retired at seventy he could claim up to £50 from the income of his last benefice as pension, while the widow might claim a small pension from Queen Anne's Bounty; but both would depend heavily on charitable grants which (to their everlasting credit) a number of City Companies paid to the poorer clergy and their widows. A few dioceses had started a pension scheme. In April 1890 the Revd J. Taylor, MA retired from the vicarage of St John's-in-the-Vale after a service of 34 years. He had been a fine country parson; he had been a Trustee of Sir John Bankes' Charity, a Governor of Keswick High School, Secretary to the Diocesan Church Building Society in the deanery of Keswick, and not least for more than 25 years Acting Manager of the Keswick Savings Bank. In the last capacity he had attended regularly to transact the business of the Bank, and by 1890 the Bank held about £20,000 of people's savings. The presentations to Mr & Mrs Taylor were presided over by Canon Rawnsley vicar of Crosthwaite. Apart from his general congratulations, Brunskill took the opportunity to ventilate his own anxieties:

> There was another evil in this unfortunate diocese, which told particularly against the elder clergyman. Not only were they left, the oldest man in the smallest living, so that the Act to promote retirement could not be applied; but even when they helped them-

selves by paying largely into the new Clergy Pensions' Institution there was in Carlisle Diocese, so far as he knew, no effort made to promote the necessary augmentation fund. Money to aid the retirement of enfeebled clergy was freely given in York Diocese, and in Liverpool they had collected more for these pensions than they had claims. However he congratulated his good neighbour, Mr Taylor, in being able to retire while some vigour remained, and he hoped that he would the longer pay cheering visits to his old friends now that he was released from overwork.

Earlier in his speech he had had a dig at Diocesan Patronage which now goes to those who spend their money and time in travelling about to make up meetings at Carlisle or Barrow. What would Brunskill have made of our present costly middle-class talking-shop the General Synod of the Church of England? But it seems that he was finding work at Threlkeld tiring, and he began to look for relief. On the 21 October 1892 the following notice appeared in the *Carlisle Patriot*:

> The Living of Hutton-in-the-Forest.
> The vacant living of Hutton-in-the-Forest has been offered by the Right Reverend the Lord Bishop of Carlisle (J.W. Bardsley) to the Reverend J. Brunskill, rector of Threlkeld, and accepted by him.[9]

Bishop Bardsley had only been at Carlisle a few months; and early in 1893 the rectory of Ormside also fell vacant, and, as the stipend was slightly better, Brunskill applied for that, and the bishop agreed. Hutton-in-the-Forest was £123 gross a year, while Ormside was £169 gross, and in 1902 £101 net. The population at Hutton was 255, and that at Ormside 212. The difference of £68 between the gross and net income at Ormside would be due to mortgage charges on the benefice, either for the repair of glebe farm buildings, or on the rectory house. Not till the mid-1930s did the church make any effort to relieve the clergy of dilapidations charges by augmentations by the Church Commissioners. It was by no means a bed of roses, and even in his last parish Brunskill was almost at the bottom rung of preferment, and that after over 40 years' service in the diocese of Carlisle. His one advantage was that the Midland Railway (that glory of railway construction) was opened in 1876, and Brunskill was able to go to meetings at Carlisle, whenever his crusading spirit required his attendance. The present day clergy have no idea of the soul-corroding loneliness which destroyed the hope of the country clergy of those days. Apart from the small railway station, Ormside was a dead end![10]

NOTES TO CHAPTER SIXTEEN

1. Letter of John Langhorne 10.5.1989,

2. L.M. Certificate of Education Department 29 Oct. 1896 recognising Miss Isabelle Maud Brunskill as a certified teacher.

3. Letter of John Langhorne 19.5.1989.

4. Letter of John Langhorne 22.5.1989.
   W.M. Typed lists of family births, marriages and deaths.
   Information of John Langhorne.

5. Letter of the Very Revd A.B. Webster 4th June 1989.
   W.M. Typed lists of family births, marriages and burials.

6. W.M. Two press cuttings. *Penrith Observer* 14. Oct. 1884
   W.M. n.d. Anniversary of Queen's Access, at Threlkeld.

7. W.M. Two letters of Leonardo Cattermole; 16 Nov. 1889 & 27 Nov. 1889.
   The second only asks for the return of papers.

8. L.M. The English (?*Lakes Advertiser*) 3 May 1890.

9. W.M. Folder of press cuttings. *Carlisle Patriot*. 21.10.1892.

10. Clergy List. 1872. Hutton-in-the-Forest. W. Whitelock had been there from 1855 to 1892 when he died.
    Crockford. 1902. Revd Joseph Brunskill.

17

Ormside
1893–1903

WHEN BRUNSKILL was appointed to Ormside in 1893 he was 67. Isabelle was 21 and Lydia 17. It was virtually a retirement parish, about four miles from Appleby off the back road from Appleby to Soulby, very quiet, remote and pastoral. Its very ancient church was built on a pre-Christian burial mound, and the antiquities of the place were a constant source of interest to him. He still had his pony and phaeton, and was able to take Rebecca or Lydia for shopping expeditions in Appleby, while stabling his horse at one of the inns. For longer expeditions he had the Midland Railway to Carlisle, and on horseback he was able to visit the local clergy, or the workhouse at Kirkby Stephen. In the rectory there was of course no central heating, with frost ferns on the windows on winter mornings, no street lamps, and candles and paraffin lamps in the house. When winter nights descended the village was very dark, and chinks of light from the houses, and the stars were the only relief from the mantle of the night. The church was lit by paraffin lamps and candles; and one of my warmest memories is of harvest festivals in remote Westmorland churches, with the tortoise stove at the back, the smell of the lamps, and the flowers and vegetables combining the fragrances of field, garden, paraffin, and moth-balls of 'the Sunday best' in a warm greenhouse atmosphere. I remember one Harvest Festival at Selside near Kendal where the wreaths and flowers of a recent funeral were also added to the mixture. I also remember (and this is an irrelevance) one country organist who felt very strongly that no psalm should exceed 20 verses. No matter how strong the view of the vicar, if he chose a long psalm it was firmly closed by the organist at verse 20, with the Gloria ending the singing. If that left the Israelites sinking in the middle of the Red Sea, that was their back luck; they should not have been so careless!

Ormside church had been restored in 1885–6, after long years of neglect. This was achieved through the intervention of Bishop

Harvey Goodwin of Carlisle who obtained the services of C. J. Ferguson FSA as the architect. £743 was spent on repairs and improvements; but when Brunskill went there in 1893 the tower was still unrestored, and he had to attend to its being reslated.

There is a strange story attached to Ormside church which I heard when I was vicar of Warcop. It came from the first part of this century, and after Brunskill's day, when the parish still had its resident rector. One evening the then rector went into church to say his Evensong on his own. During the course of his devotions he happened to look down the church, and saw the figure of an old-time clergyman coming up the church towards him. He was rather surprised, and more startled when the figure walked right through him up to the chancel. After this fright the rector confined his weekday devotions to his house. But it is my impression and experience that these very ancient places have their presences and influences.

Though Brunskill had been a member of the Cumberland & Westmorland Antiquarian Society since 1873, his Plumpton days, he did not appear in the transactions until 1883 when he reported the finding of a bronze palstave (hoe or digging tool) on Askham Fell; he also took part in a visit to Ravenstonedale in 1888. He is also referred to in a history of Threlkeld Hall in 1897. His best claim to attention came from the discovery of a Danish sword, and the umbo of a shield in a freshly dug grave in February 1898. This was immediately reported to Chancellor R. S. Ferguson, and it was realised that this was part of the finding of the Ormside Bowl, which is now in the York Museum. In 1823 the Bowl was in the possession of Mr John Bland of Ormside Lodge, who presented it to the York Philosophic Society for safe keeping.[1] Brunskill seems to have gone to York to photograph it. He gave copies of the photograph to the Revd W. S. Calverly the vicar of Aspatria, the authority on early crosses. His papers were later acquired by Professor W. G. Collingwood, with the Ormside photographs. When Collingwood wrote an article on the bowl for the 1899 transactions he published Brunskill's photos without acknowledgement! Brunskill brooded on this, and in 1901 mentioned this to Collingwood who replied rather tartly from Coniston:

'I'm not a conjurer! Behold your photographs! (Enclosed). But I did not know they were yours. I got them long ago with other scraps when I was editing Calverly, or perhaps earlier, and I never had the least idea that they were yours.'[2]

In 1897 Brunskill determined to celebrate the diamond jubilee of Queen Victoria in a suitable and loyal fashion. Many years before, the socket and steps of the ancient churchyard cross had been removed for building material by the tenant of Ormside Hall. Brunskill persuaded the son to return them to the churchyard, and Brunskill had them reconstructed, with a new cross in the socket. He first obtained the permission of Mr R. B. Barrett, Lord Hothfield's agent, to recover the stones. On the 22 June 1897 the restored cross was dedicated as part of the loyal Jubilee celebrations. Also as both of the medieval bells were cracked, and as he was not allowed to have them recast, he accepted the gift of a small new bell from Mr John Brunskill, of Holliwell, Asby. After he had been at Ormside for 7 years, lovingly caring for the old church, Brunskill published a short history in the Antiquarian Society transactions of 1901:

'Ormshed and its Church'.
By the Revd J. Brunskill, Rector of Ormshed.[3]

The article is an act of devotion.

For the first eight years at Ormside Brunskill was alert and still an effective pastor. He still read the church and local papers, and from time to time rushed off a letter to the press, though not with the frequency of his Threlkeld days. One year the Bishop of Bristol was at odds with the vicar and parishioners of the parish of St Simon, and he persuaded the Curates' Aid Society to withdraw its curate's grant, thus leaving an overworked vicar without help. In a letter to the *Church Times* Brunskill said that 'It was open to the bishop to do his best or worst to enforce his opinions; but in official business he ought to keep within the law of the Church of England.' He then cited his own experiences as curate of Ocker Hill when at the instance of Bishop Prince Lee of Manchester he lost his grant of £40 from the Curates' Aid Society who persuaded the aristocratic subscribers to the Society to transfer their support either to the evangelical Church Pastoral Aid Society, or to parishes of the bishop's choosing. 'Is it too late to hope that the Bishop of Bristol will reconsider his decision?'[4]

There was one press cutting which Brunskill stored with great glee. This account in a church paper was dated 3.4.97:

Extraordinary scene in a church.
All in the name of religion.

An extraordinary scene took place at Gorleston Church on Wednesday, where the Bishop of Norwich attended for the annual confirmation service. When his Lordship emerged from the vestry with the clergy and choir, and entered the chancel, he observed lighted candles on the altar, and at once asked the Vicar, the Rev. Forbes Phillips, to remove them. The Vicar curtly declined, and asserted his supreme authority in his own church.

The Bishop – I shall not proceed with the service unless the lights be removed.

Vicar – You may please yourself, but the lights shall remain. His Lordship then directed the churchwardens to extinguish the candles. These officials, however, ranged themselves at the side of the Vicar, and one of them declared, 'We are not the servants of the Bishop, and have no authority beyond the altar rails'.

Bishop – I have a grave objection to lighted candles on the altar in the daytime, and probably the congregation share my views.

Vicar – I invite any such to declare themselves.

Bishop – I shall not conduct the service.

Vicar – (taking out his watch) – I shall give you one minute to make up your mind, and if you then still refuse I shall conduct the service myself, ascend the pulpit, and declare the candidates members of the Church of England, throwing upon you the responsibility of rejecting them afterwards.

Before the minute had elapsed the Bishop, who seemed intensely annoyed, elected, as he said, for the sake of peace, and to spare the feelings of the congregation, to proceed with the service; but the influences of the scene were painfully evident throughout the service. At the close, instead of joining in the recessional procession, his Lordship sat in solitary state in the chancel.[5]

A cutting from the *Penrith Observer* of 15 September 1896 said:

The harvest festival for Ormside was held on Sunday, when the fine old church was skilfully decorated with various fruits, beautiful hothouse plants, and some rare flowers contributed from London. The venerable rector was able to take all the three services, preaching twice to large congregations. The alms collected as thank offerings were for this year devoted to home or church expenses, because of some arrear of debt in providing a new stove, repairing the tower, cleaning the interior of walls etc.[6]

A week later he preached at a similar festival at Newton Reigny, where he greatly interested the congregation with his reminiscences of Newton Reigny and its church 45 years ago. 'Miss Horn presided at the organ, and the choir, assisted by Mr Harrison and Messrs J. & W. Tatters, sang the harvest hymns and an anthem with much spirit and care.'[7] In 1898 (Aug.) he preached a long sermon at Ormside on behalf of the S.P.C.K.; 'how that church people through their gifts and collections had helped the Society to distribute cheap Bibles and Prayer Books with an authority which might be safely trusted. ... There was also a better prospect that the unjust attacks upon the schools founded by Churchmen would cease, and a brighter future was opening for the solid missionary labour of the S.P.C.K.'[8]

In 1898 a new Benefice Bill came up for consideration in Parliament. In May the archdeacon of Carlisle held his visitation at the Cathedral Fratry in Carlisle. To these medieval courts the churchwardens and clergy are still summoned by writs as peremptory as those of a bygone age. In the diocese of Ely the clergy and wardens are summoned 'unless any impediment is alleged': – and this to men and women who give free time and service to the church! After the swearing in of the wardens, and archdeacon's allocution, the clergy adjourned to consider the Benefices Bill. A previous Bill laid it down that if an incumbent had been disciplined or deprived by his bishop, the incumbent had no right of appeal against an alleged injustice. 'It had been discovered in the Court of Appeal that a bishop might escape punishment, though H.M. Judges declared that he had been guilty of treating his brother minister with a severity which they could not believe it possible he deserved.' The new bill proposed that there should be a right of appeal to the archbishop. The Parliamentary committee said that an appeal to a superior clergyman of the same order was not the best provision, but suggested that the right of appeal should be to a civil court presided over by one of H.M. Judges. Brunskill went up by train to the meeting, and spoke forcibly in favour of the amended draft, proposing the resolution that the meeting give its hearty approval to the Bill. In a letter to the *Carlisle Patriot* of 20 May he added these remarks:

> Respecting a now almost forgotten scandal, I wrote that 'Mr Sedgwick, a priest, who, without stipend, has laboured with remarkable ministerial success in Manchester during eleven years, is silenced and ruined by Bishop (Prince) Lee without even a hearing. Of course this is wrong, which follows on a political nomination to an office endowed by the voluntary subscriptions of churchmen; may it soon be remedied. But to exaggerate the way in which clergymen bite and devour one another cannot promote peace. The Papacy is an embodied contradiction of the judicious advice of Hooker – that in the orders of the ministry each should respect the rights of the other.[9]

Apart from the injustices of the old system against which Brunskill had written for so many years, he aimed at a constitutional form of church government in which the bishops acted as 'constitutional rulers, working harmoniously with the Parliament of Presbyters and properly constituted House of Laymen.'[10] That was prophetic!

By 1902 it appears from the letters of Cyril in Natal to Lydia at Ormside that their father's health was failing. They found it very difficult in their remote hamlet to obtain a servant, and at one point Rebecca determined to take Brunskill for a short visit to Silloth to see if a change would improve him. Also in 1902 they received news that Cyril had been in hospital at Maritsberg, and was being sent home on sick leave. This account appeared in the local paper:

ORMSIDE AND THE WAR.
Return of Corporal Brunskill.

Last week a large crowd mustered at Ormside Railway Station to welcome home from South Africa Corporal Brunskill, younger son of the Revd J. Brunskill, rector, after serving with the Royal Dragoons. Corporal Brunskill went out as a reservist with the earliest drafts landing in Natal. As orderly on the staff of General Sir Redvers Buller, he shared in the battles of the Natal Field Force, and as a compensation for the long endured hardships near the Tugela, Spion Kop, and along the Drakenberg range of mountains, he was in the front of the victories at Bulwana, which was

followed presently by the relief of Ladysmith, the advance north-
wards by Dundee, and the capture of Allman's Nek, the victory at
Bergendal, and advance by Lyndenberg to the hardly won top of
the mountain of Mauchberg.

Having lately been in hospital at Maritzberg, he was invalided
home on furlough to recruit [recover].

The welcome given by his neighbours was most enthusiastic.
Apparently the whole of the population had turned out, and
many friends mustered from Appleby, bringing the town's band.
Triumphal arches and flags gave a very gay appearance to the village as the cheering procession, led by the band, marched to the
fine old church on the hill by the Eden. The venerable building
was crowded beyond standing room while a short thanksgiving
service was led by the Revd J. G. Leonard, Kirkby Stephen. Two
suitable hymns were heartily sung, and an eloquent address was
given by the Revd Seymour Shaw, Warcop. From the church the
visitor was conducted to the neighbouring rectory, where in a
spirited speech, Sergeant-Major Clear, Westmorland and
Cumberland Yeomanry, showed, how important for the nation
was such an encouragement to the military spirit. By volunteering
soldiers old England might continue to escape the impoverishing
burden of enforced conscription. Sergeant-Major Clear wore his
Cavalry uniform.

The Rector expressed his gratitude and pleasure at the friendli-
ness thus shown by his parishioners. The village decorations had
been the ready work of Messrs. Taylor, R. Braithwaite, Allan,
Ellwood, and many ladies.[11]

Bishop Bardsley was a strong evangelical, and an eloquent
preacher; he won the trust of the majority of his clergy by working hard to raise the level of clergy sustentation. Both he and his
predecessor Harvey Goodwin did much to make a bad system
fairer, and avoid the bigotry and unfairness of Waldegrave and
Villiers. Brunskill seems to have liked and respected Bardsley;
for, when in 1902 the bishop (who had never recovered from an
illness he contacted some years earlier in an Egyptian hotel) was
ordered six weeks' rest, he wrote to Brunskill from Folkestone
on the 3 October 1902. He had been reading the last Will of the
Black Prince (a.d.1376) in Norman French as preserved in the
Registry at Lambeth, and reprinted by Dean Stanley in his
Edward the Black Prince. The bishop's letter to Brunskill began
'My Dear Mr Brunskill', and after giving the above facts he
continued:

to my great interest I found these words (p.174) 'Ego Johannes de
Ormshevede, clericus Karliolensis dioceis publicus notarius autori-
tate apostolica premissis omnibus et singulis dum sic etc.' ... Can
you tell me anything more about him than the facts thus attested
by the Will?

    Yours very sincerely,
    John W. Carlisle.[12]

During his last years Brunskill made some attempt to dis-
cover the origins of his family. The majority of Westmorland
Brunskills lived in the extensive parish of Brough-under-
Stainmore, where the parish registers contain many references
to them. The search was inconclusive; but he delivered a paper
to the Cumberland & Westmorland Antiquarian Society meeting at Appleby on the 28 August 1902 on 'The Brunskills'. It
was published in 1903, and he seems to suggest that the scattering of Brunskills in the upper Eden Valley derived from
Brough. He printed the poem on Brough bells naming John
Brunskill who gave them as a thank-offering for recovering his
lost cattle.[13] He also corresponded with Mr H. Oliver Brunskill
of 58 Upper Mount Street, Dublin, whose family derived from
Brough. But apart from naming the hamlet of Sandford where
his father was brought up, there is no firm conclusion from the
article as to the origin of the family.

The answer probably lies in the 1829 printed *Gazetteer of
Westmorland*. In Brough parish the following names occur:

    Sarah Brunskill, Borrenthwaite
    Mr Edmund Brunskill, Upman How
    John Brunskill, Gillies
    Richard Brunskill, Calvaloads
    Robert Brunskill, Oxenthwaite.

In other parts of Westmorland in 1849 there were John Brun-
skill, master of the Grammar School at Asby; John Brunskill at
Grange Hall Farm, Milburn; Anthony Brunskill at Crosby
Garrett, and Christopher Brunskill in Mallerstang.[14]

In November 1902 Brunskill made a pilgrimage to Stainmore
probably to look for Brunskill sites, for in a letter to his sister
Isabella at Hale Vicarage of the 7 November 1902 he wrote:

My own dear Sister,

If the letter from Admiral Buckle will give to you any of the interest I have had it may be worth this penny.

In my isolation, of course I am not cheered that all my life's work for church schools is to be discarded as a hindrance. The Leeds letter is from a forward defender of the Bill in Parl.

The so-called *Court*! Martial is sadly confirmatory of my old fears as to oppression in the Army. And I am increasingly proud & thankful that Cyril has borne the hateful ordeal & survived with a good character. I should like a fuller report; but there is enough to show why he chose to shrink from increasing the harrows.

H. keeps very well & busy. Ma returns tonight. My pilgrimage to Stainmoor somewhat damaged the health of your mo[st] aff[ect.] Brother.

J. Brunskill.

Mrs B.
Hale,
Altrincham.[15]

It is not clear what was the nature of Cyril Brunskill's brush with the Army authorities.

The readers of Brunskill's diary in his All Hallows day will remember his brush with dean A. C. Tait of Carlisle in June 1856 at a meeting of the Carlisle Diocesan Education Society.[16] Tait died as archbishop of Canterbury in 1882, and Brunskill kept a photograph of his alabaster tomb in Canterbury Cathedral. He also kept a press cutting about Tait, which makes one ask why?

The Late Archbishop on 'Divisions'.

Speaking at the Swansea Church Congress, Archbishop Tait said:-

'It is now many years since, I remember, this happened to me:-I was travelling a whole day in the mail in company with a great historian, politician, and literary man, well known in that day, and well remembered still, who had then but recently returned from a lengthened sojourn in India. We were talking of the divisions which at that time distracted the kingdom of Scotland in religious matters, and he said, "When a man has lived a long time in a country in which people worship cows, he comes to think less of the divisions which separate Christians".

'I presume there was a great moral lesson in this random saying. I confess it made a great impression of my heart. I have never forgotten it, and it has been the endeavour of my life to profit by

it. A godly bishop said to me once of a brother as godly as himself, but much given to controversy:- Poor man, he is always writing about the three orders of the ministry, when those to whom
he is writing are doubting whether there be a God in heaven.'[17]

In the autumn of 1902 his health began to fail, but he continued in harness until shortly before his death, which took place
on 10 March 1903. The funeral took place at Ormside on the
13 March at 3 pm. The service was conducted by the Revd E.
P. Powell of Leeds who had taken duty for the past fortnight,
the Revd Seymour Shaw vicar of Warcop who read the lesson,
and the Revd S. B. Burrell vicar of Hilton conducted the com-
mittal. There was a large congregation of clergy, relations,
friends and parishioners. Rebecca, John, Cyril, Isabelle, and
Lydia were the immediate mourners; while Brunskill's sister did
not come from Bowden but sent a wreath. At the burial the rain
fell in sheets, and the congregation dispersed quickly.[18]

According to the then law of the church the family had to
leave the rectory within a matter of weeks. Rebecca took a
house at Battlebarrow in Appleby near to the Grammar School.
Among the effects which she kept was Brunskill's phaeton,
which she lodged at the inn where they had stabled the horse in
former days. After some time the innkeeper sold the phaeton,
and Rebecca conducted a brisk correspondence with the innkeeper; but to no avail: – the deed was done. John Langhorne
used to visit her on a cycle from Hutton, and describes her as a
'fierce old lady'. Lydia, who had remained at Ormside for the
ten years they were there left to join her brother for a time at
Bowden, and then went to do parish work at Ewhurst, near
Bodiam Castle in Sussex. John returned to his parish work, and
Cyril emigrated to Canada. Rebecca died on the 5 August 1922
aged 85, and was buried at Ormside. The funeral hymn sung at
Joseph Brunskill's funeral at Ormside opened with these words:

> Now the labourer's task is o'er;
>   Now the battle day is past;
> Now upon the farther shore
>   Lands the voyager at last.
> Father, in Thy gracious keeping
> Leave we now Thy servant sleeping.

What was the judgement of his contemporaries? How did they remember this great battler? There were warm, but not uncritical tributes in the *Penrith Observer*, and the *Carlisle Patriot* to which he had sent letters and articles for fifty years. One old pupil H. T. Plumer of Catford in Kent wrote:

> Joseph Brunskill was no ordinary man. He was in many respects, nay, perhaps in all, a character – often, in the general opinion of his neighbours, and even of his friends, wrong-headed and obstinate in holding unpopular opinions; yet he could always give a good reason for the faith that was in him. I knew him well from 1857 [sic], when he became headmaster of Hackthorpe School, till the famous day (I use 'famous' in its original sense, without prejudice), Saturday, October 6th, 1900, when North Westmorland electors discarded Sir Joseph Savory for Mr Richard Rigg. On that day the late Rector of Ormside and I lunched together at the King's Head, and spent a happy hour or two afterwards in and about the ancient town. It was to be our last meeting.
>
> I always found him the same honest, cheerful, good-hearted friend, mostly engaged in some old or new crusade against what he held to be wrong. For example, in his efforts, many years ago, to persuade the Cumberland farmers to let the young children of the poor in their parishes have some of the milk which they were keeping for their calves, he used to take long and wearying rides in rough places, and, I fear, earned no little ill-will, but he did not mind that; he took it as one of the inevitable consequences of trying to do his duty.

After mentioning his encouraging boys at Lowther to take up cricket, Mr Plumer concluded:

> To sum up my recollections of my old friend, I should say that his distinguishing characteristics were courage and honesty. I cannot think it even possible that he would ever tell a lie, and what he held to be right and true I firmly believe he would have defended, if need be, with his life.[19]

Among the other tributes was one from the Revd Joseph Whiteside, the son of his old friend Stephen Whiteside, both vicars of Shap.[20] But the best came from the pen of an unknown friend, which appeared in a church paper:

Revd J. Brunskill

The Revd J. Brunskill, who had been Rector of Ormside since 1893, died at the Rectory on March 10th (aged 77), and though he had been in failing health for some months, he continued in harness to within a short time of the end. His removal lessens the number of the band of the old-fashioned High Churchmen who still survive from the fifties, and of which he was a fearless, consistent, and devout member.

His ministerial life was mostly spent in Northern villages from which the enthusiasm of the earlier Evangelical movement had evaporated, and only the prejudices against anything 'Churchy' remained. In his efforts to overcome the general indifference to religion and the restoration of seemly order in the services, he encountered much, and sometimes very bitter, opposition. His transparent sincerity, devotion to duty, and unvarying kindliness in the long run, however, overcame hostility and won the respect and love of his parishioners. In his several parochial charges his constancy, simple faith, and adherence to his principles, were great object lessons to those who at first misunderstood him.

He was thus, in the course of his long ministerial life, enabled by the best of all arguments to convince them of his absolute religious sincerity, and that he was everybody's friend and nobody's enemy. This was a task which those who are acquainted with the steadfast and conservative character of the North Country villager will allow to be by no means an easy one. From his earliest days he was always much interested in education, and for a considerable period acted as local organising Secretary for the National Society, and to the end of his life was a generous supporter of Church schools and scholars.

Many of those he assisted have risen up and called him blessed as they learned to appreciate the sterling qualities of his character.[21]
R.I.P.

NOTES TO CHAPTER SEVENTEEN

1. Early references to Revd J. Brunskill.
   Cumberland & Westmorland Antiq. Soc. Old Series:
   1881. Visit to Maiden Castle & Ray Cross, Stainmore, on 18 Aug. 1880. Brunskill appears in the Ray Cross photo, with Canon Simpson LLD.
   1883, 510. The bronze palstave found on Askham fell.
   1888, 395. The visit to Ravenstonedale.
   1897, 272. The hist. of Threlkeld Hall.
   1899, 325, 379, 381, 386. The discovery of the broken sword & umbo of a shield in a grave in Ormside churchyard.

2. W.M. Prof. W.G. Collingwood at Coniston to Revd J. Brunskill at Ormside 22 Nov. 1901. The disputed photos are returned!

3. W.M. C & W Antiq. trans. offprint N.S. XVII, 1901, p.155. Ormshed & its Church. Revd J. Brunskill.

The Ejected of 1662 in Cumberland & Westmorland, B. Nightingale, Manchester U.P. 1911, vol. II, p. 1143. Ormside parish, mentions the cross.

W.M. Letter of R.B. Barrett at Skipton Castle to Revd Joseph Brunskill at Ormside 13 May, 1897 giving permission to remove the remains of the churchyard cross to the churchyard.

4. W.M. Folder of Press Cuttings. J. Brunskill at Ormside to *Church Times* 26 Feb. [the year missing].

5. W.M. ditto. dated by Brunskill 3.4.1897.

6. W.M. ditto. *Penrith Observer* 15.9.1896.

7. W.M. ditto. *Penrith Observer* 22.9.1896.

8. W.M. ditto. *The Carlisle Patriot* 12 Aug 1898.

9. W.M. ditto. *The Carlisle Patriot* 20 May 1898.

10. W.M. ditto. Press cutting 20 Feb (no year given) to a church paper. Letter from 'Only a Country Parson' on the Church Reform League. Brunskill has marked the last paragraph on constitutional church government.

11. W.M. Press cutting, prob. in *Penrith Observer*. n.d. 'Ormside and the War; the return of Corporal Brunskill.'

12. W.M. Bishop J.W. Bardsley of Carlisle to Brunskill. 3 Oct., 1902. The bishop has quoted the latin word notarius in a different order in his two refs. to the text.
    Press cutting of J. Breay given to L.M. The obituary of Bishop Bardsley in *The Times* 15 Sept. 1904 mentions the disease contracted in Egypt in earlier years.

13. W.M. The Brunskills by Revd J. Brunskill, rector of Ormside. Cumberland Westmorland Antiq. Soc. offprint 1903.
    W.M. Letter of H. Oliver Brunskill of 58 Upper Mount Street, Dublin, 22 Oct. (1902).

14. *Hist. Topog & Directory of Westmorland*, P.J. Mannex, 1849, pp.140, 147, 151, 167.
    Hist. Topog & Gazetteer of Cumberland, Mannix & Whellan 1847 gives the information (under Penrith) that John Brunskill attended the Tuesday market in Great Dockray, selling bacon and butter. This is probably John from Newton.
    The printed Brough parish registers also contain this burial 29 May 1794: Revd John Brunskill of Upmanhowe aged 26. I have not established his origin, nor ordination.

15. L.M. Revd J. Brunskill at Ormside to his sister Mrs Isabella Brunskill at Hale, 7.11.1902.

16. Chapter 6, June 1856.

17. W.M. Folder of press cuttings. n.d. (post 1882). The late Archbishop Tait on divisions.

18. W.M. Memorial notice and funeral hymns in purple ink: In Memory of the Revd Joseph Brunskill Rector of Ormside, born 22 Feb. 1826. At Rest 10 March 1903.

19 L.M. Black-edged envelope containing memorials to the Revd J. Brunskill: *Penrith Observer* March 1903. The death of the Revd J. Brunskill.

20. *Shappe in Bygone Days*. Revd Joseph Whiteside, Kendal 1904, p.74/5. Cumberland & Westmorland Antiq. Soc trans. 1903, p. 360. In Memoriam, the Revd Joseph Brunskill.

21. L.M. Press cutting (see (19) above) from a church paper (? *The Guardian*) 27 March 1903. This excellent tribute was possibly by his old friend Revd Joseph Whiteside of Shap. Whiteside and his father Stephen had known Brunskill since 1857.

ANCESTORS AND DESCENDANTS OF JOSEPH BRUNSKILL 1826-1903

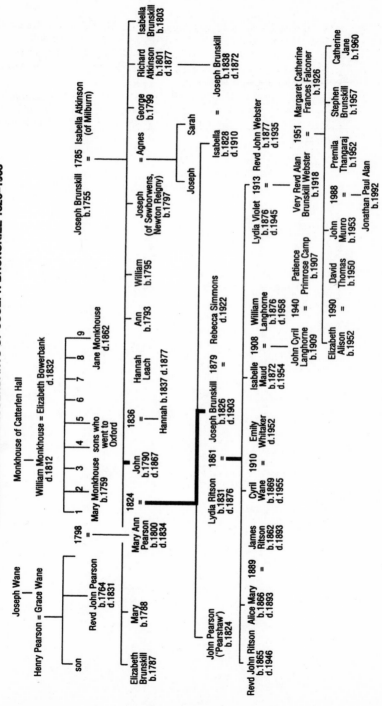

Index

INDEX